TRENDS IN INTERNET RESEARCH

TRENDS IN INTERNET RESEARCH

B. G. KUTAIS
EDITOR

Nova Science Publishers, Inc.
New York

For permission to use material from this book please contact us:
Telephone 631-231-7269; Fax 631-231-8175
Web Site: http://www.novapublishers.com

LIBRARY OF CONGRESS CATALOGING-IN-PUBLICATION DATA

Trends in Internet research / editor, B.G. Kutais.
p. cm.
Includes index.
ISBN-13: 978-1-59454-140-7 (hardcover)
ISBN-10: 1-59454-140-X
1. Web services--United States--Forecasting. 2. Internet--Law and legislation--United States. 3. Internet--Government policy--United States. 4. Internet--Social aspects--United States. 5. Telecommunication policy--United States. I. Kutais, B. G.
TK5105.88813.T74 2009
303.48'33--dc22

2009032685

Published by Nova Science Publishers, Inc. ✢ New York

CONTENTS

PREFACE

The Internet expands its wild, unpredictable reach each year as the voracious appetite of its users continues unabated. Some developments are good, while others are changing so rapidly that their significance can barely keep pace with their own evolution. This new book brings together the leading issues which have surfaced and left an impact among notable Internet trends.

Chapter 1 - Spam, also called unsolicited commercial email (UCE) or "junk email," aggravates many computer users. Not only can spam be a nuisance, but its cost may be passed on to consumers through higher charges from Internet service providers who must upgrade their systems to handle the traffic. Also, some spam involves fraud, or includes adult-oriented material that offends recipients or that parents want to protect their children from seeing. Proponents of UCE insist it is a legitimate marketing technique that is protected by the First Amendment, and that some consumers want to receive such solicitations.

On December 16, 2003, President Bush signed into law the Controlling the Assault of Non-Solicited Pornography and Marketing (CAN-SPAM) Act, P.L. 108-187. It went into effect on January 1, 2004. The CAN-SPAM Act does not ban UCE. Rather, it allows marketers to send commercial email as long as it conforms with the law, such as including a legitimate opportunity for consumers to "opt-out" of receiving future commercial emails from that sender. It preempts state laws that specifically address spam, but not state laws that are not specific to email, such as trespass, contract, or tort law, or other state laws to the extent they relate to fraud or computer crime. It does not require a centralized "Do Not Email" registry to be created by the Federal Trade Commission (FTC), similar to the National Do Not Call registry for telemarketing. The law requires only that the FTC develop a plan and timetable for establishing such a registry, and to inform Congress of any concerns it has with regard to establishing it. The FTC submitted a report to Congress on June 15, 2004, concluding that a Do Not Email registry could actually increase spam.

Proponents of CAN-SPAM have argued that consumers are most irritated by *fraudulent* email, and that the law should reduce the volume of such email because of the civil and criminal penalties included therein. Opponents counter that consumers object to *unsolicited* commercial email, and since the law legitimizes commercial email (as long as it conforms with the law's provisions), consumers actually may receive more, not fewer, UCE messages. Thus, whether or not "spam" is reduced depends in part on whether it is defined as only fraudulent commercial email, or all unsolicited commercial email. Many observers caution that consumers should not expect any law to solve the spam problem — that consumer education and technological advancements also are needed.

Chapter 2 - To produce revenue, websites have placed advertisements on their sites. Advertisers will pay a premium for greater assurance that the advertisement they are purchasing will be seen by users that are most likely to be interested in the product or service offered. As a result, technology has been developed which enables online advertisements to be targeted directly at individual users based on their web surfing activity. This practice is widely known as "behavioral" or "e-havioral" advertising.

This individual behavioral targeting has raised a number of privacy concerns. For instance, questions have been asked whether personally identifiable information is being collected; how the information collected is being protected; and whether current laws are being violated if data are being collected without the consent of the parties involved. It is often unclear whether current laws, such as the Electronic Communications Privacy Act and the Communications Act, apply to online advertising providers that are collecting data through click tracking, capturing search terms, and other methods. However, it is likely that in many cases these laws could be held to apply to such activities and that these methods of data collection would be forbidden unless consent is obtained from one of the parties to the communication. This report will examine the application of these statutes to online behavioral advertising in more detail.

There are no current federal regulations specific to online behavioral advertising. The FTC maintains that self-regulation is preferable to agency regulations, because the state of the industry is fluid and complex. To aid the industry in self-regulation of online behavioral advertising, in 2009, the FTC released a set of self-regulatory principles for the use of web sites and behavioral advertisers. The principles set forth guidance for the industry regarding the information that may be collected online and how companies should notify their customers about the collection. The FTC also applauded the efforts of industry groups to develop more detailed guidance on the issue. Organizations such as the Network Advertising Initiative have created policies, similar to the FTC's recent release, which many online advertising providers have pledged to follow that represent industry best practices for protecting the privacy of web users.

Chapter 3 - The Google Book Search Library Project, announced in December 2004, raised important questions about infringing reproduction and fair use under copyright law. Google planned to digitize, index, and display "snippets" of print books in the collections of five major libraries without the permission of the books' copyright holders, if any. Authors and publishers owning copyrights to these books sued Google in September and October 2005, seeking to enjoin and recover damages for Google's alleged infringement of their exclusive rights to reproduce and publicly display their works. Google and proponents of its Library Project disputed these allegations. They essentially contended that Google's proposed uses were not infringing because Google allowed rights holders to "opt out" of having their books digitized or indexed. They also argued that, even if Google's proposed uses were infringing, they constituted fair uses under copyright law.

The arguments of the parties and their supporters highlighted several questions of first impression. First, does an entity conducting an unauthorized digitization and indexing project avoid committing copyright infringement by offering rights holders the opportunity to "opt out," or request removal or exclusion of their content? Is requiring rights holders to take steps to stop allegedly infringing digitization and indexing like requiring rights holders to use meta-tags to keep search engines from indexing online content? Or do rights holders employ sufficient measures to keep their books from being digitized and indexed online by publishing in print? Second, can unauthorized digitization, indexing, and display of "snippets" of print works constitute a fair use? Assuming unauthorized indexing and display of "snippets" are fair uses, can digitization claim to be a fair use on the grounds that apparently *prima facie* infringing activities that facilitate legitimate uses are fair uses?

On October 28, 2008, Google, authors, and publishers announced a proposed settlement, which, if approved by the court, could leave these and related questions unanswered. However, although a court granted preliminary approval to the settlement on November 17, 2008, final approval is still pending. Until final approval is granted, any rights holder belonging to the proposed settlement class—which includes "all persons having copyright interests in books" in the United States— could object to the agreement. The court could also reject the agreement as unfair, unreasonable, or inadequate. Moreover, on July 2, 2009, the U.S. Department of Justice confirmed that it is investigating whether the terms of the proposed settlement violate antitrust law.

Chapter 4 - The Federal Election Campaign Act (FECA) regulates "federal election activity," which is defined to include a "public communication" (i.e., a broadcast, cable, satellite, newspaper, magazine, outdoor advertising facility, mass mailing, or telephone bank communication made to the general public) or "any other form of general public political advertising." In 2006, in response to a federal district court decision, the FEC promulgated regulations amending the definition of "public communication" to include paid Internet advertisements placed on another individual or entity's website. As a result, a key element of online political activity—*paid* political advertising—is subject to federal campaign finance law and regulations.

During the 110th Congress, the regulation of political communications on the Internet was not the subject of major legislative action. H.R. 894 (Price, NC) would have extended "stand by your ad" disclaimer requirements to Internet communications, among others. H.R. 5699 (Hensarling) would have exempted from treatment as a contribution or expenditure any uncompensated Internet services by individuals and certain corporations. Similar legislation has not yet been introduced in the 111th Congress. This report will be updated in the event of major legislative, regulatory, or legal developments.

Chapter 5 - Navigating the Internet requires using addresses and corresponding names that identify the location of individual computers. The Domain Name System (DNS) is the distributed set of databases residing in computers around the world that contain address numbers mapped to corresponding domain names, making it possible to send and receive messages and to access information from computers anywhere on the Internet.

The DNS is managed and operated by a not-for-profit public benefit corporation called the Internet Corporation for Assigned Names and Numbers (ICANN). Because the Internet evolved from a network infrastructure created by the Department of Defense, the U.S. government originally owned and operated (primarily through private contractors) the key components of network architecture that enable the domain name system to function. A 1998 Memorandum of Understanding (MOU) between ICANN and the Department of Commerce (DOC) initiated a process intended to transition technical DNS coordination and management functions to a private sector not-for-profit entity. While the DOC currently plays no role in the internal governance or day-to-day operations of the DNS, ICANN remains accountable to the U.S. government through a Joint Project Agreement (JPA) with the DOC.

Many of the technical, operational, and management decisions regarding the DNS can have significant impacts on Internet-related policy issues such as intellectual property, privacy, e-commerce, and cybersecurity. The ICANN-DOC Joint Project Agreement is due to expire on September 30, 2009. Congress and the Administration are assessing the appropriate federal role with respect to ICANN and the DNS, and examining to what extent ICANN is presently positioned to ensure Internet stability and security, competition, private and bottom-up policymaking and coordination, and fair representation of the Internet community. A related issue is whether the U.S. government's unique authority over the DNS root zone should continue indefinitely. Foreign governments have argued that it is inappropriate for the U.S. government to have exclusive authority over the worldwide DNS, and that technical coordination and management of the DNS should be accountable to international governmental entities. On the other hand, many U.S. officials argue that it is critical for the U.S. government to maintain authority over the DNS in order to guarantee the stability and security of the Internet.

The expiration of the JPA and the continuing U.S. authority over the DNS root zone remain two issues of keen interest to the 111th Congress, the Administration, foreign governments, and other Internet stakeholders worldwide. How these issues are addressed will likely have profound impacts on the continuing evolution of ICANN, the DNS, and the Internet.

Chapter 6 - Congress is involved in issues of state and local taxation of Internet transactions because commerce conducted by parties in different states over the Internet falls under the Commerce Clause of the Constitution. Currently, the "Internet Tax Moratorium" prohibits (1) new taxes on Internet access services and (2) multiple or discriminatory taxes on Internet commerce. The moratorium was created by the Internet Tax Freedom Act (ITFA) of 1998 (112 Stat. 2681) and has been extended twice. The original moratorium expired on October 21, 2001. Congress extended the moratorium through November 1, 2003, with the Internet Tax Nondiscrimination Act, P.L. 107-75. The moratorium was extended for an additional four years, through November 1, 2007, by the Internet Tax Nondiscrimination Act, P.L. 108-435. On October 31, 2007, P.L. 110-108, the Internet Tax Freedom Act Amendments Act of 2007 was passed extending the moratorium through November 1, 2014. Generally, taxes on Internet access that have continued in place since before October 1, 1998, are protected by a grandfather clause.

An issue previously raised in connection with the Internet tax moratorium concerned states streamlining their sales taxes in order to gain remote tax collection authority. In the 110th Congress, S. 34 and H.R. 3396 would grant states that comply with the Streamlined Sales and Use Tax Agreement the authority to require remote sellers to collect state and local taxes on interstate sales. Another related issue is whether and how to have Congress set the nexus standards under which a state is entitled to impose a business activity tax (BAT, e.g., corporate net income tax, franchise tax, business and occupation tax, gross receipts tax) on a company located outside the state, but with some business activities in the state. In the 110th Congress, S. 1726 and its twin H.R. 5267 would establish more-uniform standards — generally higher standards — for the level of business activity that would create nexus and thus state corporate income taxability. For more on state corporate income taxes, see CRS Report RL3 2297, *State Corporate Income Taxes: A Description and Analysis*, by Steven Maguire.

Chapter 7 - The Unlawful Internet Gambling Enforcement Act (UIGEA) seeks to cut off the flow of revenue to unlawful Internet gambling businesses. It outlaws receipt of checks, credit card charges, electronic funds transfers, and the like by such businesses. It also enlists the assistance of banks, credit card issuers and other payment system participants to help stem the flow. To that end, it authorizes the Treasury Department and the Federal Reserve System (the Agencies), in consultation with the Justice Department, to promulgate implementing regulations. Proposed regulations were announced with a comment period that ended on December 12, 2007, 72 *Fed. Reg.* 56680 (October 4, 2007). After taking into consideration the public comments on the proposed rule, the Agencies adopted a final rule implementing the provisions of the UIGEA, 73 *Fed. Reg.* 69382 (November 18, 2008); the rule is effective January 19, 2009, with a compliance date of December 1, 2009.

The final rule substantially resembles the proposed rule, with several modifications in response to public comments. It addresses the feasibility of identifying and interdicting the flow of illicit Internet gambling proceeds in five payment systems: card systems, money transmission systems, wire transfer systems, check collection systems, and the Automated Clearing House (ACH) system. It suggests that, except for financial institutions that deal directly with illegal Internet gambling operators, tracking the flow of revenue within the wire transfer, check collection, and ACH systems is not feasible at this point. It therefore exempts them from the regulations' requirements. It charges those with whom illegal Internet gambling operators may deal directly within those three systems, and participants in the card and money transmission systems, to adopt policies and procedures to enable them to identify the nature of their customers' business, to employ customer agreements barring tainted transactions, and to establish and maintain remedial steps to deal with tainted transactions when they are identified. The final rule provides non¬exclusive examples of reasonably designed policies and procedures to prevent restricted transactions. The rule also explains why the Agencies rejected a check-list-of-unlawful-Internet-gambling-operators approach, asserting that such a list of businesses would not be practical, efficient, or effective in preventing unlawful Internet gambling. Rather, the Agencies argued that flexible, risk-based due diligence procedures conducted by participants in the payment systems, in establishing and maintaining commercial customer relationships, is the most effective method to prevent or prohibit the restricted transactions.

Several bills have been introduced in the 111th Congress related to Internet gambling. H.R. 2266 (Reasonable Prudence in Regulation Act) would delay the implementation of the UIGEA regulations by one year, establishing an effective date of December 1, 2010. H.R. 2267 (Internet Gambling Regulation, Consumer Protection, and Enforcement Act) would establish a federal licensing program, administered by the Treasury Department, under which Internet gambling companies may lawfully operate and accept bets or wagers from individuals located in the United States. H.R. 2268 (Internet Gambling Regulation and Tax Enforcement Act of 2009) would establish a licensing fee regime within the Internal Revenue Code for Internet gambling operators.

Chapter 8 - Hyperlinking, in-line linking, caching, framing, thumbnails. Terms that describe Internet functionality pose interpretative challenges for the courts as they determine how these activities relate to a copyright holder's traditional right to control reproduction, display, and distribution of protected works. At issue is whether basic operation of the Internet, in some cases, constitutes or facilitates copyright infringement. If so, is the activity a "fair use" protected by the Copyright Act? These issues frequently implicate search engines, which scan the web to allow users to find content for uses, both legitimate and illegitimate.

In 2003, the Ninth Circuit Court of Appeals decided *Kelly v. Arriba Soft Corp.*, holding that a search engine's online display of "thumbnail" images was a fair use of copyright protected work. More recently, a U.S. district court considered an Internet search engine's caching, linking, and the display of thumbnails in a context other than that approved in *Kelly*. In *Field v. Google*, the district court found that Google's system of displaying cached images did not infringe the content owner's copyright. And in *Perfect 10 v. Amazon.com Inc.*, the Ninth Circuit revisited and expanded upon its holding in *Kelly*, finding that a search engine's use of thumbnail images and practice of in-line linking, framing, and caching were not infringing. But it left open the question of possible secondary liability for contributory copyright infringement and possible immunity under the Digital Millennium Copyright Act.

Taken together, these cases indicate a willingness by the courts to acknowledge the social utility of online indexing, and factor it into fair use analysis; to adapt copyright law to the core functionality and purpose of Internet, even when that means requiring content owners to affirmatively act, such as by the use of meta-tags; and to consider and balance conflicts between useful functions, such as online indexing and caching, against emerging, viable new markets for content owners.

Chapter 9 - It has been proposed that there be a domain on the Internet exclusively for websites that contain sexually explicit material; it might be labeled ".xxx" to complement the current ".com," ".org," and others. Some propose making use of a ".xxx" domain voluntary, and a June 26, 2008, decision by the Internet Corporation for Assigned Names and Numbers (ICAAN) to allow a virtually unlimited number of top-level domain names may make the voluntary use of ".xxx" possible in 2009. Others propose that Congress make use of ".xxx" mandatory for websites that contain sexually explicit material. This proposal raises the question whether a mandatory separate domain would violate the First Amendment, and this report focuses on that question.

It is unclear whether making a ".xxx" domain mandatory would violate the First Amendment. Whether it would be constitutional might depend upon whether a court viewed it as a content-based restriction on speech or as analogous to the zoning of adult theaters, or even as a mere disclosure requirement that did not raise a significant First Amendment issue. If a court viewed it as a content-based restriction on speech, then it would be constitutional only if the court found that it served a compelling governmental interest by the least restrictive means. Other factors that could affect its constitutionality might be whether it imposed criminal penalties and whether it were limited to websites that are predominantly pornographic.

Chapter 10 - Internet "harassment" presents new challenges for legislators in terms of defining and prosecuting such activity. Definitions for these terms vary based upon jurisdiction. Internet harassment usually encompasses "cyberstalking," "cyberharassment," and/or "cyberbullying." If one were to categorize these offenses based on danger or greatest potential harm, cyberstalking would be the most dangerous, followed by cyberharassment and then cyberbullying. Generally, cyberstalking includes a credible threat of harm, while the other two do not. Cyberharassment and/or cyberbullying may cause embarrassment, annoyance, or humiliation to the victim. Some individuals use the terms cyberharassment and cyberbullying interchangeably, while others reserve the term cyberbullying to describe harassment between minors, usually within the school context.

While laws that address cyberstalking exist at both the federal and state levels, the question of how to handle situations that do not involve a credible threat of harm against minors has drawn congressional interest. Recent high-profile cases involving teen suicides illustrate the harmful effects of Internet harassment on young people. To address the problem, H.R. 1966 was introduced in the 111th Congress. This bill would amend title 18 of the United States Code by making cyberbullying a federal crime with a punishment of up to two years of imprisonment and/or a fine.

Legislators have traditionally enacted laws prohibiting child pornography, child luring, and child sexual exploitation. However, Internet harassment potentially causes emotional harm to its victims as opposed to the physical harm inflicted by the aforementioned activities. In addressing these concerns, legislators strive to maintain a balance between enacting statutes broad enough to cover undesirable behavior, while simultaneously narrow enough to prevent infringement upon an individual's right to express oneself under the First Amendment.

The First Amendment protects certain forms of speech, but this protection is limited within the school environment. While school administrators have more flexibility in disciplining children whose speech disrupts the learning environment, this flexibility does not cover all forms of Internet harassment. As Internet harassment is a relatively new phenomenon, courts are just beginning to determine the constitutionality and scope of these school policies and statutes. This report discusses Internet crimes, such as cyberbullying, cyberharassment, and cyberstalking, along with the limitations of such laws in the current environment. It will be updated as events warrant.

Chapter 11 - In the decade between 1994 and 2004, the number of U.S. adults using the Internet increased from 15% to 63%, and by 2005, stood at 78.6%. From electronic mail to accessing information to watching videos to online purchasing, the Internet touches almost every aspect of modern life. The extent to which use of the Internet continues to grow, however, may be affected by a number of technology policy issues being debated in Congress.

First is the availability of high-speed — or "broadband" — Internet access. Broadband Internet access gives users the ability to send and receive data at speeds far greater than "dial-up" Internet access over traditional telephone lines. With deployment of broadband technologies accelerating, Congress is seeking to ensure fair competition and timely broadband deployment to all sectors and geographical locations of American society.

Next are a range of issues that reflect challenges faced by those who do use the Internet, such as security, privacy (including spyware and identity theft), unsolicited commercial electronic mail ("spam"), protecting children from unsuitable material (such as pornography), and computer security, including the vulnerability of the nation's critical infrastructures to cyber attacks.

Other issues include the Internet's domain name system (DNS), which is administered by a nonprofit corporation called the Internet Corporation for Assigned Names and Numbers (ICANN). With the Department of Commerce currently exercising legal authority over ICANN, Congress continues to monitor the administration of the DNS, particularly with respect to issues such as privacy, governance, and protecting children on the Internet.

The evolving role of the Internet in the political economy of the United States also continues to attract congressional attention. Among the issues are what changes may be needed at the Federal Communications Commission in the Internet age, federal support for information technology research and development, provision of online services by the government ("e-government"), and availability and use of "open source" software by the government.

A number of laws already have been passed on many of these issues. Congress is monitoring the effectiveness of these laws, and assessing what other legislation may be needed. Other CRS reports referenced in this document track legislation, and the reader should consult those reports, which are updated more frequently than this one, for current information.

In: Trends in Internet Research
Editor: B.G. Kutais
ISBN: 978-1-59454-140-7

Chapter 1

"SPAM": AN OVERVIEW OF ISSUES CONCERNING COMMERCIAL ELECTRONIC MAIL

Patricia Moloney Figliola*

ABSTRACT

Spam, also called unsolicited commercial email (UCE) or "junk email," aggravates many computer users. Not only can spam be a nuisance, but its cost may be passed on to consumers through higher charges from Internet service providers who must upgrade their systems to handle the traffic. Also, some spam involves fraud, or includes adult-oriented material that offends recipients or that parents want to protect their children from seeing. Proponents of UCE insist it is a legitimate marketing technique that is protected by the First Amendment, and that some consumers want to receive such solicitations.

On December 16, 2003, President Bush signed into law the Controlling the Assault of Non-Solicited Pornography and Marketing (CAN-SPAM) Act, P.L. 108-187. It went into effect on January 1, 2004. The CAN-SPAM Act does not ban UCE. Rather, it allows marketers to send commercial email as long as it conforms with the law, such as including a legitimate opportunity for consumers to "opt-out" of receiving future commercial emails from that sender. It preempts state laws that specifically address spam, but not state laws that are not specific to email, such as trespass, contract, or tort law, or other state laws to the extent they relate to fraud or computer crime. It does not require a centralized "Do Not Email" registry to be created by the Federal Trade Commission (FTC), similar to the National Do Not Call registry for telemarketing. The law requires only that the FTC develop a plan and timetable for establishing such a registry, and to inform Congress of any concerns it has with regard to establishing it. The FTC submitted a report to Congress on June 15, 2004, concluding that a Do Not Email registry could actually increase spam.

Proponents of CAN-SPAM have argued that consumers are most irritated by *fraudulent* email, and that the law should reduce the volume of such email because of the civil and criminal penalties included therein. Opponents counter that consumers object to

---

* This is an edited, reformatted and augmented version of a Congressional Research Service Publication, Order Code RL31953, Prepared for Members and Committees of Congress, Updated May 14, 2008.

unsolicited commercial email, and since the law legitimizes commercial email (as long as it conforms with the law's provisions), consumers actually may receive more, not fewer, UCE messages. Thus, whether or not "spam" is reduced depends in part on whether it is defined as only fraudulent commercial email, or all unsolicited commercial email. Many observers caution that consumers should not expect any law to solve the spam problem — that consumer education and technological advancements also are needed.

Note: This report was originally written by Marcia S. Smith; the author acknowledges her contribution to CRS coverage of this issue area.

INTRODUCTION

One aspect of increased use of the Internet for electronic mail (e-mail) has been the advent of unsolicited advertising, also called "unsolicited commercial e-mail" (UCE), "unsolicited bulk e-mail," "junk e-mail, "or "spam."[1] Complaints often focus on the fact that some spam contains, or has links to, pornography; that much of it is fraudulent; and the volume of spam is steadily increasing.[2] However, recent research shows that Internet users' concerns about spam are actually decreasing, even while the volume of spam continues to increase. For example, in a survey conducted by the Pew Internet & American Life Project during February and March 2007, respondents stated that they were "less bothered by [spam]" now than they reported being in the previous survey, conducted in June 2003. Specifically, in the 2003 survey, 25% of respondents stated that spam was a "big problem"; in the 2007 survey, that figure had dropped to 18%. Even more striking is that the percentage of participants who responded that spam was "not a problem at all" rose from 16% to 28% between 2003 and 2007. The percentage of respondents stating that spam is "an annoyance, but not a big problem" has stayed roughly the same at 57% and 51% in 2003 and 2007, respectively.[3]

One reason for this change in attitude towards spam is attributed to Internet users' growing savvy with identifying spam on their own as well as their increased use of spam filters (whether provided by their Internet service provider (ISP) or purchased on their own). In 2007, 71% of Internet users use filters, up from 65% in 2005.[4]

DEFINING SPAM

One challenge in debating the issue of spam is defining it.[5] To some, it is any commercial e-mail to which the recipient did not "opt-in" by giving prior *affirmative consent* to receiving it. To others, it is commercial e-mail to which *affirmative* or *implied consent* was not given, where implied consent can be defined in various ways (such as whether there is a pre-existing business relationship). Still others view spam as "unwanted" commercial e-mail. Whether or not a particular e-mail is unwanted, of course, varies per recipient. Since senders of UCE do find buyers for some of their products, it can be argued that at least some UCE is reaching interested consumers, and therefore is wanted, and thus is not spam. Consequently, some argue that marketers should be able to send commercial e-mail messages as long as they allow each recipient an opportunity to indicate that future such e-mails are not desired (called "opt-out"). Another group considers spam to be only fraudulent commercial e-mail, and believe that commercial e-mail messages from "legitimate" senders should be permitted. The DMA, for example, considers spam to be only fraudulent UCE.

The differences in defining spam add to the complexity of devising legislative or regulatory remedies for it. Some of the bills introduced in the 108th Congress took the approach of defining commercial e-mail, and permitting such e-mail to be sent to recipients as long as it conformed with certain requirements. Other bills defined *unsolicited* commercial e-mail and prohibited it from being sent unless it met certain requirements. The final law, the CAN-SPAM Act (see below), took the former approach, defining and allowing marketers to send such e-mail as long as they abide by the terms of the law, such as ensuring that the e-mail does not have fraudulent header information or deceptive subject headings, and includes an opt-out opportunity and other features that proponents argue will allow recipients to take control of their in-boxes. Proponents of the law argue that consumers will benefit because they should see a reduction in fraudulent e-mails. Opponents of the law counter that it legitimizes sending commercial e-mail, and to the extent that consumers do not want to receive such e-mails, the amount of unwanted e-mail actually may increase. If the legislation reduces the amount of fraudulent e-mail, but not the amount of unwanted e-mail, the extent to which it reduces "spam" would depend on what definition of that word is used.

On December 16, 2004, the FTC issued its final rule defining the term "commercial electronic mail message," but explicitly declined to define "spam."

Avoiding and Reporting Spam

Tips on avoiding spam are available on the FTC website[6] and from Consumers Union.[7] Consumers may file a complaint about spam with the FTC by visiting the FTC website and choosing "File a Complaint" at the bottom of the page.[8] The offending spam also may be forwarded to the FTC, at spam@uce.gov, to assist the FTC in monitoring spam trends and developments. The September 2004 issue of *Consumer Reports* has a cover story about spam, including ratings of commercially available spam filters consumers can load onto their computers. Also, individual ISPs use spam filters (though the filters may not catch all spam) and have mechanisms available for subscribers to report spam.

Foreign Spam

Controlling spam is complicated by the fact that some of it originates outside the United States and thus is not subject to U.S. laws or regulations. Spam is a global problem, and a 2001 study by the European Commission concluded that Internet subscribers globally pay 10 billion Euros a year in connection costs to download spam.[9] Some European officials complain that the United States is the source of most spam, and the U.S. decision to adopt an opt-out approach in the CAN-SPAM Act (discussed below) was not helpful.[10] In April 2005, a British anti-spam and anti-virus software developing company, Sophos, listed the United States as the largest spam producing country, exporting 35.7% of spam (down from 42.1% in December 2004); South Korea was second, at 25% (up from 13.4% in December 2004).[11]

Tracing the origin of any particular piece of spam can be difficult because some spammers route their messages through other computers (discussed below) that may be located anywhere on the globe.

THE FEDERAL CAN-SPAM ACT: SUMMARY OF MAJOR PROVISIONS

The 108th Congress passed the CAN-SPAM Act, S. 877, which merged provisions from several House and Senate bills.[12] Signed into law by President Bush on December 16, 2003 (P.L. 108-187), it went into effect on January 1, 2004.[13] P.L. 108-187 includes the following major provisions.

- Commercial e-mail may be sent to recipients as long as the message conforms with the following requirements:
    - transmission information in the header is not false or misleading;
    - subject headings are not deceptive;
    - a functioning return e-mail address or comparable mechanism is included to enable recipients to indicate they do not wish to receive future commercial e-mail messages from that sender at the e-mail address where the message was received;
    - the e-mail is not sent to a recipient by the sender, or anyone acting on behalf of the sender, more than 10 days after the recipient has opted-out, unless the recipient later gives affirmative consent to receive the e-mail (i.e., opts back in); and
    - the e-mail must be clearly and conspicuously identified as an advertisement or solicitation (although the legislation does not state how or where that identification must be made).

- Commercial e-mail is defined as e-mail, the primary purpose of which is the commercial advertisement or promotion of a commercial product or service (including content on an Internet website operated for a commercial purpose). It does not include transactional or relationship messages (see next bullet). The act directs the FTC to issue regulations within 12 months of enactment to define the criteria to facilitate determination of an e-mail's primary purpose. The FTC did so on December 16, 2004.
- Some requirements (including the prohibition on deceptive subject headings, and the opt-out requirement) do not apply if the message is a "transactional or relationship message," which include various types of notifications, such as periodic notifications of account balance or other information regarding a subscription, membership, account, loan or comparable ongoing commercial relationship involving the ongoing purchase or use by the recipient of products or services offered by the sender; providing information directly related to an employment relationship or related benefit plan in which the recipient is currently involved, participating, or enrolled; or delivering goods or services, including product updates or upgrades, that the

recipient is entitled to receive under the terms of a transaction that the recipient has previously agreed to enter into with the sender. The act allows, but does not require, the FTC to modify that definition.

- Sexually-oriented commercial e-mail must include, in the subject heading, a "warning label" to be prescribed by the FTC (in consultation with the Attorney General), indicating its nature. The warning label does not have to be in the subject line, however, if the message that is initially viewable by the recipient does not contain the sexually oriented material, but only a link to it. In that case, the warning label, and the identifier, opt-out, and physical address required under section 5 (a)(5) of the act; must be contained in the initially viewable e-mail message as well. Sexually oriented material is defined as any material that depicts sexually explicit conduct, unless the depiction constitutes a small and insignificant part of the whole, the remainder of which is not primarily devoted to sexual matters. These provisions do not apply, however, if the recipient has given prior affirmative consent to receiving such e-mails.
- Businesses may not knowingly promote themselves with e-mail that has false or misleading transmission information.
- State laws specifically related to spam are preempted, but not other state laws that are not specific to electronic mail, such as trespass, contract, or tort law, or other state laws to the extent they relate to fraud or computer crime.
- Violators may be sued by FTC, state attorneys general, and ISPs (but not by individuals).
- Violators of many of the provisions of the act are subject to statutory damages of up to $250 per e-mail, to a maximum of up to $2 million, which may be tripled by the court (to $6 million) for "aggravated violations."
- Violators may be fined, or sentenced to up to 3 or five years in prison (depending on the offense), or both, for accessing someone else's computer without authorization and using it to send multiple commercial e-mail messages; sending multiple commercial e-mail messages with the intent to deceive or mislead recipients or ISPs as to the origin of such messages; materially falsifying header information in multiple commercial e-mail messages; registering for five or more e-mail accounts or online user accounts, or two or more domain names, using information that materially falsifies the identity of the actual registrant, and sending multiple commercial e-mail messages from any combination of such accounts or domain names; or falsely representing oneself to be the registrant or legitimate successor in interest to the registrant of five of more Internet Protocol addresses, and sending multiple commercial e-mail messages from such addresses. "Multiple" means more than 100 e¬mail messages during a 24-hour period, more than 1,000 during a 30-day period, or more than 10,000 during a one-year period. Sentencing enhancements are provided for certain acts.
- The Federal Communications Commission, in consultation with the FTC, must prescribe rules to protect users of wireless devices from unwanted commercial messages. (The rules were issued in August 2004. See CRS Report RL3 1636, *Wireless Privacy and Spam: Issues for Congress*, by Marcia S. Smith, for more on this topic.)

Conversely, the act does not —

- Create a "Do Not Email registry" where consumers can place their e-mail addresses in a centralized database to indicate they do not want commercial e-mail. The law required only that the FTC develop a plan and timetable for establishing such a registry and to inform Congress of any concerns it has with regard to establishing it. (The FTC released that report in June 2004; see next section.)
- Require that consumers "opt-in" before receiving commercial e-mail.
- Require commercial e-mail to include an identifier such as "ADV" in the subject line to indicate it is an advertisement. The law does require the FTC to report to Congress within 18 months of enactment on a plan for requiring commercial e-mail to be identifiable from its subject line through use of "ADV" or a comparable identifier, or compliance with Internet Engineering Task Force standards, or an explanation of any concerns FTC has about such a plan.
- Include a "bounty hunter" provision to financially reward persons who identify a violator and supply information leading to the collection of a civil penalty, although the FTC must submit a report to Congress within nine months of enactment setting forth a system for doing so. (The study was released in September 2004.)

Opt-In, Opt-Out, and A "Do Not Email" Registry

Much of the debate on how to stop spam focuses on whether consumers should be given the opportunity to "opt-in" (where prior consent is required) or "opt-out" (where consent is assumed unless the consumer notifies the sender that such e-mails are not desired) of receiving UCE or all commercial e-mail. The CAN-SPAM Act is an "opt out" law, requiring senders of all commercial e-mail to provide a legitimate[14] opt-out opportunity to recipients.

During debate on the CAN- SPAM Act, several anti-spam groups argued that the legislation should go further, and prohibit commercial e-mail from being sent to recipients unless they opt-in, similar to a policy adopted by the European Union (see below). Eight U.S. groups, including Junkbusters, the Coalition Against Unsolicited Commercial Email (CAUCE), and the Consumer Federation of America, wrote a letter to several Members of Congress expressing their view that the opt-out approach (as in P.L. 108-187) would "undercut those businesses who respect consumer preferences and give legal protection to those who do not."[15] Some of the state laws (see below) adopted the opt-in approach, including California's anti-spam law.

The European Union adopted an opt-in requirement for e-mail, which became effective October 31, 2003.[16] Under the EU policy, prior affirmative consent of the recipient must be obtained before sending commercial e-mail unless there is an existing customer relationship. In that case, the sender must provide an opt-out opportunity. The EU directive sets the broad policy, but each member nation must pass its own law as to how to implement it.[17]

As noted, Congress chose opt-out instead of opt-in, however. One method of implementing opt-out is to create a "Do Not Email" registry where consumers could place their names on a centralized list to opt-out of all commercial e-mail instead of being required to respond to individual e-mails. The concept is similar to the National Do Not Call registry where consumers can indicate they do not want to receive telemarketing calls. During consideration of the CAN-SPAM Act, then-FTC Chairman Timothy Muris and other FTC officials repeatedly expressed skepticism about the advisability of a Do Not Email registry despite widespread public support for it.[18] One worry is that the database containing the e-mail addresses of all those who do not want spam would be vulnerable to hacking, or spammers otherwise might be able to use it to obtain the e-mail addresses of individuals who explicitly do not want to receive spam. In an August 19, 2003, speech to the Aspen Institute, Mr. Muris commented that the concept of a Do Not Email registry was interesting, "but it is unclear how we can make it work" because it would not be enforceable.[19] "If it were established, my advice to consumers would be: Don't waste the time and effort to sign up."

Following initial Senate passage of S. 877, an unnamed FTC official was quoted by the *Washington Post* as saying that the FTC's position on the registry is unchanged, and "Congress would have to change the law" to require the FTC to create it.[20] After the House passed S. 877, Mr. Muris released a statement complimenting Congress on taking a positive step in the fight against spam, but cautioned again that legislation alone will not solve the problem.[21]

CAN-SPAM Act Provision

The CAN-SPAM Act did not require the FTC to create a Do Not Email registry.[22] Instead, it required the FTC to submit a plan and timetable for establishing a registry, authorized the FTC to create it, and instructed the FTC to explain to Congress any concerns about establishing it.

FTC Implementation

The FTC issued its report to Congress on June 15, 2004.[23] The report concluded that without a technical system to authenticate the origin of e-mail messages, a Do Not Email registry would not reduce the amount of spam, and, in fact, might increase it.

The FTC report stated that "spammers would most likely use a Registry as a mechanism for verifying the validity of e-mail addresses and, without authentication, the Commission would be largely powerless to identify those responsible for misusing the Registry. Moreover, a Registry-type solution to spam would raise serious security, privacy, and enforcement difficulties." (p. I) The report added that protecting children from "the Internet's most dangerous users, including pedophiles," would be difficult if the Registry identified accounts used by children in order to assist legitimate marketers from sending inappropriate messages to them. (p. I) The FTC described several registry models that had been suggested, and computer security techniques that some claimed would eliminate or alleviate security and privacy risks. The FTC stated that it carefully examined those techniques — a centralized scrubbing of marketers' distribution lists, converting addresses to one- way hashes (a cryptographic approach), and seeding the Registry with "canary" e-mail addresses — to determine if they could effectively control the risks "and has concluded that none of them would be effective." (p. 16)

The FTC concluded that a necessary prerequisite for a Do Not Email registry is an authentication system that prevents the origin of e-mail messages from being falsified, and proposed a program to encourage the adoption by industry of an authentication standard. If a single standard does not emerge from the private sector after a sufficient period of time, the FTC report said the Commission would initiate a process to determine if a federally mandated standard is required. If the government mandates a standard, the FTC would then consider studying whether an authentication system, coupled with enforcement or other mechanisms, had substantially reduced the amount of spam. If not, the Commission would then reconsider whether or not a Do Not Email registry is needed.

On August 1, 2005, the FTC issued a press release summarizing the results of testing it had conducted to determine if online retailers were honoring opt-out requests. The FTC found that 89% of the merchants it tested did, in fact, stop sending e-mails when requested to do so.[24]

Labels

Another approach to restraining spam is requiring that senders of commercial e-mail use a label, such as "ADV," in the subject line of the message, so the recipient will know before opening an e-mail message that it is an advertisement. That would also make it easier for spam filtering software to identify commercial e-mail and eliminate it. Some propose that adult-oriented spam have a special label, such as ADV-ADLT, to highlight that the e-mail may contain material or links that are inappropriate for children, such as pornography.

CAN-SPAM Act Provision

The CAN-SPAM Act: (1) requires clear and conspicuous identification that a commercial e-mail is an advertisement, but is not specific about how or where that identification must be made; (2) requires the FTC to prescribe warning labels for sexually-oriented e-mails within 120 days of enactment; and (3) requires the FTC to submit a report within 18 months of enactment setting forth a plan for requiring commercial e-mail to be identifiable from its subject line using ADV or a comparable identifier, or by means of compliance with Internet Engineering Task Force standards. However, the clear and conspicuous identification that a commercial e-mail is an advertisement, and the warning label for sexually-oriented material, are not required if the recipient has given prior affirmative consent to receipt of such messages.

FTC Implementation

On May 19, 2004, an FTC rule regarding labeling of sexually oriented commercial e-mail went into effect. The rule was adopted by the FTC (5-0) on April 13, 2004. A press release and the text of the ruling are available on the FTC's website.[25] The rule requires that the mark "SEXUALLY-EXPLICIT" be included both in the subject line of any commercial e-mail containing sexually oriented material, and in the body of the message in what the FTC called the "electronic equivalent of a 'brown paper wrapper.'" The FTC explained that the "brown paper wrapper" is what a recipient initially sees when opening the e-mail, and it may not contain any other information or images except what the FTC prescribes. The rule also clarifies that the FTC interprets the CAN-SPAM Act provisions to include both visual images and written descriptions of sexually explicit conduct.

On July 20, 2005, the FTC announced that it had charged seven companies with violating federal laws requiring these labels. Four of the companies settled with the FTC, which imposed a total of $1.159 million in civil penalties. U.S. District Court suits were filed against the other three companies.[26]

The act also required the FTC to submit a report to Congress on a plan for making commercial e-mail identifiable from its subject line, or to explain what concerns would lead the FTC to recommend against such a plan. That report was submitted in June 2005. It concluded that requiring UCE senders to use a prefix such as ADV probably would not result in less spam.

> Experience with subject line labeling requirements in the states and in other countries does not support the notion that such requirements are an effective means of reducing spam.... Indeed, spam filters widely available at little or no cost ... more effectively empower consumers to set individualized email preferences to reduce unwanted UCE from both spammers and legitimate marketers. Mandatory subject line labeling, by comparison, would be an imprecise tool ... that, at best, might make it easier to segregate *labeled* UCE from *unlabeled* UCE. ... [I]t is extremely unlikely that outlaw spammers would comply with a requirement to label the email messages they send. By contrast, legitimate marketers likely *would* comply.... As a result ... labeled UCE messages sent by law-abiding senders would be filtered out. Meanwhile, unlabeled UCE messages sent by outlaw spammers would still reach consumers' in-boxes.[27] (Italics in original.)

Other Implementation Actions

The act required the FTC or the Federal Communications Commission (FCC) to take a number of other actions with regard to implementing the CAN-SPAM Act. The FTC routinely issues Notices of Proposed Rulemaking or the results thereof regarding this act, which are too numerous to include in this report. Selected issues are addressed below. See the FTC's spam website [http://www.ftc.gov/spam] for more information.

Wireless Spam

The act required the FCC to issue regulations concerning spam on wireless devices such as cell phones. The FCC issued those regulations in August 2004.[28]

"Bounty Hunter" Provision

The act required the FTC to conduct a study on whether rewarding persons who identify a spammer and supply information leading to the collection of a civil penalty could be an effective technique for controlling spam (the "bounty hunter" provision). The study was released on September 15, 2004.[29] The FTC concluded that the benefits of such a system are unclear because, for example, without large rewards (in the $100,000 to $250,000 range) and a certain level of assurance that they would receive the reward, whistleblowers might not be willing to assume the risks of providing such information. The FTC offered five recommendations if Congress wants to pursue such an approach:

- tie eligibility for a reward to imposition of a final court order, instead of to collecting a civil penalty;
- fund the rewards through congressional appropriations, instead of through collected civil penalties;
- restrict reward eligibility to insiders with high-value information;

- exempt FTC decisions on eligibility for rewards from judicial or administrative review; and
- establish reward amounts high enough to attract insiders with high- value information.

Definition of "Primary Purpose"

The act required the FTC to issue regulations, within one year of enactment, defining the relevant criteria to facilitate determination of an e-mail's "primary purpose." The FTC issued its final rule on December 16, 2004, exactly one year after the law was enacted. According to the FTC's press release,[30] the final rule clarifies that the Commission does not intend to regulate non-commercial speech. It differentiates between commercial content and "transactional or relationship" content in defining the primary purpose of an e-mail message.

- If an e-mail contains only a commercial advertisement or promotion of a commercial product or service, its primary purpose is deemed to be commercial.
- If an e-mail contains both commercial content and transactional or relationship content, the primary purpose is deemed to be commercial if the recipient would likely conclude that it was commercial through reasonable interpretation of the subject line, or if the transactional and relationship content does not appear in whole or in substantial part at the beginning of the body of the message.
- If an e-mail contains both commercial content, and content that is neither commercial content nor transactional or relationship content, the primary purpose is deemed to be commercial if the recipient would likely conclude that it was commercial through reasonable interpretation of the subject line, or if the recipient would likely conclude the primary purpose was commercial through reasonable interpretation of the body of the message.
- If an e-mail contains only transactional or relationship content, it is not deemed to be a commercial e-mail message.

"Commercial" content is defined in the final rule as "the commercial advertisement or promotion of a commercial product or service," which includes "content on an Internet website operated for a commercial purpose." That is the same as the definition in the CAN-SPAM Act.[31]

The FTC specifically declined to define the term "spam" because the act sets forth a regulatory scheme built around the terms "commercial electronic mail message" and "transactional or relationship message."[32]

Related Legislation

On December 22, 2006, President Bush signed the Undertaking Spam, Spyware, And Fraud Enforcement With Enforcers beyond Borders Act of 2005 (U.S. SAFE WEB Act, (P.L. 109-455). The law allows the FTC and parallel foreign law enforcement agencies to share information while investigating allegations of "unfair and deceptive practices" that involve foreign commerce, but raised some privacy concerns because the FTC would not be required to make public any of the information it obtained through foreign sources.

Legal Actions Based on the CAN-SPAM Act

Many lawsuits have been brought against spammers. The following discussion is illustrative, not comprehensive.

On October 10, 2007, the FTC announced that it had filed a civil lawsuit against an international enterprise, with defendants in the United States, Canada, and Australia, that used spam to drive traffic to websites selling pills that the FTC alleges do not work.[33] The FTC's spam database received over 175,000 spam messages sent on behalf of the operation. The action, announced at an international meeting of government authorities and private industry about spam, spyware, and other online threats, is the first brought by the agency using the U.S. SAFE WEB Act to share information with foreign partners. In addition, the FTC alleges that the operation violated the CAN-SPAM Act by initiating commercial e-mails that contained false "from" addresses and deceptive subject lines, and failed to provide an opt-out link or physical postal address.

On April 29, 2004, the FTC announced that it had filed a civil lawsuit against a Detroit-based spam operation, Phoenix Avatar, and the Department of Justice (DOJ) announced that it had arrested two (and were seeking two more) Detroit-area men associated with the company who are charged with sending hundreds of thousands of spam messages using false and fraudulent headers.[34] The FTC charged Phoenix Avatar with making deceptive claims about a diet patch sold via the spam in violation of the FTC Act, and with violations of the CAN- SPAM Act because the spam did not contain a valid opt-out opportunity and the "reply to" and "from" addresses were fraudulent. The DOJ filed criminal charges against the men under the CAN-SPAM Act for sending multiple commercial e-mails with materially false or fraudulent return addresses. According to the FTC, from January 1, 2004 until the lawsuit was filed, about 490,000 of the spam messages forwarded by consumers to the FTC were linked to Avatar Phoenix.

The FTC simultaneously announced that it had filed a legal action against an Australian spam enterprise operating out of Australia and New Zealand called Global Web Promotions. The FTC stated that it was assisted by the Australian Competition and Consumer Commission and the New Zealand Commerce Committee in bringing the case. According to the FTC, since January 1, 2004, among the spam forwarded by consumers to the FTC, about 399,000 are linked to Global Web Promotions. The FTC charges that a diet patch, and human growth hormone products, sold by Global Web Promotions are deceptive and in violation of the FTC Act. The products are shipped from within the United States. The FTC further charges that the spam violates the CAN-SPAM Act because of fraudulent headers.

The FTC also filed a complaint against six companies and five individuals who, the FTC alleges, acting as a single business enterprise, sent e-mails containing sexually-explicit content without the required warning label and violated other provisions of the Adult Labeling Rule, the CAN-SPAM Act, and the FTC Act.[35] A federal district court issued a Temporary Restraining Order against the defendants.

Separately, four of the largest ISPs — AOL, Earthlink, Microsoft, and Yahoo! — working together as part of the Anti-Spam Alliance, filed civil suits under the CAN-SPAM

Act against hundreds of alleged spammers in March 2004.[36] The suits were filed in federal courts in California, Georgia, Virginia and Washington. A number of other suits since have been filed.

The Massachusetts Attorney General filed the first state CAN-SPAM case against a Florida business called DC Enterprises, and its proprietor William T. Carson in July 2004, which also was filed under the Massachusetts Consumer Protection Act.[37] That case was settled by DC Enterprises and Mr. Carson, who agreed to pay $25,000, halt further violations of the CAN-SPAM Act, and comply with state regulations regarding mortgage brokers.[38]

It should be noted, however, that some ISPs are having difficulty recovering monetary judgments from spam cases (though not necessarily cases brought under the CAN-SPAM Act). Microsoft, for example, reportedly has won $620 million in judgments, but has collected only $500,000.[39]

Federal Trade Commission Activity

The FTC enforces the CAN- SPAM Act and conducts other consumer-education initiatives related to combating spam.

May 2008 Rules on CAN-SPAM Compliance

On May 12, 2008, the FTC approved new four new provisions clarifying the requirements of the CAN-SPAM Act. The provisions are intended to clarify the Act's requirements.

The new rule provisions address four topics: (1) an e-mail recipient cannot be required to pay a fee, provide information other than his or her e-mail address and opt-out preferences, or take any steps other than sending a reply e-mail message or visiting a single Internet Web page to opt out of receiving future e-mail from a sender; (2) the definition of "sender" was modified to make it easier to determine which of multiple parties advertising in a single e-mail message is responsible for complying with the Act's opt-out requirements; (3) a "sender" of commercial e-mail can include an accurately-registered post office box or private mailbox established under United States Postal Service regulations to satisfy the Act's requirement that a commercial e-mail display a "valid physical postal address"; and (4) a definition of the term "person" was added to clarify that CAN-SPAM's obligations are not limited to natural persons.

In addition, the Commission's Statement of Basis and Purpose (SBP) accompanying the final rule addresses a number of topics that are not the subject of any new rule provisions. These include: CAN-SPAM's definition of "transactional or relationship message"; the Commission's decision not to alter the length of time a "sender" of commercial e-mail has to honor an opt-out request; the Commission's determination not to designate additional "aggravated violations" under the Act; and the Commission's views on how CAN-SPAM applies to forward-to-a-"friend" e-mail marketing campaigns, in which someone either receives a commercial e-mail message and forwards the e-mail to another person, or uses a Web-based mechanism to forward a link to or copy of a Web page to another person. The

SBP explains that, as a general matter, if the seller offers something of value in exchange for forwarding a commercial message, the seller must comply with the Act's requirements, such as honoring opt-out requests.

December 2007 Staff Report on Malicious Spam and Phishing

In this staff report, the FTC describes findings from its July 2007 workshop, "Spam Summit: The Next Generation of Threats and Solutions" and proposes follow- up action steps that stakeholders can adopt to mitigate the harmful effects of malicious spam and phishing. In addition to proposing action steps for stakeholders, the report provides an overview of the agency's role in protecting consumers from the threats of fraudulent spam and phishing. The report also announces results from the FTC's 2007 Harvesting and Filtering Study, which suggest that Internet service providers' spam filters continue to serve an integral role in reducing the amount of spam that reaches consumers' in-boxes.

July 2007 Spam Summit

In July 2007, the FTC hosted "Spam Summit: The Next Generation of Threats and Solutions."[40] This event was a follow-on effort of the FTC's 2003 Spam Forum. Issues included defining the problem; new methods for sending spam; the "covert economy" (e.g., to what extent does stolen information, such as government-issued identity numbers, credit cards, bank cards and personal identification numbers, user accounts, and e-mail addresses, play a role in spam?); deterring malicious spammers and cybercriminals; emerging threats (e.g., what emerging threats are occurring in media other than e-mail including spam over instant messaging, etc.?); putting consumers back in control (how can we empower consumers and businesses in the fight against spam and malware?); and stakeholder best practices.

December 2005 Assessment of the CAN-SPAM Act

Under the law, the FTC was required to provide Congress with an assessment of the act's effectiveness, and recommend any necessary changes. The FTC submitted its report in December 2005.[41] The FTC concluded that the act has been effective in terms of adoption of commercial e-mail "best practices" that are followed by "legitimate" online marketers, and in terms of providing law enforcement agencies and ISPs with an additional tool to use against spammers. Additionally, the FTC concluded that the volume of spam has begun to stabilize, and the amount reaching individuals' inboxes has decreased because of improved anti-spam technologies.[42] However, it also found that the international dimension of spam has not changed significantly, and that there has been a shift toward the inclusion of "increasingly malicious" content in spam messages, such as "malware," which is intended to harm the recipient. Other negative changes noted by the FTC are that spammers are using increasingly complex multi-layered business arrangements to frustrate law enforcement, and are hiding their identities by providing false information to domain registrars (the "Whois" database).

The FTC did not recommend any changes to the CAN-SPAM Act, but encouraged Congress to pass the US SAFE WEB Act (S. 1608, see next paragraph), noted that continued consumer education efforts are needed, and called for improved anti-spam technologies, particularly domain-level authentication (discussed later in this report).

STATE LAWS REGULATING SPAM

Thirty-eight states have passed laws regulating spam: Alaska, Arizona, Arkansas, California, Colorado, Connecticut, Delaware, Florida, Georgia, Idaho, Illinois, Indiana, Iowa, Kansas, Louisiana, Maine, Maryland, Michigan, Minnesota, Missouri, Nevada, New Mexico, North Carolina, North Dakota, Ohio, Oklahoma, Oregon, Pennsylvania, Rhode Island, South Dakota, Tennessee, Texas, Utah, Virginia, Washington, West Virginia, Wisconsin, and Wyoming.[43]

The CAN-SPAM Act preempts state spam laws, but not other state laws that are not specific to electronic mail, such as trespass, contract, or tort law, or other state laws to the extent they relate to fraud or computer crime. California passed an anti-spam law that would have become effective January 1, 2004 and was considered relatively strict. It required opt-in for UCE unless there was a prior business relationship, in which case, opt-out is required. The anticipated implementation of that California law is often cited as one of the factors that stimulated Congress to complete action on a less restrictive, preemptive federal law before the end of 2003.[44]

A number of lawsuits have been filed under the state laws. Two notable cases involve the Maryland and Virginia laws. In December 2004, a Maryland judge ruled that Maryland's anti-spam law is unconstitutional, because it seeks to regulate commerce outside of the state.[45] An individual, Eric Menhart, who was a resident of the District of Columbia, but had a business in Maryland whose domain name was "maryland-state-resident.com," filed suit against a New York-based spammer. According to the spamlaws.com website, the Maryland law prohibits sending commercial e-mail that uses a third party's domain name without permission, or that contains false or missing routing information, or with a false or misleading subject line. The law applies, *inter alia*, to e-mail sent from within Maryland, or if the sender knows that the recipient is a Maryland resident. Mr. Menhart reportedly is appealing the ruling.

A lawsuit brought under Virginia's anti-spam law, however, led to a conviction of two North Carolina residents: Jeremy Jaynes, and his sister, Jessica DeGroot. According to the spamlaws.com website, the Virginia law makes it illegal, *inter alia*, to send unsolicited bulk e-mails containing falsified routing information, and allows the court to exercise personal jurisdiction over a nonresident who uses a computer or computer network located in Virginia. The case reportedly is the first felony spam case in the country. According to press accounts, Mr. Jaynes and Ms. DeGroot were convicted of misrepresenting the origin of e-mails that sold software and other products (a third defendant was acquitted). The e-mails went through AOL servers located in Virginia. Ms. DeGroot's conviction was later overturned, and Mr. Jaynes, who was sentenced to nine years in prison, appealed his conviction;[46] his conviction was upheld by a three-judge panel for the Virginia Court of Appeals on September 5, 2006. Jaynes plans to appeal this decision, as well, but Virginia Attorney General Robert McDonnell said in a statement that his office plans to ask the court to revoke bond and order Jaynes to begin serving his sentence.[47]

End Notes

[1] The origin of the term spam for unsolicited commercial e-mail was recounted in *Computerworld*, April 5, 1999, p. 70: "It all started in early Internet chat rooms and interactive fantasy games where someone repeating the same sentence or comment was said to be making a 'spam.' The term referred to a Monty Python's Flying Circus scene in which actors keep saying 'Spam, Spam, Spam and Spam' when reading options from a menu."

[2] This report does not address junk mail or junk fax. See CRS Report RL32 177, *Federal Advertising Law: An Overview*, by Henry Cohen, or CRS Report RS2 1647, *Facsimile Advertising Rules Under the Junk Fax Prevention Act of 2005*, by Patricia Moloney Figliola, respectively, for information on those topics

[3] Pew Internet & American Life Project. Pew Internet Project Data Memo. May 2007. Available at [http://www.pewinternet.org/pdfs/PIP_Spam_May_2007.pdf].

[4] Pew Internet & American Life Project. Pew Internet Project Data Memo. May 2007. Available at [http://www.pewinternet.org/pdfs/PIP_Spam_May_2007.pdf].

[5] "Spam" generally refers to e-mail, rather than other forms of electronic communication. The term "spim," for example, is used for unsolicited advertising via Instant Messaging. "Spit" refers to unsolicited advertising via Voice Over Internet Protocol (VOIP). Unsolicited advertising on wireless devices such as cell phones is called "wireless spam."

[6] See [http : //www .ftc .gov/bcp], [http : //onguardonline .gov/index.html], and [http://www.ftc.gov/spam/].

[7] See [http://www.consumersunion.org/pub/core_product_safety/0002 1 0.html]. Additional spam information is available from CU online at [http://www.consumerreports.org/cro/ electronics-computers/computers/internet-and-other-services/net-threats-9-07/spam/0709_net_spam.htm?resultPageIndex=1resultIndex=1&searchTerm=spam].

[8] The webpage to file a complaint is [https://rn.ftc.gov/pls/dod/wsolcq$.startup? Z_ORG_CODE=PU0 1].

[9] See [http://ec.europa.eu/justice_home/fsj/privacy/studies/spam_en.htm].

[10] For example, see Mitchener, Brandon. "Europe Blames Weaker U.S. Law for Spam Surge." *Wall Street Journal*, February 3, 2004, p. B1 (via Factiva).

[11] Sophos Reveals Latest "Dirty Dozen" Spam Producing Countries. Press release, April 7, 2005. The other countries on the list are: China (9.7%), France (3.2%), Spain (2.7%), Canada (2.7%), Japan (2.1%), Brazil (2%), United Kingdom (1.6%), Germany (1.2%), Australia (1.2%), and Poland (1.2). [http://www.sophos.com/pressoffice/news/articles/2005/ 04/sa_dirtydozen05 .html].

[12] Nine bills were introduced in the 108th Congress prior to passage of the CAN-SPAM Act: H.R. 1933 (Lofgren), H.R. 2214 (Burr-Tauzin-Sensenbrenner), H.R. 2515 (Wilson-Green), S. 877 (Burns-Wyden), S. 1052 (Nelson-FL), and S. 1327 (Corzine) were "opt-out" bills. S. 563 (Dayton) was a "do not e-mail" bill. S. 1231 (Schumer) combined elements of both approaches. S. 1293 (Hatch) created criminal penalties for fraudulent e-mail.

[13] The Senate originally passed S. 877 on October 22, 2003, by a vote of 97-0. As passed at that time, the bill combined elements from several of the Senate bills. The House passed (392-5) an amended version of S. 877 on November 21, 2003, melding provisions from the Senate-passed bill and several House bills. The Senate concurred in the House amendment, with an amendment, on November 25, through unanimous consent. The Senate amendment included several revisions, requiring the House to vote again on the bill. The House agreed with the Senate amendment by unanimous consent on December 8, 2003.

[14] Some spam already contains instructions, usually to send a message to an e-mail address, for how a recipient can opt-out. However, in many cases this is a ruse by the sender to trick a recipient into confirming that the e-mail has reached a valid e-mail address. The sender then sends more spam to that address and/or includes the e-mail address on lists of e-mail addresses that are sold to bulk e-mailers. It is virtually impossible for a recipient to discern whether the proffered opt-out instructions are genuine or duplicitous.

[15] See [http://www.cauce.org/node/57].

[16] See [http://www.europa.eu.int/scadplus/leg/en/lvb/l24120.htm].

[17] Not all EU nations have yet passed such legislation. According to the Associated Press (December 7, 2003, 12:30), the EU asked nine countries (Belgium, Germany, Greece, Finland, France, Luxembourg, the Netherlands, Portugal, and Sweden) to provide within two months an explanation of when they will pass such legislation. AP identified six countries that have taken steps to implement the EU law: Austria, Britain, Denmark, Ireland, Italy, and Spain. Sweden reportedly adopted spam legislation in March 2004.

[18] A survey by the ePrivacy Group found that 74% of consumers want such a list. Bowman, Lisa. "Study: Do-Not-Spam Plan Winning Support," c|net news.com, July 23, 2003, 12:28 PM PT.

[19] Muris, Timothy. The Federal Trade Commission and the Future Development of U.S. Consumer Protection Policy. Remarks to the Aspen Summit, Aspen, CP, August 19, 2003. [http://www.ftc.gov/speeches/muris/0308 1 9aspen.htm].

[20] Krim, Jonathan. "Senate Votes 97-0 to Restrict E-Mail Ads; Bill Could Lead to No-Spam Registry." *Washington Post*, October 23, 2003, p. A1 (via Factiva).

[21] U.S. Federal Trade Commission. Statement of Timothy J. Muris Regarding Passage of the Can-Spam Act of 2003. November 21, 2003. [http://www.ftc.gov/opa/ 2003/1 1/spamstmt.htm]

[22] The FTC issued a warning to consumers in February 2004 that a website (unsub.us) promoting a National Do Not Email Registry is a sham and might be collecting e-mail addresses to sell to spammers. See [http://www.ftc.gov/opa/2004/02/spamcam.htm].

[23] U.S. Federal Trade Commission. National Do Not Email Registry: A Report to Congress. Washington, FTC, June 2004. A press release, and a link to the report, is available at [http://www.ftc.gov/opa/2004/06/canspam2.htm].

[24] FTC Survey Tests Top E-Tailers' Compliance with Can-spam's Opt-Out Provisions. August 1, 2005. See [http://www.ftc.gov/opa/2005/08/optout.htm].

[25] See [http://www.ftc.gov/opa/2004/04/adultlabel.htm].

[26] FTC Cracks Down on Illegal "X-Rated" Spam. July 20, 2005. [http://www.ftc.gov/opa/2005/07/alrsweep.htm]

[27] FTC. Subject Line Labeling As A Weapon Against Spam: A Report to Congress. June 17, 2005. p. i-ii. [http://www.ftc.gov/reports/canspam05/0506 1 6canspamrpt.pdf]

[28] See CRS Report RL3 1636, *Wireless Privacy and Spam: Issues for Congress*, for more information.

[29] A press release is available at [http://www.ftc.gov/opa/2004/09/bounty.htm], and the report, A CAN-Spam Informant Reward System, is available at [http://www.ftc.gov/ reports/rewardsys/0409 1 6rewardsysrpt.pdf].

[30] FTC press release, FTC Issues Final Rule Defining What Constitutes a "Commercial Electronic Mail Message," December 16, 2004.

[31] The FTC's notice of proposed rulemaking had a slightly different definition. The final rule emphasizes that, in the final rule, the definition is the same as in the act.

[32] This explanation is offered on p. 11 of the text of the *Federal Register* notice as it appears on the FTC website at [http://www.ftc.gov/opa/2005/0 1/primarypurp.htm].

[33] "HoodiaLife" and "HoodiaPlus," was supposed to contain hoodia gordonii and cause significant weight loss; the other, called "HGHLife" and "HGHPlus," was supposed to be a "natural human growth hormone enhancer" that would dramatically reverse the aging process.

[34] (1) FTC Announces First Can-Spam Act Cases. [http://www.ftc.gov/opa/2004/ 04/040429canspam.htm]; (2) Department of Justice Announces Arrests of Detroit-Area Men on Violations of the 'Can-Spam' Act. [http://www.usdoj .gov/opa/pr/2004/April/ 04 _crm _28 1 .htm].

[35] FTC press release, Court Stops Spammers From Circulating Unwanted Sexually-Explicit E-mails, January 11, 2005. [http://www.ftc.gov/opa/2005/0 1/globalnetsolutions.htm].

[36] Mangalindan, Mylene. "Web Firms File Spam Suit Under New Law." *Wall Street Journal*, March 11, 2004, p. B4 (via Factiva).

[37] Hines, Matt. "Massachusetts Files Suit Under Can-Spam." C|NET News.com, July 2, 2004, 11:54 am PDT.

[38] Bray, Hiawatha. "Spammer to Pay $25,000 Settlement." *Boston Globe*, October 8, 2004, p. D3 (via Factiva).

[39] "ISPs Push to Collect Money from Spammers." *Communications Daily*, February 18, 2005, p. 9.

[40] The Spam Summit webpage is online at [http://www.ftc.gov/bcp/workshops/ spamsummit/]. The page includes links to both days' transcripts.

[41] FTC. Effectiveness and Enforcement of the CAN-SPAM Act: A Report to Congress. December 2005 [http://www.ftc.gov/reports/canspam05/05 1 220canspamrpt.pdf].

[42] A November 2005 FTC report concluded that anti-spam technologies used by ISPs are very effective in preventing spam from reaching recipients. A press release summarizing the report is available at [http://www.ftc.gov/opa/2005/1 1/spam3.htm].

[43] National Council for State Legislatures website, [http://www.ncsl.org/ programs/lis/legislation/spamlaws02.htm].

[44] For example, see Glanz, William. "House Oks Measure Aimed at Spammers; Senate Likely to Approve Changes." *Washington Times*, November 22, 2003, p. A1 (via Factiva).

[45] Baker, Chris. "Maryland Spam Law Ruled Illegal." *Washington Times*, December 15, 2004, p. C6 (via Factiva).

[46] Bruilliard, Karin. "Woman's Spam Conviction Thrown Out." *Washington Post*, March 2, 2005, p. E01 (via Factiva).

[47] Rondeaux, Candace. "Anti-Spam Conviction Is Upheld." *Washington Post*, September 6, 2006, p. B03. Online at [http://www.washingtonpost.com/wp-dyn/content/article/ 2006/09/05/AR200609050 11 66_pf.html].

In: Trends in Internet Research
Editor: B.G. Kutais
ISBN: 978-1-59454-140-7

Chapter 2

PRIVACY LAW AND ONLINE ADVERTISING: LEGAL ANALYSIS OF DATA GATHERING BY ONLINE ADVERTISERS SUCH AS DOUBLE CLICK AND NEBUAD*

Kathleen Ann Ruane†

ABSTRACT

To produce revenue, websites have placed advertisements on their sites. Advertisers will pay a premium for greater assurance that the advertisement they are purchasing will be seen by users that are most likely to be interested in the product or service offered. As a result, technology has been developed which enables online advertisements to be targeted directly at individual users based on their web surfing activity. This practice is widely known as "behavioral" or "e-havioral" advertising.

This individual behavioral targeting has raised a number of privacy concerns. For instance, questions have been asked whether personally identifiable information is being collected; how the information collected is being protected; and whether current laws are being violated if data are being collected without the consent of the parties involved. It is often unclear whether current laws, such as the Electronic Communications Privacy Act and the Communications Act, apply to online advertising providers that are collecting data through click tracking, capturing search terms, and other methods. However, it is likely that in many cases these laws could be held to apply to such activities and that these methods of data collection would be forbidden unless consent is obtained from one of the parties to the communication. This report will examine the application of these statutes to online behavioral advertising in more detail.

There are no current federal regulations specific to online behavioral advertising. The FTC maintains that self-regulation is preferable to agency regulations, because the state of the industry is fluid and complex. To aid the industry in self-regulation of online

---

* This is an edited, reformatted and augmented version of a Congressional Research Service Publication, Order Code RL34693, Prepared for Members and Committees of Congress, February 20, 2009.

† kruane@crs.loc.gov, 7-9135

behavioral advertising, in 2009, the FTC released a set of self-regulatory principles for the use of web sites and behavioral advertisers. The principles set forth guidance for the industry regarding the information that may be collected online and how companies should notify their customers about the collection. The FTC also applauded the efforts of industry groups to develop more detailed guidance on the issue. Organizations such as the Network Advertising Initiative have created policies, similar to the FTC's recent release, which many online advertising providers have pledged to follow that represent industry best practices for protecting the privacy of web users.

INTRODUCTION AND TECHNICAL BACKGROUND

Many website operators produce income by selling advertising space on their sites. Advertisers will pay a premium for ads that are more likely to reach their target demographic. In other media, such as broadcasting, advertisers engage in targeting by purchasing advertising time during programs that those who buy their products are most likely to watch. The Internet presented new challenges and opportunities for advertisers to reach their target audiences. Technology has been developed that allows advertisers to target advertising to individual web users. This is seen as an advantage for advertisers, because, rather than aiming their ads at groups of people who visit a particular site, their ads are aimed at the individual user. This maximizes the odds that the user who sees the ad will be interested in the product or service it touts. Targeting advertising to individuals involves gathering information about that individual's web surfing habits. The collection of this information has raised concerns among some over the privacy of web activity, particularly if the data collected are personally identifiable. Some have alleged that online advertisers are violating privacy laws by collecting these data.

In online advertising's simplest form, a commercial website rents out "space" on its site to another website which places a hot link banner advertisement in that space.[48] The banner ad, when clicked, sends the user directly to the advertiser's website. In this scenario, no matter who visits a particular website, that user will see the same advertisement, regardless of whether he/she may be interested in that product or service. However, many advertisers will pay a premium for the increased likelihood that users viewing their advertisement would be interested in the product or service offered. As a result, technology has developed to more accurately target online ads to the desired audience.

Online advertising providers, such as DoubleClick and NebuAd, have developed the ability to target ads to individual Internet users who would be most interested in seeing those ads. These techniques are known generally as "behaviorally targeted advertising." Behaviorally targeted advertising delivers ads that are geared toward specific Internet users by tracking certain, though not necessarily all, web activity of each user and inferring each user's interests based on that activity. Most online advertising providers monitor individual Internet users by placing a "persistent cookie" on that user's computer. "Cookies" are small text files that can store information. "Persistent cookies" reside on a hard drive indefinitely, unlike most "cookies" which expire when a browser window is closed. Generally, online advertisers give the "cookies" they place on user computers a unique alphanumeric code that identifies that user to the advertising company purportedly without revealing any personally identifiable information. "Cookies" may be placed on an individual's computer when an individual visits a website affiliated with the online advertisement supplier; however, the exact moment of "cookie" placement may be different when the relevant advertising partnership is between a user's Internet Service Provider (ISP) and an online advertising provider.

Once the cookie is in place, it gathers certain information related to that user's online activity on a continuous basis and relays that information to the online advertising provider. The advertising provider assembles that data into an individual profile that is then used to target advertising to that user's interests. This process is ongoing, but, in general, the user may opt out of continued monitoring at any point, assuming they are aware that it is occurring. In most types of behaviorally targeted advertising technology, the advertising firm gathers information about user activities on websites that are affiliated with the advertising firm. The behavioral advertiser DoubleClick, for instance, operates on this model. Information on individual users is transmitted to DoubleClick by DoubleClick's clients. In a newly emerging behavioral advertising model, the advertising provider is attempting to partner with the users' ISP. This partnership will presumably grant the advertising provider access to all web activity in which an ISP's subscribers engage. Both of these types of potential partnerships raise a number of questions regarding potential violations of existing privacy protections in federal law.

ELECTRONIC COMMUNICATIONS PRIVACY ACT

Concerns have been raised that online advertising providers, websites, and ISPs that agree to collect certain data generated by Internet traffic to behaviorally target advertising may be violating the Electronic Communications Privacy Act (ECPA)100 Stat. 1848, 18 U.S.C. 2510-2521.[49] ECPA is an amendment to Title III of the Omnibus Crime Control and Safe Streets Act of 1968, 87 Stat. 197, 18 U.S.C. 2510-2520 (1970 ed.), which prohibits the interception of electronic communications unless an exception to the general prohibition applies.[50] ECPA also prohibits electronic communications service providers from intentionally divulging information while in transit to third parties, unless an exception applies. This section will discuss the potential application of ECPA to online advertising providers and the potential application of ECPA to ISPs.

The Online Advertising Provider

The first question that must be addressed is whether ECPA applies to the activities of online advertising providers. Online advertising providers are acquiring information such as the fact that a user clicked on a particular link (an action which is the equivalent of asking the site providing the link to send the user information), and they are acquiring that information while the communication is in transit.[51] Furthermore, these advertisers may acquire information, such as words entered into a search engine or answers to online forms, while it is in transit.[52] Under ECPA, it is illegal, with certain enumerated exceptions, for any person to "intentionally intercept, endeavor to intercept, or procure any other person to intercept or endeavor to intercept, any wire, oral or electronic communication."[53] It is important to lay out the statutory definitions of each of the key terms in order to assess whether the ECPA prohibition and/or any of its exceptions applies to activities conducted by online behavioral advertisers.

- "Intercept" means the aural or other acquisition of the contents of any wire, electronic, or oral communication through the use of any electronic, mechanical, or other device.[54]
- "Contents" when used with respect to any wire, oral, or electronic communication includes any information concerning the substance, purport, or meaning of that communication.[55]
- "Electronic Communication" means any transfer of signs, signals, writing, images, sounds, data, or intelligence of any nature transmitted in whole or in part by a wire, radio, electromagnetic, photoelectronic, or photo optical system that affects interstate or foreign commerce.[56]

Because the advertisers record that a particular user requested information from a website by clicking on a particular link or sent information to a website via a search entry or other method, the advertisers appear to be "intercepting" the "contents" of those "electronic communications." Therefore, the interceptions are likely covered by ECPA.[57]

Merely determining that this type of data acquisition by online advertisers is an interception for the purposes of ECPA does not end the analysis. ECPA excepts certain communication interceptions from its prohibition. The exception to ECPA that would most likely apply to these types of interceptions is the exception that allows for interception of communications with the consent of one of the parties.[58] The question of when and how consent to the interception may be given is addressed below.

The Internet Service Provider

The second question to be addressed is whether ECPA applies to ISP providers that would allow online advertising providers to gather data from traffic over the ISP's network. ECPA prohibits any person or entity providing an electronic communications service from intentionally divulging the "contents of any communications ... while in transmission on that service to any person or entity other than an addressee or intended recipient of such communications or an agent of such addressee or intended recipient."[59] This section seems to apply to ISPs that would agree to allow online advertising providers to acquire portions of the web traffic of ISP customers, because the ISP would be allowing the advertising providers to acquire the contents of communications while they are in transmission and neither the advertising provider nor the ISP would, in most cases, be the addressee or intended recipient of the communications.

Again, determining that the data collection is likely covered by ECPA does not end the analysis. An ECPA exception may apply. ISPs are allowed to divulge the contents of communications while in transit if the divulgence is part of "any activity which is a necessary incident to the rendition of [that service] or to the protection of the rights or property of the provider of that service."[60] It does not seem likely that this exception applies to ISPs when contracting with online advertising providers. Though the service for which they contract may help keep the websites of the advertising provider's clients free to the public by producing advertising revenue, the interception is not necessary to maintain an ISP's proper function or solvency and, therefore, likely is not necessary to the rendition of Internet access service.[61] ISPs also are allowed to divulge the contents of a communication in transit "with the lawful consent of the originator or any addressee or intended recipient of such communication."[62] If the ISPs obtain the consent of their customers to intercept some of their online activities, this exception to ECPA would seem to apply. Again, the questions of how and when consent may be obtained and what constitutes "lawful consent" arise and are addressed in the following section.

The Consent Exception to ECPA

As noted above, interception of electronic communications is not prohibited by ECPA if one of the parties to the communications has consented to the interception. Consent is not defined by ECPA; nor do precise instructions of how and when consent may be obtained under ECPA appear in regulation. Therefore, it has been left largely to the courts to determine when consent to intercept a communication otherwise covered by ECPA's prohibitions has been granted.[63] There have been few cases dealing with ECPA's application to online advertising providers and none examining ECPA's application to agreements between ISP providers and online advertising providers. As a result, many open-ended questions exist regarding how to obtain adequate consent. This section first will examine whether the consent exception to ECPA applies to data collection agreements between online advertising providers and website operators. It will then examine whether and how the consent exception applies to data collection agreements between ISPs and online advertising providers.

Data Collection Agreements Between Website Operators and Online Advertising Providers

Agreements for online advertising providers to monitor certain web traffic may be between the online advertising provider and the website operators seeking to have ads placed on their sites. The advertising providers receive information about user activity on participating websites and aggregate that data to better target ads. In litigation against the online advertising provider DoubleClick for violations of ECPA, the court examined whether websites were "users" of electronic communications services under ECPA.[64] ECPA defines a "user" as "any person or entity who (A) uses an electronic communication service; and (B) is duly authorized by the provider of such service to engage in such use."[65] The court reasoned that websites are "users" (and, therefore, "parties to the communications" at issue) because they actively respond to requests they receive over electronic communications services by deciding whether to send the requested document, breaking the document down into TCP/IP protocol, and sending the packets over the Internet.[66] Because websites are "users" of electronic communications, the court found that websites are also "parties to the communications" in dispute; therefore, website owners have the ability to consent to a communication's interception.[67]

The court also held that the website operators had consented, by virtue of their contract with DoubleClick, to allow the company to intercept certain traffic on their websites in order to target advertising to website visitors.[68] Consent for private interceptions of electronic communications cannot be granted if the purpose of the interception is the commission of criminal or tortious conduct.[69] The court noted that the focus of the determination of criminal or tortious purpose under ECPA is "not upon whether the interception itself violated another law; it is upon whether the purpose for the interception—its intended use—was criminal or tortious."[70] Applying that standard, the court found that the plaintiffs had not alleged that DoubleClick's primary motivation for intercepting communications was to injure plaintiffs tortiously. In the court's view, even if DoubleClick's actions ultimately proved tortious or criminal, there was no evidence that DoubleClick was motivated by tortious intent. As a result, the court found that the consent exception to ECPA was satisfied.[71]

In a similar suit against online advertising provider Pharmatrak, the court outlined limitations to the consent exception regarding these types of agreements. In that case, Pharmatrak had contracted with certain drug companies to provide advertising on their websites. Included in the agreement was permission for the advertising provider to record certain web traffic that did not include personally identifiable information.[72] Perhaps inadvertently, the online advertising provider did collect a small amount of personally identifiable information though it had pledged not to do so. The advertiser argued that consent had been granted for such interception. The court disagreed. According to the court, it is for the party granting consent to define its scope, and the parties in this case had not consented to the collection of personally identifiable information.[73] In collecting personally identifiable information by intercepting data without the consent of one of the parties, the online advertiser potentially had violated ECPA, but may have lacked the requisite intent to be found liable under the statute.[74] The appeals court directed the trial court to conduct further investigation into the matter.

Given the conclusions in the above cases, it appears that online advertising providers, like DoubleClick, that partner to collect data from individual websites generally are not violating ECPA, because the websites are "parties to the communication" with the ability to consent to interception. Based on these cases, the advertising providers will not be seen as running afoul of ECPA so long as the data the advertising providers collect do not fall outside the scope of the data the advertising providers' clients have agreed to disclose.

Data Collection Agreements between ISPs and Online Advertising Providers

On the other hand, when the partnership is between the ISP and the online advertising provider, neither of the parties to the agreement to intercept web traffic is a party to the communications that are being intercepted. Therefore, it would appear that consent for the interceptions must be obtained from individual customers of the ISPs. The questions, in these circumstances, are whether consent must be "affirmative," or if it can be "implied," and if consent must be "affirmative" what process must be used to obtain such consent from individual users.

"Affirmative" or "Implied" Consent

Consent to interceptions has been implied by the surrounding circumstances of communications. While consent may be implied, it may not be "casually inferred."[75] It seems unlikely, as a result, that merely by using an ISP's service, a customer of that service has implied her consent to the interception of her electronic communications by online advertising providers. If consent likely may not be implied simply from use of an ISP's service, then a form of affirmative consent from the ISP's customer would be necessary.

"Opt-in" v. "Opt-out" Consent

In other statutes requiring consent for certain types of disclosure, regulatory regimes have developed to define when and how affirmative consent should be obtained.[76] A similar debate is occurring now involving how ISPs should obtain consent from their customers to share data about their online activities with online advertising providers. The debate centers around whether ISPs and advertisers must obtain "opt-in" consent or if they may continue to obtain "opt-out" consent for these interceptions.

"Opt-in" consent is obtained when a party to the communication is notified that his or her ISP has agreed to allow an online advertiser to track that person's online activity in order to better target advertising to that person. The advertiser, however, may not begin to track that individual's web activity until the individual responds to the notification granting permission for such activity.[77] If the individual never responds, interception can never begin. "Opt-out" consent, by contrast, is obtained when a party to the communication is notified that his or her ISP has agreed to allow an online advertiser to track that person's online activity and the advertising provider will begin such tracking *unless* the individual notifies the ISP or the advertiser that he or she does not grant permission for such activity.[78] If the individual never responds, interception will begin. Currently, it appears that companies such as NebuAd are obtaining or planning to obtain "opt-out" consent for the information gathering they engage in with ISPs.[79] The present question is whether "opt-out" consent is sufficient to satisfy the ECPA consent requirement. This question has yet to be addressed by a federal court or clarified by legislation or regulation. However, as discussed below, if Section 631 of the Communications Act applies to this type of data collection, "opt-in" consent may already be required for cable companies acting as ISPs (though this may not be required of telco companies such as Verizon or AT&T that operate as ISPs).

SECTION 631 OF THE COMMUNICATIONS ACT

It is also possible that privacy provisions of the Communications Act apply to agreements between cable operators acting as ISPs and online advertising providers.[80] Section 631 of the Communications Act provides basic privacy protections for personally identifiable information gathered by cable operators.[81] Specifically, cable operators must provide notice to subscribers, informing them of the types of personally identifiable information the cable operator collects, how it is disclosed, how long it is kept, etc.[82] Cable operators are prohibited from collecting personally identifiable information over the cable system without a subscriber's prior written or electronic consent.[83] Cable operators are also forbidden to disclose personally identifiable information without prior written or electronic consent of subscribers and must take action to prevent unauthorized access to personally identifiable information by anyone other than the subscriber or cable operator.[84] NebuAd has argued that Section 631 does not apply to the activities of cable operators when cable operators are acting as cable modem service providers.[85]

Section 631 governs the protection of information about subscribers to "any cable service or other service" provided by a cable operator. "Other service" is defined as "any wire or radio communications service provided using any of the facilities of a cable operator that are used in the provision of cable service."[86] In its order classifying cable modem services as "information services," the FCC stated the belief that "cable modem service would be included in the category of 'other service' for the purposes of section 631."[87] Furthermore, in 1992, Congress added the term "other services" to Section 631 as part of the Cable Television and Consumer Protection and Competition Act.[88] The House Conference Report on the law clarified that provisions redefining the term "other services" were included in order "to ensure that new communications services provided by cable operators are covered by the privacy protections" of Section 631.[89]

Section 631 is judicially enforced, however, and it is for the courts to interpret the scope of its application absent more specific guidance from Congress.[90] It is unclear whether all of the provisions of Section 631 encompass Internet services. "Other services" have been interpreted by at least one district court to encompass Internet services.[91] On the other hand, in 2006, the Sixth Circuit Court of Appeals found that the plain language of Section 631(b) precluded its application to broadband Internet service.[92] Section 631(b) prohibits cable operators from using their cable systems to collect personally identifiable information without the consent of subscribers.[93] The court based its decision that Internet services were not covered by this prohibition on its interpretation of the definition of "cable systems."[94] The court found that the systems that deliver Internet services are not the systems that Section 631(b) addresses, and therefore, cable operators were not prohibited by Section 631(b) from collecting personally identifiable information over systems that delivered Internet access services. The Supreme Court has yet to rule on this issue.

Even if Section 631(b) does not prevent cable operators from collecting personally identifiable information over broadband Internet services, Section 631(c) may prohibit the disclosure of such information to third parties regardless of whether the information was collected over the cable system.[95] Section 631(c) of the Communications Act states that "a cable operator shall not disclose personally identifiable information concerning any subscriber without the prior written or electronic consent of the subscriber concerned and shall take such actions as are necessary to prevent unauthorized access to such information by a person other than the subscriber or cable operator."[96] If a cable operator, as an ISP, agrees to allow an online advertising provider to inspect traffic over its cable system and to acquire some of that information, it seems that the cable operator/ISP is disclosing information to the online advertising provider. Such disclosure would apparently be a violation of the Communications Act if (1) the information disclosed is personally identifiable information and (2) the cable operator/ISP is disclosing it without the prior written or electronic consent of the subscribers to whom the information pertains.

Whether online advertising providers are gathering personally identifiable information in order to provide their services is a matter of much debate. Section 631 does not define what personally identifiable information is; it defines what personally identifiable information is not. According to 631, Personally Identifiable Information (PII) does not include "any record of aggregate data which does not identify particular persons."[97] Online advertising providers claim that they do not collect any personally identifiable information.[98] Public interest groups and other commentators disagree, citing scenarios in which data which was not supposed to contain personally identifiable information was used to identify individuals.[99] Because Section 631 is judicially enforced, it is likely that whether online advertisers are acquiring personally identifiable information as opposed to aggregate data that do not identify particular persons will be a determination made by a federal trial court. To date, there have been no cases addressing this question.

Assuming even that online advertising providers are gathering personally identifiable information, cable operators are allowed to disclose personally identifiable information as long as they obtain the prior written or electronic consent of the relevant subscribers, essentially an "opt-in" standard.[100] In the event that online advertising companies are determined to be gathering personally identifiable information and that Section 631(c) applies to cable operators in their provision of cable modem services, cable operators would be required to obtain consent for such disclosure under an "opt-in" regime.

FEDERAL TRADE COMMISSION ONLINE ADVERTISING SELF-REGULATORY PRINCIPLES

In February of 2009, the FTC released a new set of Self Regulatory Principles for Online Behavioral Advertising.[101] These principles represent the most recent step in the FTC's ongoing examination of behavioral advertising practices, which began with the release of proposed self-regulatory principles for public comment in December of 2007.[102] Among other things, the finalized principles clarified the types of advertising to which they should be applied and discussed what types of Non-PII should be included when notifying a consumer about what types of data the site or advertiser is collecting about him/her. A brief sketch of the principles follows.[103]

- The FTC's principles cover only online behavioral advertising. Online behavioral advertising means "the tracking of a consumer's online activities ***over time***." The principles make clear that so-called "first party" advertising (where no information is shared with a third party) and contextual advertising (where the ad is based on a single page visit or search) are not covered by the principles.
- According to the principles, websites engaged in online behavioral advertising should provide clear notification to consumers regarding the types of data being collected on the site and why, as well as the opportunity for consumers to choose whether their data may be collected for such purposes.
- Companies collecting the data should provide reasonable security for the data. The security measures should be concomitant with the sensitivity of the data (the more sensitive the data, the more protected it should be). The data should be retained only so long as necessary to fulfill a legitimate business purpose or as required by law.
- Companies must keep the promises they make to their customers. If the company decides to use *previously* collected data for purposes that differ materially from the

uses the company described to the customer at the time data collection began, the company should obtain the affirmative express consent of affected customers.
- Companies should collect sensitive data (e.g., social security number, medical information, financial account information, etc.) for behavioral advertising only after obtaining affirmative express consent from the consumer.

The FTC noted that the release of these principles is a step in the ongoing process of evaluating the online behavioral advertising industry. The principles do not absolve the companies of their responsibilities under other governing laws (i.e., Section 5 of the Federal Trade Commission Act). The FTC pledged to continue to monitor online behavioral advertising issues and its affect on consumer privacy.

NETWORK ADVERTISING INITIATIVE STANDARDS

The Network Advertising Initiative (NAI) is an industry group composed of online advertising providers that has developed voluntary privacy, notice, and consent standards that are considered to represent industry best practices for the protection of data gathered for the purposes of behavioral advertising.[104] These standards do not have the force of law, but a number of online advertising providers have pledged to abide by them.

In December of 2008, the NAI released a new "Self-Regulatory Code of Conduct."[105] Under these standards, members of the NAI must post clear and conspicuous notice on their websites describing their data collection, transfer, and use practices. The Code instructs NAI members to require the sites with which they contract for behavioral advertising to post conspicuous notice of, among other things, the types of data collected by the company and how that data is used or transferred to third parties. Members also must contractually require any third parties to whom they provide personally identifiable information to comply with the Self-Regulatory Code of Conduct.

The Self-Regulatory Code creates three tiers of information that may be collected for behavioral advertising: non-personally identifiable information (Non-PII),[106] personally identifiable information (PII),[107] and Sensitive Consumer Information.[108] The code requires "opt-out" consent for the use of Non-PII. The prospective use of PII that is to be merged with Non-PII requires "opt-out" consent accompanied by a "robust notice"[109] that occurs prior to data collecion. The use of PII that is to be merged with previously collected Non-PII requires "opt-in" consent. The use of Sensitive Consumer Information always requires "opt-in" consent. Members must provide reasonable security for the data that they collect, and they may only retain the data collected "as long as necessary to fulfill a legitimate business need, or as required by law." Behavioral advertising that targets children under the age of thirteen (regardless of the type of information) is prohibited.

End Notes

[48] For a basic description of the technology involved in delivering behaviorally targeted advertising, please see the following source material: In re DoubleClick, Inc. Privacy Litigation, 154 F.Supp. 2d 497 (S.D.N.Y. 2001), In re Pharmatrak Privacy Litigation, 329 F.3d 9 (1st Cir. 2003), and Paul Lansing and Mark Halter, *Internet Advertising and Right to Privacy Issues*, 80 U. Det. Mercy L. Rev. 181 (2003). *See also*, Testimony of Mr. Robert R. Dykes, CEO of NebuAd Inc., *Privacy Implications of Online Advertising: Hearing Before the S.*

Comm. On Commerce, Science, and Transportation, 110th Cong. (2008)(hereinafter NebuAd Testimony), available at http://commerce.senate.gov/public/ _files/RobertDykesNebuAdOnlinePrivacyTestimony.pdf.

[49] Testimony of Ms. Leslie Harris, CEO of the Center for Democracy and Technology, *Privacy Implications of Online Advertising: Hearing Before the S. Comm. On Commerce, Science, and Transportation*, 110th Cong. (2008)(hereinafter CDT Testimony), available at http://commerce.senate.gov/public/_files/LeslieHarrisCDTOnlinePrivacyTestimony.pdf.

[50] For a more detailed discussion of the history of ECPA, see CRS Report 98-326, *Privacy: An Overview of Federal Statutes Governing Wiretapping and Electronic Eavesdropping*, by Gina Marie Stevens and Charles Doyle.

[51] *See e.g.*, NebuAd Testimony at 3-4.

[52] *See id.*; In re DoubleClick, Inc. Privacy Litigation, 154 F.Supp. 2d 497 (S.D.N.Y. 2001).

[53] 18 U.S.C. §2511(1)(a).

[54] 18 U.S.C. §2510(4).

[55] 18 U.S.C. §2510(8).

[56] 18 U.S.C. §2510(12).

[57] It is worth noting that there has yet to be a court case to decide definitively that ECPA applies to this type of data collection. In the cases cited here, the online advertising providers made their cases by assuming, but not conceding, that ECPA applied to the data collection. *See* In re Pharmatrk, Inc. Privacy Litigations, 329 F.3d 9 (1st Cir. 2003); In re DoubleClick, Inc. Privacy Litigation, 154 F.Supp. 2d 497 (S.D.N.Y. 2001).

[58] "It shall not be unlawful under this chapter for a person not acting under color of law to intercept a wire, oral, or electronic communication where such person is a party to the communication or where one of the parties to the communications has given prior consent to such interception unless such communication is intercepted for the purpose of committing any criminal or tortious act in violation of the Constitution or laws of the United States or any State." 18 U.S.C. §2511(2)(d).

[59] 18 U.S.C. §2511(3)(a). It is worth noting that this section does not require that the divulgence of information while it is in transit by an electronic communications service be an "interception" in order for it to be prohibited. Data acquisition can only be categorized as an "interception" for the purposes of ECPA "through the use of any electronic, mechanical, or other device." 18 U.S.C. §2510(4). The statute makes clear that "electronic, mechanical, or other device" does not mean the equipment or facilities of a wire or electronic communications service that are used in the ordinary course of the provider's business. 18 U.S.C. 2510(5). Therefore, it is possible that when an ISP allows a third party to collect data that is in transit over its network the ISP may not be "intercepting" that data as the term "intercept" is defined by ECPA. Nonetheless, "intentionally divulging the contents of any communication while in transmission" over an ISP's network is prohibited by 18 U.S.C. §2511(3)(a), unless it meets one of the exceptions outlined in 18 U.S.C. § 2511(3)(b).

[60] 18 U.S.C. §2511(2)(a)(i).

[61] *See, e.g.*, U.S. Census 2006 Annual Survey (Information Sector), *Internet Service Providers—Estimated Sources of Revenue and Expenses for Employer Firms: 2004 Through 2006* at 32, Table 3.4.1 (April 15, 2006) (indicating that internet access service are responsible for the greatest percentage of revenue earned by ISPs) available at http://www.census.gov/svsd/www/services/sas/sas_data/51/2006_NAICS51.pdf; Comcast Corporation, Quarterly Report (Form 10-Q) (June 30, 2008) (reporting that 95% of Comcast Corporation's consolidated revenue is derived from its cable operations, which includes the provision of high-speed internet services) available at http://sec.gov/ Archives/edgar/data/1166691/000119312508161385/d10q.htm.

[62] 18 U.S.C. 2511(3)(b)(ii).

[63] *See e.g.*, United States v. Friedman, 300 F.3d 111, 122-23 (2d Cir. 2002)(inmate use of prison phone);United States v. Faulkner, 439 F.3d 1221, 1224 (10th Cir. 2006)(same); United States v. Hammond, 286 F.3d 189, 192 (4th Cir. 2002) (same); *United States v. Footman*, 215 F.3d 145, 154-55 (1st Cir. 2000) (same); Griggs-Ryan v. Smith, 904 F.2d 112, 116-17 (1st Cir. 1990) (use of landlady's phone); United States v. Rivera, 292 F. Supp. 2d 838, 843-45 (E.D. Va. 2003)(inmate use of prison phone monitored by private contractors). For a discussion of the consent exception to the Wiretap Act as it is applied in other contexts, see, CRS Report 98-326, *Privacy: An Overview of Federal Statutes Governing Wiretapping and Electronic Eavesdropping*, by Gina Marie Stevens and Charles Doyle.

[64] In re DoubleClick, Inc. Privacy Litigation, 154 F.Supp. 2d 497 (S.D.N.Y. 2001).

[65] 18 U.S.C. §2510(13).

[66] In re DoubleClick, Inc. Privacy Litigation, 154 F.Supp. 2d at 508-09.

[67] *Id.* at 514.

[68] *Id.* at 509-513.

[69] 18 U.S.C. §2511(2)(d).

[70] In re DoubleClick, Inc. Privacy Litigation, 154 F.Supp. 2d at 516 (quoting Sussman v. ABC, 196 F.3d 1200, 1202 (9th Cir. 1999)).

[71] *Id.* at 518-19.

[72] In re Pharmatrk, Inc. Privacy Litigations, 329 F.3d 9 (1st Cir. 2003).

[73] *Id.* at 20.

---

[74] *Id.* at 23.

[75] Williams v. Poulos, 11 F.3d 271, 281 (1st Cir. 1993)(finding that defendant corporation violated the Wiretap Act, because it did not have implied consent or a business necessity to place wiretaps).

[76] See e.g., *In the Matter of Implementation of the Telecommunications Act of 1996; Telecommunications Carriers; Use of Customer Proprietary Network Information and Other Customer Information; IP-Enabled Services*, 22 FCC Rcd 6927 (2007)(outlining under what circumstances voice service providers must obtain "opt-in" v. "opt-out" consent in order to disclose Customer Proprietary Network Information(CPNI)). For a discussion of the FCC's CPNI disclosure regulations, see CRS Report RL34409, *Selected Laws Governing the Disclosure of Customer Phone Records by Telecommunications Carriers*, by Kathleen Ann Ruane.

[77] *See* The Network Advertising Initiative's Self-Regulatory Code of Conduct for Online Behavioral Advertising, Draft: For Public Comment, available at http://networkadvertising.org/networks/NAI_Principles_2008_Draft_for_Public.pdf (last visited July 28, 2008). *See* also, 47 C.F.R. §2003(k)(defining "opt-in" approval in the CPNI context).

[78] *See* The Network Advertising Initiative's Self-Regulatory Code of Conduct for Online Behavioral Advertising, Draft: For Public Comment, available at http://networkadvertising.org/networks/NAI_Principles_2008_Draft_for_Public.pdf (last visited July 28, 2008). See also, 47 C.F.R. §2003(l)(defining "opt- out" approval in the CPNI context).

[79] NebuAd Testimony at 4.

[80] Testimony of Ms. Leslie Harris, CEO of the Center for Democracy and Technology, *Privacy Implications of Online Advertising: Hearing Before the S. Comm. On Commerce, Science, and Transportation*, 110th Cong. (2008).

[81] Codified at 47 U.S.C. §55 1. It is important to note that those providing DSL Internet service over phone lines, such as Verizon or AT&T, would not be subject to the provisions of Section 631, because they are not cable operators. Testimony of Ms. Gigi B. Sohn, President, Public Knowledge, *Broadband Providers and Consumer Privacy: Hearing Before the S. Comm. On Commerce, Science, and Transportation*, 110th Cong. (2008)(hereinafter Public Knowledge Testimony), available at http://commerce.senate.gov/public/_files/SohnTestimony.pdf.

[82] 47 U.S.C. §551(a).

[83] 47 U.S.C. §551(b).

[84] 47 U.S.C. §551(c).

[85] Memorandum from NebuAd, Inc., Legal and Policy Issues Supporting NebuAd's Services at 6.

[86] 47 U.S.C. Sec. §551(a)(2)(B).

[87] *In the Matter of Inquiry Concerning High-Speed Access to the Internet Over Cable and Other Facilities; Internet Over Cable Declaratory Ruling; Appropriate Regulatory Treatment for Broadband Access to the Internet Over Cable Facilities*, 17 FCC Rcd at 4854, ¶ 112.

[88] Cable Television and Consumer Protection and Competition Act, P.L. 102-385.

[89] H.Rept. 102-862.

[90] *See* 47 U.S.C. 551(f).

[91] *See* Application of the United States of America for an Order Pursuant to 18 U.S.C. Sec. 2703(D), 157 F. Supp. 2d 286, 291 (SDNY 200 1)(finding that the notice requirement for the disclosure of personally identifiable information under 47 U.S.C. §551 included Internet services, except under 47 U.S.C. §551(h), which was exempt specifically from the broad definition of "other services").

[92] Klimas v. Comcast Cable, Inc., 465 F.3d 271, 276 (6th Cir. 2006).

[93] 47 U.S.C. §551(b)(1).

[94] *Klimas*, 465 F.3d at 276.

[95] 47 U.S.C. §551(c)(1).

[96] 47 U.S.C. §551(c)(1). Cable operators, however, may collect such information without consent for the purposes of obtaining information necessary to provide cable services or other services provided to the subscriber or to detect unauthorized reception of cable communications. Cable operators may disclose personally identifiable information without consent when it is necessary to render cable services or other services provided by the cable operator to the subscriber, pursuant to a valid court order, and in other limited circumstances. 47 U.S.C. 551 (c)(2). These exemptions do not appear to apply in this case.

[97] 47 U.S.C. §551(a)(2)(A).

[98] *See, e.g.,* NebuAd Testimony.

[99] *See, e.g.,* CDT Testimony.

[100] 47 U.S.C. §551(c).

[101] FTC Staff, *Self-Regulatory Principles for Online Behavioral Advertising* (Feb. 12, 2009), *available at* http://www.ftc.gov/os/2009/02/P085400behavadreport.pdf.

[102] FTC Staff, *Online Behavioral Advertising: Moving the Discussion Forward to Possible Self-Regulatory Principles* (Dec. 20, 2007), *available at* http://www.ftc.gov/os/2007/12/P859900stmt.pdf.

[103] FTC Staff, *Self-Regulatory Principles for Online Behavioral Advertising, at 46-47* (Feb. 12, 2009), *available at* http://www.ftc.gov/os/2009/02/P085400behavadreport.pdf.

[104] Network Advertising Initiative, http://networkadvertising.org/index.asp.

[105] The Network Advertising Initiative's Self-Regulatory Code of Conduct, available at http://www.networkadvertising.org/networks/2008%20NAI%20Principles_final%20for%20Website.pdf (last visited January 13, 2009).

[106] Non-PII is information that is not PII or Sensitive Consumer Information.

[107] "PII includes name, address, telephone number, email address, financial account number, government-issued identifier, and any other data used or intended to be used to identify contact or precisely locate a person." The Network Advertising Initiative's Self-Regulatory Code of Conduct, Section II, available at http://www.networkadvertising.org/ networks/2008%20NAI%20Principles_final%20for%20Website.pdf (last visited January 13, 2009).

[108] "Sensitive Consumer Information includes: Social Security Number or other Government-issued identifier; insurance plan numbers, financial account numbers; information that describes the precise real-time geographic location of an individual derived through location-based services such as through GPS-enabled services; precise information about past, present, or potential future health or medical conditions or treatments, including genetic, genomic, and family medical history." It seems that some of the information included in the definition of PII is also included in the definition for Sensitive Consumer Information. The Code of Conduct indicates that the definition of Sensitive Consumer Information will be further developed in the coming implementation guidelines. The Network Advertising Initiative's Self-Regulatory Code of Conduct, Section II, available at http://www.networkadvertising.org/networks/ 2008%20NAI%20Principles_final%20for%20Website.pdf (last visited January 13, 2009).

[109] Robust Notice is defined by the Code of Conduct. "For the notice to be robust the consumer must be afforded clear and conspicuous notice about the scope of any non-PII to be merged with PII, and how the merged data would be used for [behavioral advertising]. Such notice must be provided immediately above or before the mechanism used to authorize submission of any PII." The Network Advertising Initiative's Self-Regulatory Code of Conduct, Section II, available at http://www.networkadvertising.org/networks/2008%20NAI%20Principles_final%20for%20Website.pdf (last visited January 13, 2009).

In: Trends in Internet Research
Editor: B.G. Kutais
ISBN: 978-1-59454-140-7

Chapter 3

THE GOOGLE LIBRARY PROJECT: IS DIGITIZATION FOR PURPOSES OF ONLINE INDEXING FAIR USE UNDER COPYRIGHT LAW?*

Kate M. Manuel†

ABSTRACT

The Google Book Search Library Project, announced in December 2004, raised important questions about infringing reproduction and fair use under copyright law. Google planned to digitize, index, and display "snippets" of print books in the collections of five major libraries without the permission of the books' copyright holders, if any. Authors and publishers owning copyrights to these books sued Google in September and October 2005, seeking to enjoin and recover damages for Google's alleged infringement of their exclusive rights to reproduce and publicly display their works. Google and proponents of its Library Project disputed these allegations. They essentially contended that Google's proposed uses were not infringing because Google allowed rights holders to "opt out" of having their books digitized or indexed. They also argued that, even if Google's proposed uses were infringing, they constituted fair uses under copyright law.

The arguments of the parties and their supporters highlighted several questions of first impression. First, does an entity conducting an unauthorized digitization and indexing project avoid committing copyright infringement by offering rights holders the opportunity to "opt out," or request removal or exclusion of their content? Is requiring rights holders to take steps to stop allegedly infringing digitization and indexing like requiring rights holders to use meta-tags to keep search engines from indexing online content? Or do rights holders employ sufficient measures to keep their books from being digitized and indexed online by publishing in print? Second, can unauthorized digitization, indexing, and display of "snippets" of print works constitute a fair use? Assuming unauthorized indexing and display of "snippets" are fair uses, can digitization claim to be a fair use on the grounds that apparently *prima facie* infringing activities that facilitate legitimate uses are fair uses?

---

* This is an edited, reformatted and augmented version of a Congressional Research Service Publication, Order Code R40194, Prepared for Members and Committees of Congress, July 6, 2009.

† Kate M. Manuel, Legislative Attorney, kmanuel@crs.loc.gov, 7-4477

On October 28, 2008, Google, authors, and publishers announced a proposed settlement, which, if approved by the court, could leave these and related questions unanswered. However, although a court granted preliminary approval to the settlement on November 17, 2008, final approval is still pending. Until final approval is granted, any rights holder belonging to the proposed settlement class—which includes "all persons having copyright interests in books" in the United States— could object to the agreement. The court could also reject the agreement as unfair, unreasonable, or inadequate. Moreover, on July 2, 2009, the U.S. Department of Justice confirmed that it is investigating whether the terms of the proposed settlement violate antitrust law.

INTRODUCTION

Authors and publishers sued Google Inc. in 2005, shortly after Google announced plans to digitize books in the collections of several major libraries, index them in its search engine (http://www.google.com), and allow searchers to view "snippets" of the digitized books. Google's proposed reproduction and display of copyrighted books was not authorized by the rights holders, who alleged that the Google Library Project infringed their copyrights. Google's counterarguments—that allowing rights holders to "opt out" of having their books digitized or indexed kept its proposed uses from being infringing, or that, if found to be infringing, its proposed uses were fair—raised important questions about reproduction and fair use under copyright law. Namely, does an entity engaged in unauthorized digitization and indexing avoid committing copyright infringement by offering rights holders the opportunity to request removal or exclusion of their content? And, assuming unauthorized indexing and display of "snippets" are fair uses, can digitization claim to be a fair use on the grounds that apparently *prima facie* infringing activities that facilitate legitimate uses are fair uses? The proposed settlement agreement between Google and rights holders could mean that litigation over the Library Project does not help to answer these questions. However, final court approval of the settlement is still pending, and future digitization and indexing projects may raise similar questions.

This report provides background on the Library Project, legal issues raised by digitization and indexing projects, and the proposed settlement. It will be updated as developments warrant. It supersedes CRS Report RS22356, *The Google Book Search Project: Is Online Indexing a Fair Use Under Copyright Law?*, by Robin Jeweler.

THE GOOGLE LIBRARY PROJECT

In December 2004, Google initiated its Library Project by announcing partnerships with five libraries.[110] Under the partnership agreements, the libraries would allow Google to digitize the print books in their collections, and Google would (1) index the contents of the books; (2) display at least "snippets" of the books among its search results; and (3) provide partner libraries with digital copies of the print books in their collections.[111] Google and its partners never planned to make the full text of any digitized and indexed books that are still within their terms of copyright protection available to searchers.[112] Rather, by digitizing and indexing books, Google and its partners sought to make the contents of print books more accessible to searchers, who could potentially buy or borrow books after seeing "snippets" of them among the results of Google searches.[113] Google also intended to sell advertising "keyed" to results lists incorporating the digitized books.[114]

Google's Library Project was itself part of a larger initiative initially known as Google Print and later renamed Google Book Search.[115] The Google Partner Program was also part of this initiative.[116] The Partner Program allowed authors and publishers to submit copies of their books for indexing in Google's search engine.[117] However, because rights holders affirmatively chose to have their books digitized or indexed through the Partner Program, the Program was not subject to allegations of copyright infringement like those made against the Library Project.

THE LITIGATION AND THE PARTIES' POSITIONS

Authors and publishers objected to the Google Library Project from its inception on the grounds that it infringed their copyrights.[118] Generally, copyrights in books initially vest in the books' authors.[119] Many authors later transfer their copyrights to publishers under contract in exchange for payment and the publisher's manufacturing and selling copies of the book.[120] Regardless of whether they are the books' authors or publishers, however, copyright holders have exclusive rights "to reproduce the copyrighted work in copies," or, in the case of literary works such as books, "to display the copyrighted work publicly."[121] The authors and publishers who objected to the Library Project claimed that Google infringed these exclusive rights by making digital copies of print books and presenting snippets from the digitized books without rights holders' permission.[122] Google initially responded to these concerns by allowing rights holders who did not want their books included in Google Book Search to "opt out."[123] If rights holders notified Google, Google would ensure that digitized versions of their books were not included in its database.

The ability to "opt out" of the Library Project did not satisfy authors and publishers, however. They sued to enjoin Google's digitization and indexing and to recover monetary damages for Google's alleged copyright infringement. In September 2005, the Authors Guild filed a class action suit in U.S. District Court for the Southern District of New York on behalf of "all persons or entities that hold the copyright to a literary work that is contained in the library of the University of Michigan."[124] Shortly thereafter, five publishing companies also sued in the Southern District of New York.[125] The suits were consolidated, and additional plaintiffs, including the Association of American Publishers, joined the suit. Because the consolidated case was a class action, the court must approve any settlement of it.[126]

In responding to the suit, Google essentially contended that its conduct was not infringing because it gave rights holders the opportunity to "opt out" of having their books digitized and indexed.[127] Google also claimed that, even if a court found its conduct to be infringing, this conduct represented a fair use of the rights holders' works.[128] Google and supporters of its Library Project specifically cited the decision by the U.S. Court of Appeals for the Ninth Circuit in *Kelly v. Arriba Soft Corporation* as support for the proposition that the indexing activities of Internet search engines constitute fair uses.[129]

LEGAL ISSUES RAISED BY THE LITIGATION

The litigation over the Google Library Project raised important questions about infringing reproduction and fair use under copyright law. Namely, can an entity engaging in unauthorized digitization and indexing avoid liability for copyright infringement by offering rights holders the opportunity to request removal or exclusion of their content from its database? And, assuming unauthorized indexing and display of "snippets" of digitized works are fair uses, can digitization itself claim to be a fair use on the grounds that apparently *prima facie* infringing activities that facilitate legitimate uses are fair uses? These questions will arguably persist, and their answers remain important, even if the parties ultimately settle the litigation over the Library Project.

"Opt Out" Programs and Liability for Infringement

Google's first line of defense against the authors and publishers was essentially that it was not liable for copyright infringement because it gave rights holders the opportunity to "opt out" of having their works digitized and indexed. In making this argument, Google relied on the related claim that no one would conduct multi-library digitization and indexing projects like the Library Project if they had to clear the copyrights for every book with the rights holders.[130] Identifying and locating the rights holder(s) for one book can be difficult enough, supporters of the Google Library Project noted, without repeating this process millions of times, as would be necessary with a major library collection.[131] The publishers, in contrast, noted that Google's offer to let rights holders "opt out" of having their books digitized and indexed "stands copyright law on its head."[132] They argued that one cannot generally announce one's intention to infringe multiple copyrighted works and collectively offer rights holders the opportunity not to have their works infringed.[133]

It is impossible to predict what a court would find based on such arguments, and this report does not attempt to do so. This report does, however, highlight some of the considerations that could factor in the court's consideration of the issue. On the one hand, the requirement that a copyright owner act affirmatively to stop non-willful infringement is not without precedent. The "notice and takedown" procedures of the Digital Millennium Copyright Act (DMCA),[134] for example, require content owners to notify Internet Service Providers (ISPs) of the existence of infringing content and can immunize ISPs from liability for infringement when they serve as "passive conduits" for infringing content transmitted by third parties.[135] Similarly, at least one court has found that content owners are responsible for taking affirmative measures, such as using meta-tags within the computer code of a Web page, to prevent Internet search engines from automatically indexing and displaying their content.[136] On the other hand, plaintiffs could argue that comprehensive digitization projects, like that proposed by Google, willfully infringe copyright[137] and differ from the "passive conduits" protected by the DMCA. Likewise, rights holders in print books could argue that their situations differ from that of Web page authors because Google had to digitize their books before indexing them. They could claim that they took sufficient affirmative measures to protect their works by not making them available for free on the Web.[138]

Digitization, Indexing, and Display as Fair Uses

Google also attempted to defend against the rights holders' allegations of copyright infringement by claiming that the Library Project, if found to be infringing, constituted a fair use.[139] The "fair use" exemption within copyright law limits rights holders' exclusive rights by providing that uses for "certain purposes"—including, but not limited to, criticism, comment, news reporting, teaching, scholarship, and research—do not infringe copyright *even if* they are made without the rights holders' consent.[140] In determining whether challenged conduct constitutes a fair use, a court considers the following factors, which were developed under the common law and later codified in the Copyright Act of 1976:

(1) the purpose and character of the use, including whether such use is of a commercial nature or is for nonprofit educational purposes;
(2) the nature of the copyrighted work;
(3) the amount and substantiality of the portion used in relation to the copyrighted work as a whole; and
(4) the effect of the use upon the potential market for or value of the copyrighted work.141

These four factors must not be "treated in isolation, one from another."[142] Rather, "[a]ll are to be explored, and the results weighed together, in light of the purposes of copyright,"[143] which is to "Promote the Progress of Science and useful Arts" and serve the public welfare.[144] Also, because fair use is an "equitable rule of reason" to be applied in light of copyright law's overall purposes, other relevant factors may be considered.[145] The court hearing the case makes findings of fact and assigns relative value and weight to each of the fair use factors. The court can also look to prior cases for guidance even though determining whether a challenged activity constitutes a fair use "calls for a case-by-case analysis."[146]

Although it is impossible to predict what a court would find when confronted with an actual case, and this report will not attempt to do so, it does highlight some of the many questions that the Google Library Project raised regarding each of the four statutory "fair use" factors. The report does so in order to illustrate the potential importance of the Library Project—or similar digitization and indexing projects—in establishing the scope of infringing reproduction and fair use under copyright law.

The Purpose and Character of the Use

First, as regards the purpose and character of the use, copyright law generally presumes that commercial uses are not fair,[147] and that transporting a work to a new medium is not a fair use.[148] These presumptions would seem to work against digitization and indexing projects like the Library Project. The Project was implemented by a for-profit corporation that proposed, among other things, to sell ads "keyed" to the digitized content. The Project was also intended to migrate content from print to digital format. These presumptions can, however, be overridden when the use is sufficiently transformative.[149] A copy's use of the original is transformative when the copy does not "merely supersede[]" the original but rather "adds something new, with a further purpose or a different character" to the original.[150]

The transformative nature of the Library Project would arguably be more easily established if it merely indexed books and displayed "snippets" of them. Were Google's uses so limited, it could probably rely on the precedent of two cases from the U.S. Court of Appeals for the Ninth Circuit which found that indexing and abridged displays of copyrighted content were fair uses. In the first case, *Kelly v. Arriba Soft Corporation*, the court held that a company operating a search engine, which had indexed a rights holder's online photographs and displayed "thumbnail" versions of them, was not liable for copyright infringement because its uses were fair.[151] Key to this holding was the court's finding that indexing represented a transformative use of the original photographs. While the original photographs were intended "to inform and to engage the viewer in an aesthetic experience," Arriba used its copies of them for a different function: "improving access to information on the internet."[152] The court also emphasized that Arriba indexed and displayed "thumbnail" versions of the photographs.[153] The thumbnails had much lower resolution than the originals and thus could not substitute for them because "enlarging them sacrifices their clarity."[154] The Ninth Circuit reached a similar conclusion in Perfect 10, *Inc. v. Amazon.com, Inc.*[155] There, the court also considered a use's benefit to society in finding the use to be transformative. The court noted that "a search engine provides social benefit by incorporating an original work into a new work, namely, an electronic reference tool."[156]

The digitization involved in the Library Project complicates the analysis, however. Admittedly, the prior cases that found indexing and abridged displays of copyrighted content to be fair uses also involved copying of originals.[157] However, in these cases, the copying was of originals posted on the Internet and resulted in copies that were "inferior" to the originals for all purposes except their use in indexing. The first difference is potentially significant because courts have held that rights holders confer limited licenses to copy their content for purposes of indexing and abridged display by posting it on the Internet without taking affirmative measures to prevent copying.[158] The second difference could also be significant because digitized books are arguably superior to print ones when it comes to locating specific information within them.[159]

Because digitization was so central to the Library Project, and arguably could not be directly paralleled to the copying in cases involving indexing and display of Internet materials, Google might have had to rely on the proposition that apparently *prima facie* infringing activities (such as digitization) that facilitate legitimate uses (such as indexing and limited displays) are fair uses. The Supreme Court's decision in *Sony Corporation of America v. Universal City Studios* could arguably provide broad support for this principle.[160] In *Sony*, the Court held that the sale of the video recording machine, which was used to "time shift" broadcast television for personal home viewing, was not contributory copyright infringement.[161] Although the factual underpinnings and legal precedent of *Sony* are not particularly relevant to or controlling in a case like Google's, the *Sony* decision itself stands as a landmark in copyright law demonstrating the willingness of the Court to balance new technological capabilities against traditional principles of copyright law and to recognize new categories of fair use. Many copyright experts saw analogies to the technological considerations inherent in *Sony* in Google's case.[162] Such experts noted that Google's allegedly infringing activity in digitizing print books was incidental to the valid and socially useful function of indexing.

The analogy to *Sony* might not be enough to persuade a court that digitizing for purposes of non-infringing indexing constitutes a fair use, however. Digitizing and indexing print books are arguably far removed from making and selling devices that consumers use to record broadcast television programming and replay it later. Additionally, courts have shown little inclination to recognize categories of judicially created fair uses other than time shifting. In *UMG Recordings v. MP3.com, Inc.*, for example, a U.S. district court rejected out-of-hand the defendant's proffered fair use defense as a justification for unauthorized copying of plaintiffs' audio CDs.[163] The defendant had claimed that its unauthorized copying enabled CD owners to "space shift" because they could access the music on their CDs from any location through MP3.com's subscription service.[164]

The Nature of the Copyrighted Work

Comprehensive digitization and indexing projects, such as the Google Library Project, raise similar questions when the second fair use factor is considered. Projects that digitize library collections potentially encompass diverse types of materials. Some of these materials may be works of fiction, which are among the creative works accorded the highest level of copyright protection.[165] Other materials may be reference books or compendiums of facts, which are afforded the "thinnest" copyright protection.[166] Yet other materials may be nonfiction and mix unprotected ideas with protected expressions of these ideas.[167] This diversity of materials makes possible the arguments of both proponents and opponents of the view that projects like Google Book Search constitute fair uses. The nature of the work can, however, be less important than the purpose and character of the use, at least in situations where the use can be clearly recognized as transformative.[168]

The Amount and Substantiality of the Portion Used

The amount and substantiality of the portion used in relation to the copyrighted work as a whole is another factor that could potentially cut either way in cases involving digitization and indexing projects. As a general rule, "[w]hile wholesale copying does not preclude fair use per se, copying an entire work militates against a finding of fair use."[169] Copying entire works can, however, be found to constitute a fair use when doing so is reasonable given the purpose and character of the use.[170] Digitization projects, such as the Google Library Project, would clearly be engaged in wholesale copying, including copying any segments comprising the "heart" of the copied work.[171] The question would thus become whether such wholesale copying was reasonable for an indexing project. Proponents of the project could argue that courts have found copying entire works in order to digitize them reasonable,[172] and that searchers would see only "snippets" of the work in any case. Opponents, in contrast, could argue that, in all cases where courts protected wholesale copying for purposes of indexing, the authors had placed their works online, thereby creating implied licenses for others to copy and index them.[173] Moreover, in at least some of these cases, the copies were deleted after the indexing was completed. [174] In no case did the copier propose to give copies to third parties, as Google did when contracting to provide digital copies of the books in their collections to libraries.

The Effect of the Use Upon the Potential Market or Value of the Work

Finally, digitization and indexing projects could be seen as either promoting or inhibiting the potential markets or values of the copyrighted works. Proponents of digitization could argue that indexing and display of "snippets" of print books increases the markets for the originals by alerting researchers to books on their topics. If researchers purchase books of which they would otherwise have been unaware, the markets for these books could potentially be improved by the unauthorized digitization. Opponents, in contrast, could argue that unauthorized digitization and indexing usurps markets that the rights holders are developing;[175] that viewing "snippets" of print books sometimes can substitute for purchases of them; and that rights holders should be free to determine whether, when, and how their print works are digitized.[176] The outcome of any findings by the court on this factor may hinge upon the degree of harm to their markets that plaintiffs must show. Some courts have required plaintiffs to show only that the markets in which they alleged harm are "likely to be developed,"[177] while others have required proof of actual losses in established markets.[178] The fact that a use is transformative can, however, outweigh even inhibition of or harm to plaintiffs' markets.[179]

THE PROPOSED SETTLEMENT AGREEMENT

On October 28, 2008, Google and the rights holders announced a proposed settlement agreement.[180] Under this agreement, Google would compensate rights holders for prior and future uses of their work.[181] Google would also fund the establishment and initial operations of a not-for-profit entity, called the Registry, which would represent rights holders in negotiating future uses of their content with Google.[182] Google, in turn, would receive a non-exclusive license[183] to (1) "Digitize all Books and Inserts" published before January 5, 2009, and (2) make certain uses of the digitized materials, including displaying "snippets" of them among its search results, subject to the terms of the agreement.[184] By allowing Google to digitize and display books, the agreement would pave the way for Google to expand Google Book Search, selling subscriptions to institutions and electronic versions of books to individuals.[185] The agreement would also create certain rights and responsibilities for libraries that allow Google to digitize their books,[186] as well as make certain provisions for institutional subscribers to, or individual users of, commercialized versions of Google's Book Search database.[187]

The agreement will not take effect until certain conditions are met, one of which requires final court approval of the settlement agreement.[188] The court granted preliminary approval of the agreement on November 17, 2008.[189] Final approval is still pending, however. Class members presently have until September 4, 2009, to file objections with the court.[190] The court will then consider these objections, as well as conduct its own review of the proposed agreement, in determining whether to grant final approval to the settlement.[191]

Commentators have voiced numerous concerns about the proposed settlement, some of which could recur in class members' objections or the court's review of the agreement. One major concern is that the settlement would effectively grant Google an exclusive license to digitize the books covered by the agreement and display them to individual users and libraries.[192] The settlement states that Google's digitization and display rights under the agreement are non-exclusive,[193] and nothing, under the settlement or otherwise, would preclude another entity from undertaking a digitization and indexing project like Google Book Search.[194] However, some commentators worry that these factors might not suffice to prevent Google's effectively monopolizing the book-search field given that the settlement agreement (1) includes a clause granting Google the right to any more favorable terms that the Registry negotiates with third-parties over the next ten years[195] and (2) protects Google from the litigation risks likely to confront those initiating new book-digitization projects. These factors could significantly diminish the willingness of potential competitors to enter the field and could result in a monopolized market where individual consumers and libraries, in particular, are vulnerable to price increases.[196] On July 2, 2009, the U.S. Department of Justice confirmed that it is conducting an antitrust investigation into the Google settlement because of such concerns. [197] The Justice Department reportedly has written a letter to the federal judge reviewing the proposed settlement indicating that the settlement's terms could violate the Sherman Act of 1890, which prohibits, among other things, any "contract, combination ... or conspiracy" that constitutes a "restraint of trade or commerce."[198]

Another related concern focuses upon the settlement's potential effects on "orphan works," or copyrighted works whose owners are difficult or impossible to identify or locate.[199] Some commentators worry that the settlement would grant Google a "unique lock"[200] on orphan works by making the Registry, which is to be created under the agreement, the effective trustee of rights in "orphaned" books.[201] The Registry has already opted to deal with Google regarding these books, and some commentators are concerned that the absence of known or identifiable rights holders effectively means that these books could not be further used without the agreement of the Registry and/or Google.[202] Commentators concerned about orphan works also suggest that the settlement agreement's treatment of them constitutes "a kind of legislation, stepping on congressional prerogatives."[203] The 110th Congress considered, but did not enact, orphan works legislation that would have authorized use of orphan works under certain conditions and would have made the U.S. Copyright Office responsible for receiving and recording notices tracking users and uses of orphan works.[204] Similar legislation may be introduced in the 111th Congress. Some commentators feel that any "changes" involving orphan works of the magnitude allegedly made in the settlement agreement ought to be made by Congress, not the federal courts.[205]

Other concerns center upon the settlement agreement's effects on public welfare, especially its reliance on a private Registry instead of the Copyright Office and its provisions regarding user privacy.[206]

Rejection of the proposed settlement agreement could place the parties' claims and defenses back before the court. Moreover, even if eventually approved by the courts, the settlement agreement only governs claims against Google over its Library Project within the United States. Litigation in other jurisdictions remains possible. [207]

ACKNOWLEDGMENTS

Robin Jeweler, Legislative Attorney, original author of RS22356 *The Google Book Search Project: Is Online Indexing a Fair Use Under Copyright Law?*

End Note

[110]Google Checks Out Library Books, Dec. 14, 2004, *available at* http://www.google.com/press/pressrel/print_library.html. Participating libraries included those at the University of Michigan, Harvard University, Stanford University, and Oxford University, as well as the New York Public Library.

[111] *Id.*

[112] *Id.* Copyright protection for books generally lasts "for a term consisting of the life of the author and 70 years after the author's death." 17 U.S.C. § 302(a).
[113] Google Checks Out Library Books, *supra* note 1.
[114] *Id.*
[115] Association of American University Presses, Google Book Search, Neé Google Print, *available at* http://www.aaupnet.org/aboutup/issues/gprint.html.
[116] Google Books Partner Program: Promote Your Books on Google—For Free, 2009, *available at* http://books.google.com/googlebooks/book_search_tour.
[117] *Id.*
[118] *See, e.g.,* Anandashankar Mazumdar, University Press Group Expresses Concern Over Google Print's Digitization of Works, 70 *Pat., Trademark & Copyright J.* 109 (June 3, 2005).
[119] 17 U.S.C. § 20 1(a). There are exceptions to this general rule, such as when a book is "made for hire" or is a "work of the United States Government." *See* 17 U.S.C. § 105 & 201(b).
[120] See, e.g., Example Author Contract, *available at* http://www.writecontent.com/Publishing_Tools/Author_Contract_/author_contract_.html ("The Author hereby grants to the Publisher exclusive rights to reproduce and/or publish or adapt and sell, and/or license third parties to publish or adapt and sell said Work.").
[121] 17 U.S.C. § 106(1) & (5).
[122] See, e.g., Mazumdar, *supra* note 9.
[123] See, e.g., Christine Mumford, Google Library Project Temporarily Halted to Allow Copyright Owner Response, 70 *Pat., Trademark & Copyright J.* 461 (Aug. 19, 2005).
[124] Authors Guild v. Google Inc., Class Action Complaint, No. 05 CV 8136 (S.D.N.Y. Sept. 20, 2005) at ¶ 20. The University of Michigan's library was the focus because Google began digitizing its books first. Id. at ¶ 31. Under copyright law, "literary works" are any "works, other than audiovisual works, expressed in words." 17 U.S.C. § 101.
[125] McGraw Hill Cos. v. Google Inc., Complaint, No. 05 CV 8881 (S.D.N.Y. Oct. 19, 2005). These companies were McGraw-Hill Companies; Pearson Education; Penguin Group; Simon & Schuster; and John Wiley and Sons.
[126] Fed. R. Civ. P. 23(e).
[127] *See, e.g.,* Susan Wojcicki, Google Print and the Authors Guild, Sept. 20, 2005, *available at* http://googleblog.blogspot.com/2005/09/google-print-and-authors-guild.html.
[128] *Id.*
[129] See 336 F.3d 811 (9th Cir. 2003). For more background on Kelly, see CRS Report RL33810, Internet Search Engines: Copyright's *"Fair Use" in Reproduction and Public Display Rights*, by Robin Jeweler and Brian T. Yeh.
[130] See, e.g., Wojcicki, supra note 18.
[131] The Harvard University Libraries (HUL), for example, contain over 15 million books. HUL, About the HOLLIS Catalog, June 25, 2007, *available at* http://lib.harvard.edu/catalogs/hollis.html.
[132] Anandashankar Mazumdar, Publishers: Value of Book Search Project Shows That Scanning Is Not Fair Use, 71 *Pat., Trademark & Copyright J.* 94 (Nov. 25. 2005).
[133] *Id.*
[134] P.L. 105-3 04. For more information on the DMCA generally, see CRS Report 98-943, *Digital Millennium Copyright Act, P.L. 1 05-304: Summary and Analysis*, by Dorothy M. Schrader.
[135] 11 U.S.C. § 512(b)-(c).
[136] *See* Field v. Google Inc., 412 F. Supp. 2d 1106 (D. Nev. 2006).
[137] *See, e.g.,* Class Action Complaint, *supra* note 15, at ¶ 23.d and ¶ 41 (alleging Google's infringement was willful); Complaint, supra note 16, at ¶ 2 (same).
[138] *See, e.g.,* Complaint, *supra* note 16, at ¶ 29 (arguing that Web pages differ from print books because rights holders in Web pages can rely on technological measures to prevent indexing, while authors of print books can take no such measures to prevent digitization).
[139] *See, e.g.,* Wojcicki, *supra* note 18.
[140] 17 U.S.C. § 107.
[141] *Id.*
[142] Campbell v. Acuff-Rose Music, Inc., 510 U.S. 569, 578 (1994).
[143] *Id.*
[144] Perfect 10, Inc. v. Amazon.com, Inc., 487 F.3d 701, 720 (9th Cir. 2007) (quoting the U.S. Constitution, art. I, § 8, cl. 8, *as well as Sony Corp. of Am. v. Universal City Studios, Inc.*, 464 U.S. 417, 429 n. 10 (1984)).
[145] Stewart v. Abend, 495 U.S. 207, 237 (1990).
[146] Campbell, 510 U.S. at 577-78.
[147] *See, e.g.,* Sony, 464 U.S. at 451 ("Every commercial use of copyrighted materials is presumptively an unfair exploitation of the monopoly privilege that belongs to the owner of the copyright.").

[148] *See, e.g.*, Infinity Broad. Corp. v. Kirkwood, 150 F.3d 104, 108 (2d Cir. 1998) (retransmission of radio broadcast over telephone lines not a fair use); UMG Recordings, Inc. v. MP3.com, Inc., 92 F. Supp. 2d 349, 351 (S.D.N.Y. 2000) (reproducing analog audio CDs as MP3s not a fair use).
[149] Campbell, 510 U.S. at 578-79.
[150] *Id.* at 579.
[151] 336 F.3d 811 (9th Cir. 2003).
[152] *Id.* at 818-19.
[153] *Id.* at 818.
[154] *Id.* at 819.
[155] 487 F.3d 701, 721 (9th Cir. 2007), rev'g Perfect 10, Inc. v. Google Inc., 416 F. Supp. 2d 828 (C.D. Cal. 2006) (holding that Google's use of thumbnail versions of Perfect 10's copyrighted photographs was not fair, in part, because Google's thumbnails could potentially substitute for the reduced-size versions of these photographs that Perfect 10 had licensed another company to reproduce and distribute for display on cell phones).
[156] Perfect 10, Inc., 487 F.3d at 721.
[157] *See, e.g.*, Kelly, 336 F.3d at 816.
[158] Field, 412 F. Supp. 2d at 1115-16.
[159] A digital version of a print book would display poorer resolution than the original. However, it would enable researchers to locate specific content more easily by using the "search" or "find" functions of their Web browsers.
[160] 464 U.S. 417 (1984).
[161] *Id.* at 442.
[162] *See, e.g.*, Jonathan Band, The Google Print Library Project: Fair or Foul?, 9 J. of Internet L. 1, 4 (Oct. 2005); Christopher Heun, Courts Unlikely to Stop Google Book Copying, *Internet Week* (Sept. 2, 2005), *available at* http://internetweek.cmp.com/showArticle.jhtml?articleID=170700329.
[163] 92 F. Supp. 2d 349, 352 (S.D.N.Y. 2000) ("[D]efendant's 'fair use' defense is indefensible and must be denied as a matter of law.").
[164] *Id.*
[165] Kelly, 336 F.3d at 820.
[166] *See, e.g.*, Feist Publ'ns, Inc. v. Rural Tel. Serv., 499 U.S. 340 (1991) (requiring originality in the selection or arrangement of facts for copyrightability).
[167] See, e.g., Baker v. Selden, 101 U.S. 99 (1879) (distinguishing non-protectable ideas from their protectable expressions).
[168] Campbell, 510 U.S. at 577-78.
[169] Worldwide Church of God v. Philadelphia Church of God, Inc., 227 F.3d 1110, 1118 (9th Cir. 2000) (internal quotations omitted).
[170] *See, e.g.*, Kelly, 336 F.3d at 821; Sega Enters., Ltd. v. Accolade, Inc., 977 F.2d 1510, 1523 (9th Cir. 1992).
[171] *See, e.g.*, Harper & Row Publishers, Inc. v. Nation Enters., 471 U.S. 539, 564 (1985).
[172] *See, e.g.*, Kelly, 336 F.3d 811; Perfect 10, Inc., 487 F.3d 701.
[173] *See* Field, 412 F. Supp. 2d at 1115-16.
[174] *See* Kelly, 336 F.3d at 816.
[175] *See* Complaint, *supra* note 16, at ¶ 5 (noting that publishers were already making their print books available online in various ways, including a partnership with the search engine Yahoo!).
[176] *Cf.* BMG Music v. Gonzalez, 430 F.3d 888, 891 (7th Cir. 2005) ("Copyright law lets authors make their own decisions about how best to promote their works.").
[177] *See, e.g.*, Bill Graham Archives, LLC v. Dorling Kindersley, Ltd., 386 F. Supp. 2d 324, 332 (S.D.N.Y. 2005).
[178] Perfect 10, Inc., 487 F.3d at 725.
[179] *See, e.g.*, Campbell, 510 U.S. at 591.
[180] Authors Guild, Inc. v. Google Inc., Settlement Agreement, Case No. 05 CV 8136-JES (S.D.N.Y. Oct. 28, 2008).
[181] *Id.* at ¶ 2.1(a) (providing that Google would pay 70% of the net revenue earned from uses of Google Book Search in the United States to rights holders); ¶ 2.1(b) (providing that Google would pay at least $45 million into a "Settlement Fund," whose proceeds would pay rights holders whose books or "inserts" were digitized prior to January 5, 2009).
[182] *Id.* at ¶ 2.1(c). Among other functions, the Registry could negotiate the terms of "New Revenue Models" (e.g., print¬on-demand) with Google and negotiate pricing categories and percentages for sale of digitized materials to users.
[183] Because this license is non-exclusive, the Registry could license other entities to digitize, index, or display the works of rights holders. However, if the Registry were to enter into a similar agreement within 10 years of the settlement's effective date, it must extend comparable economic and other terms to Google. *Id.* at ¶ 3.8(a).
[184] *Id.* at ¶ 3.1. Google's rights to use books within their terms of copyright protection would hinge upon whether they were "commercially available," or available "for sale new through one or more then-customary channels of trade in the United States." *See id.* at ¶ 1.28. If a book is commercially available, Google could not make

"display uses" without the copyright holders' consent. *Id.* at ¶¶ 3.3-3.5. Conversely, if a book is not commercially available, Google could make "display uses" unless the rights holder objects. Id. This distinction between commercially available and non- commercially available books would significantly vary the legal protections of copyright law, which protects all works equally, regardless of their commercial availability, during their terms of copyright protection. See 17 U.S.C. § 106 and § 302.

[185] See, e.g., Settlement Agreement, *supra* note 71, at ¶ 3.7.

[186] Id. at ¶ 7.2(f)(i)-(ii) and Article X.

[187] *See, e.g.,* James Grimmelmann, Principles and Recommendations for the Google Book Search Settlement, Nov. 8, 2008, *available at* http://www.laboratorium.net/archive/2008/1 1/08/ principles_and_recommendations_for_the_google_book (noting the existence, as well as the potential inadequacy, of provisions regarding users).

[188] Settlement Agreement, *supra* note 71, at ¶ 1.49.

[189] Authors Guild, Inc. v. Google Inc., Order Granting Preliminary Settlement Approval, Case No. 05 CV 8136-JES (S.D.N.Y. Nov. 17, 2008). The final hearing is presently scheduled to be held on October 4, 2009. It was originally set for June 11, 2009, but the court changed the date in an order issued on April 28, 2009. See Court Delays Google Book Search Settlement Hearing, Extends Opt-Out Period, 78 *Pat., Trademark & Copyright J.* 9 (May 1, 2009).

[190] Court Delays Google Book Search Settlement Hearing, *supra* note 80. The deadline for filing objections was originally May 5, 2009. See Order Granting Preliminary Settlement Approval, *supra* note 80.

[191] Under the Federal Rules of Civil Procedure, judges must ensure that settlements in class action lawsuits are "fair, reasonable, and adequate." Fed. R. Civ. P. 23(e). In conducting this review, the court could reject a proposed settlement because of concerns not raised by class members or other parties to the agreement. *See, e.g.,* Muchnick v. Thompson Corp., 509 F.3d 116 (2d Cir. 2007) (quashing the proposed settlement agreement resolving the litigation in *Tasini v. New York Times* because some members of the proposed settlement class had not registered their works with the U.S. Copyright Office and so lacked standing to bring suit in federal court). The district court had previously approved the settlement, and no class member or party had raised this objection.

[192] *See, e.g.,* James Gibson, Google's New Monopoly? How the Company Could Gain by Paying Millions in Copyright Fees, *Wash. Post*, Nov. 3, 2008, at A21 ("[S]ettling probably puts Google in a better position than it would have been in if it had won its case in court. ... Google's concession has made it more difficult for *anyone* to invoke fair use for book searches [and] [b]y settling the case, Google has made it much more difficult for others to compete with its Book Search service.").

[193] See, e.g., Settlement Agreement, *supra* note 71, at ¶ 3.1(a).

[194] See, e.g., Miguel Helft, Some Raise Alarms as Google Resurrects Out-of-Print Books, *New York Times*, Apr. 4, 2009, at A1 ("Nothing prevent[s] a potential rival from following in [Google's] footsteps—namely, by scanning books without explicit permission, waiting to be sued and working to secure a similar settlement."). Microsoft, for example, has explored offering book-search capabilities in the past. See Andrea L. Foster, Microsoft's Book-Search Project Has a Surprise Ending, *Chron. of Higher Educ.*, May 29, 2008, *available at* http://chronicle.com/free/2008/05/ 3022n.htm.

[195] *See, e.g.,* Settlement Agreement, *supra* note 71, at ¶ 3.8(a) ("The Registry ... will extend economic and other terms to Google that, when taken as a whole, do not disfavor or disadvantage Google as compared to any other substantially similar authorizations granted to third parties by the Registry.").

[196] *See, e.g.,* Laura G. Mirviss, Harvard-Google Online Book Deal at Risk, *The Harvard Crimson*, Oct. 30, 2008, *available at* http://www.thecrimson.com/article.aspx?ref=524989 ("The settlement provides no assurance that the prices charged for access will be reasonable.").

[197] *See, e.g.,* Miguel Helft, U.S. Inquiry Is Confirmed into Google Books Deal, N.Y. Times, July 2, 2009, *available at* http://www.nytimes.com/2009/07/03/technology/companies/03google.html?_r=1&ref=technology.

[198] 15 U.S.C. § 1.

[199] *See, e.g.,* Anandashankar Mazumdar, Internet Archive Warns of Online Book Market Consolidation from Google Settlement, *Pat., Trademark & Copyright L. Daily*, Apr. 23, 2009. For more on orphan works generally, see CRS Report RL33392, "*Orphan Works" in Copyright Law*, by Brian T. Yeh.

[200] Grimmelmann, *supra* note 78.

[201] See, e.g., Mazumdar, *supra* note 89.

[202] *Id.*

[203] *See, e.g.,* Anandashankar Mazumdar, Google Books Settlement Prompts Questions about Effect on Readers, Libraries, Others, *Pat., Trademark & Copyright L. Daily*, Mar. 18, 2009 (quoting Marybeth Peters, Register of Copyrights).

[204] Orphan Works Act of 2008, H.R. 5889, 1 10th Cong. There was a similar bill in the Senate, but it did not include the notice requirements of the House bill. See Shawn Bentley Orphan Works Act of 2008, S. 2913, 110th Cong.

[205] *See, e.g.*, Helft, *supra* note 85 ("They are doing an end run around the legislative process.") (quoting Brewster Kahle, founder of the Internet Archive and the Open Content Alliance).

[206] *See, e.g.*, Mazumdar, *supra* note 93.

[207] *See, e.g.*, Editions du Seuil v. Google Inc., Tribunal de Grand Instance de Paris (alleging that Google Book Search infringes copyright under French law); Joe Kirwin, EU States Urge Investigation into Google's Digital Book Plan, *Pat., Trademark & Copyright L. Daily*, May 29, 2009 (noting that the Federation of European Publishers has also raised concerns about the potential anticompetitive effects of the Google Library Project with the European Commission).

In: Trends in Internet Research
Editor: B.G. Kutais
ISBN: 978-1-59454-140-7

Chapter 4

CAMPAIGN FINANCE: REGULATING POLITICAL COMMUNICATIONS ON THE INTERNET*

L. Paige Whitaker[1] *and R. Sam Garrett*[2]

ABSTRACT

The Federal Election Campaign Act (FECA) regulates "federal election activity," which is defined to include a "public communication" (i.e., a broadcast, cable, satellite, newspaper, magazine, outdoor advertising facility, mass mailing, or telephone bank communication made to the general public) or "any other form of general public political advertising." In 2006, in response to a federal district court decision, the FEC promulgated regulations amending the definition of "public communication" to include paid Internet advertisements placed on another individual or entity's website. As a result, a key element of online political activity—*paid* political advertising—is subject to federal campaign finance law and regulations.

During the 110th Congress, the regulation of political communications on the Internet was not the subject of major legislative action. H.R. 894 (Price, NC) would have extended "stand by your ad" disclaimer requirements to Internet communications, among others. H.R. 5699 (Hensarling) would have exempted from treatment as a contribution or expenditure any uncompensated Internet services by individuals and certain corporations. Similar legislation has not yet been introduced in the 111th Congress. This report will be updated in the event of major legislative, regulatory, or legal developments.

---

* This is an edited, reformatted and augmented version of a Congressional Research Service Publication, Order Code RS22272, Prepared for Members and Committees of Congress, January 26, 2009.

[1] L. Paige Whitaker, Legislative Attorney, lwhitaker@crs.loc.gov, 7-5477

[2] R. Sam Garrett, Analyst in American National Government, rgarrett@crs.loc.gov, 7-6443

BACKGROUND

The Federal Election Campaign Act

The Federal Election Campaign Act (FECA), as amended by the Bipartisan Campaign Reform Act of 2002 (BCRA),[208] regulates "federal election activity," which is defined to include (1) voter registration drives in the last 120 days of a federal election; (2) voter identification, get-out-the vote drives (GOTV), and generic activity in connection with an election in which a federal candidate is on the ballot; (3) "public communications" that refer to a clearly identified federal candidate and promote, support, attack, or oppose that candidate (regardless of whether the communications expressly advocate a vote for or against a candidate); and (4) services by a state or local party employee who spends at least 25% of paid time per month on activities in connection with a federal election.[209] FECA further defines "public communications" as broadcast, cable, satellite, newspaper, magazine, outdoor advertising facility, mass mailing, or telephone bank communications made to the general public, "or any other form of general public political advertising."[210] As a result, candidate and party committees can only use regulated federal funds to pay for such "federal election activity." Regulated federal funds, also known as "hard money," are funds that are subject to FECA's contribution limitations, source restrictions, and reporting requirements.[211]

Shays v. FEC

Shortly after enactment of the BCRA amendments to FECA in 2002, the FEC promulgated regulations that exempted Internet communications from federal campaign finance regulation altogether by excluding such communications from the definition of "public communication."[212] In response, the two primary sponsors of BCRA in the House of Representatives, Representatives Shays and Meehan, filed suit in U.S. district court against the FEC. In seeking to invalidate the regulations, the plaintiffs argued, *inter alia*, that by not regulating Internet activities, the FEC was opening a new avenue for circumvention of federal campaign finance law, contrary to Congress's intent in enacting BCRA. In 2004, in *Shays v. FEC*,[213] the U.S. District Court for the District of Columbia agreed with the BCRA sponsors and generally overturned the FEC's initial regulations governing political communications on the Internet.

The *Shays* court held that excluding all Internet communications from the FEC rule defining "public communication," at 11 CFR § 100.26, was inconsistent with Congress's use of the phrase, "or any other form of general public political advertising," in the BCRA definition of "public communication." Further, the court found that the FEC had failed to provide legislative history that would persuade the court to ignore the plain meaning of the statute.[214] While not all Internet communications fall within the phrase, "any other form of general public political advertising," the court observed that "some clearly do."[215] However, the court left it to the FEC to determine precisely what constitutes "general public political advertising" in the context of the Internet.[216] Furthermore, while the court specifically upheld the definition of "generic campaign activity" as a "public communication," it found that the FEC's 2002 Notice of Proposed Rulemaking (NPRM) failed to provide adequate notice to the public, under the Administrative Procedure Act (APA), that the FEC might establish such a definition. As the court noted, it could not "fathom how an interested party 'could have anticipated the final rulemaking from the draft rule.'"[217]

The *Shays* court also found that the FEC rule exempting Internet communications from the definition of "public communications" meant that no matter how closely such communications were coordinated with political parties or candidate campaigns, they could not be considered "coordinated communications" and hence, subject to FECA regulation.[218] As the court observed, it had long been a tenet of campaign finance law that, in order to prevent circumvention of regulation, FECA treated expenditures made "in cooperation, consultation, or concert, with or at the suggestion of a candidate" as a contribution to such candidate.[219] According to the court, the exclusion of Internet communications from coordinated communications contrasted with prior FEC rules and was contrary to Congress's intent in enacting the statute.[220] The court remanded the case to the FEC for further action consistent with its decision.[221]

FEC RULEMAKING

Background

In response to the district court's decision in *Shays v. FEC*, in April 2005, the FEC published an NPRM seeking comment on its proposal to amend the definition of "public communication" to conform to the ruling.[222] In its NPRM, the FEC requested comments on proposed rules to include paid Internet advertisements in the definition of "public communication." In addition, the FEC sought comment on the related definition of "generic campaign activity," on proposed changes to disclaimer regulations, and on proposed exceptions to the definitions of "contribution" and "expenditure" for certain Internet activities and communications that would qualify as individual volunteer activity or that would qualify for the "press exemption." According to the FEC, the proposed rules were intended to ensure that political committees properly finance and disclose their Internet communications, without impeding individual citizens from using the Internet to speak freely regarding candidates and elections (e.g., blogging).

The comment period closed and a public hearing was held in June 2005, and in anticipation of congressional action, the FEC delayed consideration of the Internet regulations. However, in the absence of congressional legislation, in March 2006, the FEC voted unanimously to approve the new regulations. In so doing, the commissioners cited the 2004 *Shays v. FEC* federal district court decision as requiring them to take such action.

Summary of Regulations

Generally, the Internet regulations reflect an attempt by the FEC to leave blogs, created and wholly maintained by individuals, free of FECA regulation, so long as such services are not performed for a fee. As stated in its NPRM:

> While drafting a proposed rule, the Commission recognized the important purpose of BCRA in preventing actual and apparent corruption and the circumvention of the Act as well as the plain meaning of "general public political advertising," and the significant public policy considerations that encourage the promotion of the Internet as a unique forum for free or low-cost speech and open information exchange. The Commission was also mindful that there is no record that Internet activities present any significant danger of corruption or the appearance of corruption, nor has the Commission seen evidence that its 2002 definition of "public communication" has led to circumvention of the law or fostered corruption or the appearance thereof. Therefore the Commission proposed to treat paid Internet advertising on another person's website as a "public communication," but otherwise sought to exclude all Internet communications from the definition of "public communication."[223]

The regulations apply only when money is exchanged for Internet-related campaign advertisements. Accordingly, the funds expended for such advertisements are subject to the limitations, source restrictions, and reporting requirements of FECA.

Key aspects of the FEC regulations include the following:

Regulation of paid Internet ads as "public communications"—The definition of "public communication" includes paid Internet ads placed on another individual or entity's website as a form of "general public political advertising," with no dollar threshold required; the advertiser, not the website operator, is considered to be making the public communication. Accordingly, the fees for such ads are subject to FECA contribution limits, source restrictions, and disclosure requirements.[224]

Disclaimer requirements—Disclaimers (statements of attribution) are required on all political committee websites available to the public. As "public communications," paid Internet ads must contain disclaimers if they expressly advocate the election or defeat of a clearly identified federal candidate or solicit contributions. Disclaimers are not required on e-mails from individuals or groups unless they are political committees, in which case disclaimers are required if more than 500 substantially similar, unsolicited e-mails are sent within a 30-day period.[225]

Disclosure of fees paid by candidates to bloggers—Payments to bloggers from candidates are required to be disclosed only on candidate disclosure statements; no such disclaimers are required on blog sites.[226]

Coordinated communications—Internet advertisements made for the purpose of influencing a federal election, placed on the website of another person or entity *for a fee*—and coordinated with a candidate or party committee—are considered "coordinated communications" and as such, constitute in-kind contributions to the candidate or committee. Accordingly, the fees for such ads are subject to FECA contribution limits, source restrictions, and disclosure requirements.[227]

Media exemption—Under the definition of "contribution," the general exemption from FECA coverage of news stories, commentaries, and editorials distributed through broadcasters, newspapers, and periodicals applies to such communications that are distributed over the Internet.[228]

Exceptions for individual or volunteer activity on the Internet—Under the definitions of "contribution" and "expenditure," an uncompensated individual or group of individuals using Internet equipment and services in order to influence a federal election, whether or not such services were known by or coordinated with a campaign, are excluded from FECA regulation.[229]

CONGRESSIONAL ACTIVITY

Brief History

During Congress's consideration of BCRA in 2001 and 2002, the subject of communications over the Internet was not addressed, but it was discussed during debate on a previous version of what became BCRA during House consideration of H.R. 417 (Shays-Meehan) in the 106th Congress.

An amendment was offered to that bill by Representative DeLay to exempt communications over the Internet from regulation under FECA, but was defeated by a vote of 160-268.[230]

During the 109th Congress, several bills were proposed to exempt all communications over the Internet from the BCRA definition of "public communication," and therefore, regulation under FECA. These proposals included H.R. 1606 (Hensarling), the Online Freedom of Speech Act, which was considered by the House under suspension of the rules but, on a 225-182 vote, failed to receive the two-thirds necessary for passage. The bill was brought up again and ordered reported favorably by the House Administration Committee on March 9, 2006, setting up consideration by the House, but the vote was postponed pending FEC regulatory action. Also during the 109th Congress, in response to concerns that the Online Freedom of Speech Act could open the door to FECA circumvention (for example, by allowing corporations and unions to finance advertisements), two additional bills were offered: H.R. 4194 (Shays-Meehan) would have excluded Internet communications from FECA regulation, but regulated communications placed on a website for a fee and those made by most corporations and unions, by any political committee, and by state and local parties; and H.R. 4900 (Allen-Bass) would have exempted from FECA regulation most individual online communications and advertisements below a dollar threshold. In the wake of the new FEC regulations approved on March 27, 2006, however, House floor action was postponed indefinitely.

110th Congress

During the 110th Congress, the regulation of political communications on the Internet was not the subject of major legislative action. H.R. 894 (Price, NC) would have extended "stand by your ad" disclaimer requirements to Internet communications, among others. It was referred to the Committee on House Administration.

H.R. 5699 (Hensarling) would have exempted from treatment as a contribution or expenditure any uncompensated Internet services by individuals and corporations that are wholly owned by individuals engaging primarily in Internet activities, which do not derive a substantial portion of revenue from sources other than income from Internet activities, except payment for (1) a public communication (other than a nominal fee), (2) the purchase or rental of an email address list made at the direction of a political committee, or (3) an email address list that is transferred to a political committee. H.R. 5699 also would have exempted blogs and other Internet and electronic publications from treatment as an expenditure by including such communications in the general media exemption applicable to broadcast stations and newspapers. It was referred to the Committee on House Administration.

111th Congress

Similar legislation has not yet been introduced in the 111th Congress.

ACKNOWLEDGMENTS

CRS specialist Joseph E. Cantor (now retired) originally co-authored this report.

End Note

[208] P.L. 107-155 (2002).
[209] 2 U.S.C. § 431(20).
[210] 2 U.S.C. § 431(22).
[211] *See* 11 C.F.R. § 300.2(k).
[212] "The term public communication shall not include communications over the Internet." 11 C.F.R. § 100.26 (2005). The FEC also determined that Internet communications should not be considered "electioneering communications," which is a specific type of broadcast, cable, or satellite advertising. According to the FEC: The Internet is included in the list of exceptions in the final rules in section 100.29(c)(1) because, in most instances, it is not a broadcast, cable, or satellite communication. BCRA's legislative history.... establishes Congress's intent to exclude communications over the Internet from the electioneering communication provisions. The Commission concludes that Congress did not seek to regulate the Internet in subtitle A of Title II of BCRA. The relatively few commenters who opposed the Internet exemption did not disagree with this conclusion; rather, they argued that as the Internet develops, aspects of it might come to be used in a manner like radio or television. To these commenters, this potential evolution of the Internet calls for a more precise approach and makes the exemption as proposed too broad a treatment of this issue. The Commission has decided to include the exemption in the final rules, rather than attempt to craft a regulation that responds to unknown, future developments. Electioneering Communications, 67 *Fed. Reg.* 65,190 (2002). *See* 11 CFR § 100.29 for the definition of "electioneering communication."
[213] 337 F. Supp. 2d 28 (D.D.C. 2004), *aff'd*, 414 F. 3d 76 (D.C. Cir. 2005), *reh'g en banc denied*, No. 04-5352 (October 21, 2005).
[214] Id. at 69.
[215] Id. at 67.
[216] Id. at 70.
[217] Id. at 112 (quoting Anne Arundel Co., Maryland v. U.S. EPA., 963 F.2d 412, 418 (D.C. Cir. 1999)).
[218] For further discussion of coordination, see CRS Report RS22644, *Coordinated Party Expenditures in Federal Elections: An Overview*, by R. Sam Garrett and L. Paige Whitaker.

[219] Shays, 337 F. Supp. 2d at 62 (quoting McConnell v. FEC, 124 S. Ct. 619, 705 (2003)).
[220] *Id.* at 65, 70.
[221] *Id.* at 130.
[222] Internet Communications, 70 Fed. Reg. 16,967 (April 4, 2005).
[223] Internet Communications, 71 Fed. Reg. 18,589, 18,593 (April 12, 2006) (codified at 11 C.F.R. pts. 100, 110, and 114).
[224] See 11 C.F.R. § 100.26.
[225] See 11 C.F.R. § 110.11.
[226] See 11 C.F.R. § 104.3(b).
[227] See 11 C.F.R. § 109.21(b).
[228] See 11 C.F.R. § 100.73.
[229] See 11 C.F.R. §§ 100.94, 100.32.
[230] Bipartisan Campaign Reform Act of 1999. 145 CONG. REC. 21526 (September 14, 1999).

In: Trends in Internet Research
Editor: B.G. Kutais ISBN: 978-1-59454-140-7

Chapter 5

INTERNET DOMAIN NAMES: BACKGROUND AND POLICY ISSUES*

Lennard G. Kruger

ABSTRACT

Navigating the Internet requires using addresses and corresponding names that identify the location of individual computers. The Domain Name System (DNS) is the distributed set of databases residing in computers around the world that contain address numbers mapped to corresponding domain names, making it possible to send and receive messages and to access information from computers anywhere on the Internet.

The DNS is managed and operated by a not-for-profit public benefit corporation called the Internet Corporation for Assigned Names and Numbers (ICANN). Because the Internet evolved from a network infrastructure created by the Department of Defense, the U.S. government originally owned and operated (primarily through private contractors) the key components of network architecture that enable the domain name system to function. A 1998 Memorandum of Understanding (MOU) between ICANN and the Department of Commerce (DOC) initiated a process intended to transition technical DNS coordination and management functions to a private sector not-for-profit entity. While the DOC currently plays no role in the internal governance or day-to-day operations of the DNS, ICANN remains accountable to the U.S. government through a Joint Project Agreement (JPA) with the DOC.

Many of the technical, operational, and management decisions regarding the DNS can have significant impacts on Internet-related policy issues such as intellectual property, privacy, e-commerce, and cybersecurity. The ICANN-DOC Joint Project Agreement is due to expire on September 30, 2009. Congress and the Administration are assessing the appropriate federal role with respect to ICANN and the DNS, and examining to what extent ICANN is presently positioned to ensure Internet stability and security, competition, private and bottom-up policymaking and coordination, and fair representation of the Internet community. A related issue is whether the U.S. government's unique authority over the DNS root zone should continue indefinitely.

* This is an edited, reformatted and augmented version of a Congressional Research Service Publication, Order Code 97-868, Prepared for Members and Committees of Congress, June 8, 2009.

Foreign governments have argued that it is inappropriate for the U.S. government to have exclusive authority over the worldwide DNS, and that technical coordination and management of the DNS should be accountable to international governmental entities. On the other hand, many U.S. officials argue that it is critical for the U.S. government to maintain authority over the DNS in order to guarantee the stability and security of the Internet.

The expiration of the JPA and the continuing U.S. authority over the DNS root zone remain two issues of keen interest to the 111th Congress, the Administration, foreign governments, and other Internet stakeholders worldwide. How these issues are addressed will likely have profound impacts on the continuing evolution of ICANN, the DNS, and the Internet.

Background and History

The Internet is often described as a "network of networks" because it is not a single physical entity but, in fact, hundreds of thousands of interconnected networks linking many millions of computers around the world. Computers connected to the Internet are identified by a unique Internet Protocol (IP) number that designates their specific location, thereby making it possible to send and receive messages and to access information from computers anywhere on the Internet. Domain names were created to provide users with a simple location name, rather than requiring them to use a long list of numbers. For example, the IP number for the location of the THOMAS legislative system at the Library of Congress is 140.147.248.9; the corresponding domain name is thomas.loc.gov. Top Level Domains (TLDs) appear at the end of an address and are either a given country code, such as .jp or .uk, or are generic designations (gTLDs), such as .com, .org, .net, .edu, or .gov. The Domain Name System (DNS) is the distributed set of databases residing in computers around the world that contain the address numbers, mapped to corresponding domain names. Those computers, called root servers, must be coordinated to ensure connectivity across the Internet.

The Internet originated with research funding provided by the Department of Defense Advanced Research Projects Agency (DARPA) to establish a military network. As its use expanded, a civilian segment evolved with support from the National Science Foundation (NSF) and other science agencies. While there were (and are) no formal statutory authorities or international agreements governing the management and operation of the Internet and the DNS, several entities played key roles in the DNS. For example, the Internet Assigned Numbers Authority (IANA), which was operated at the Information Sciences Institute/University of Southern California under contract with the Department of Defense, made technical decisions concerning root servers, determined qualifications for applicants to manage country code TLDs, assigned unique protocol parameters, and managed the IP address space, including delegating blocks of addresses to registries around the world to assign to users in their geographic area.

NSF was responsible for registration of nonmilitary domain names, and in 1992 put out a solicitation for managing network services, including domain name registration. In 1993, NSF signed a five-year cooperative agreement with a consortium of companies called InterNic. Under this agreement, Network Solutions Inc. (NSI), a Herndon, Virginia engineering and management consulting firm, became the sole Internet domain name registration service for registering the .com, .net., and .org. gTLDs.

After the imposition of registration fees in 1995, criticism of NSI's sole control over registration of the gTLDs grew. In addition, there was an increase in trademark disputes arising out of the enormous growth of registrations in the .com domain. There also was concern that the role played by IANA lacked a legal foundation and required more permanence to ensure the stability of the Internet and the domain name system. These concerns prompted actions both in the United States and internationally.

An International Ad Hoc Committee (IAHC), a coalition of individuals representing various constituencies, released a proposal for the administration and management of gTLDs on February 4, 1997. The proposal recommended that seven new gTLDs be created and that additional registrars be selected to compete with each other in the granting of registration services for all new second level domain names. To assess whether the IAHC proposal should be supported by the U.S. government, the executive branch created an interagency group to address the domain name issue and assigned lead responsibility to the National Telecommunications and Information Administration (NTIA) of the Department of Commerce (DOC). On June 5, 1998, DOC issued a final statement of policy, "Management of Internet Names and Addresses." Called the White Paper, the statement indicated that the U.S. government was prepared to recognize and enter into agreement with "a new not-for-profit corporation formed by private sector Internet stakeholders to administer policy for the Internet name and address system."[231] In deciding upon an entity with which to enter such an agreement, the U.S. government would assess whether the new system ensured stability, competition, private and bottom-up coordination, and fair representation of the Internet community as a whole.

The White Paper endorsed a process whereby the divergent interests of the Internet community would come together and decide how Internet names and addresses would be managed and administered. Accordingly, Internet constituencies from around the world held a series of meetings during the summer of 1998 to discuss how the New Corporation might be constituted and structured. Meanwhile, IANA, in collaboration with NSI, released a proposed set of bylaws and articles of incorporation. The proposed new corporation was called the Internet Corporation for Assigned Names and Numbers (ICANN). After five iterations, the final version of ICANN's bylaws and articles of incorporation were submitted to the Department of Commerce on October 2, 1998. On November 25, 1998, DOC and ICANN signed an official Memorandum of Understanding (MOU), whereby DOC and ICANN agreed to jointly design, develop, and test the mechanisms, methods, and procedures necessary to transition management responsibility for DNS functions—including IANA—to a private-sector not-for-profit entity.

On September 17, 2003, ICANN and the Department of Commerce agreed to extend their MOU until September 30, 2006. The MOU specified transition tasks which ICANN agreed to address. On June 30, 2005, Michael Gallagher, then-Assistant Secretary of Commerce for Communications and Information and Administrator of NTIA, stated the U.S. government's principles on the Internet's domain name system. Specifically, NTIA stated that the U.S. government intends to preserve the security and stability of the DNS, that the United States would continue to authorize changes or modifications to the root zone, that governments have legitimate interests in the management of their country code top level domains, that ICANN is the appropriate technical manager of the DNS, and that dialogue related to Internet governance should continue in relevant multiple fora.[232]

On September 29, 2006, DOC announced a new Joint Project Agreement (JPA) with ICANN which continues the transition to the private sector of the coordination of technical functions relating to management of the DNS. The JPA extends through September 30, 2009, and focuses on institutionalizing transparency and accountability mechanisms within ICANN.

ICANN Basics

ICANN is a not-for-profit public benefit corporation headquartered in Marina del Rey, California, and incorporated under the laws of the state of California. ICANN is organized under the California Nonprofit Public Benefit Law for charitable and public purposes, and as such, is subject to legal oversight by the California attorney general. ICANN has been granted tax-exempt status by the federal government and the state of California.[233]

ICANN's organizational structure consists of a Board of Directors (BOD) advised by a network of supporting organizations and advisory committees that represent various Internet constituencies and interests (see Figure 1). Policies are developed and issues are researched by these subgroups, who in turn advise the Board of Directors, which is responsible for making all final policy and operational decisions. The Board of Directors consists of 15 international and geographically diverse members, composed of one president, eight members selected by a Nominating Committee, two selected by the Generic Names Supporting Organization, two selected by the Address Supporting Organization, and two selected by the Country-Code Names Supporting Organization. Additionally, there are six non-voting liaisons representing other advisory committees.

The explosive growth of the Internet and domain name registration, along with increasing responsibilities in managing and operating the DNS, has led to marked growth of the ICANN budget, from revenues of about $6 million and a staff of 14 in 2000, to revenues of $60 million and a staff of 110 in 2009. ICANN is funded primarily through fees paid to ICANN by registrars and registry operators. Registrars are companies (e.g. GoDaddy, Google, Network Solutions) with which consumers register domain names.[234] Registry operators are companies and organizations who operate and administer the master database of all domain names registered in each top level domain (for example VeriSign, Inc. operates .com and .net, Public Interest Registry operates .org, and Neustar, Inc. operates .biz.).[235] In 2009, ICANN is receiving 92% of its total revenues from registry and registrar fees (41% from registry fees, 51% from registrar fees).[236]

Issues in the 111th Congress

Congressional Committees (primarily the Senate Committee on Commerce, Science and Transportation and the House Committee on Energy and Commerce) maintain oversight on how the Department of Commerce manages and oversees ICANN's activities and policies. Other Committees, such as the House and Senate Judiciary Committees, maintain an interest in other issues affected by ICANN, such as intellectual property and privacy. Specific issues of Congressional interest include ICANN's relationship with the U.S. government and the international community, the proposal to add new generic top level domains, and privacy. The

Appendix shows a complete listing of Congressional committee hearings on ICANN and the domain name system dating back to 1997.

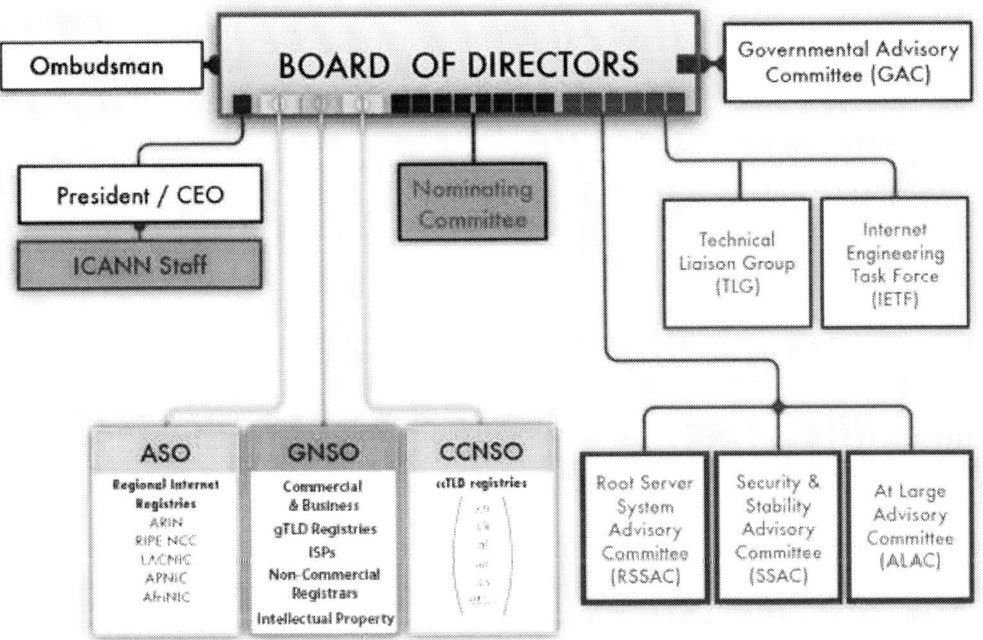

Figure 1. Organizational Structure of ICANN

Source: ICANN (http://www.icann.org/en/structure/)

ICANN's Relationship with the U.S. Government

The Department of Commerce (DOC) has no statutory authority over ICANN or the DNS. However, because the Internet evolved from a network infrastructure created by the Department of Defense, the U.S. government originally owned and operated (primarily through private contractors such as the University of Southern California, SRI International, and Network Solutions Inc.) the key components of network architecture that enable the domain name system to function. The 1998 Memorandum of Understanding between ICANN and the Department of Commerce initiated a process intended to transition technical DNS coordination and management functions to a private sector not-for-profit entity. While the DOC plays no role in the internal governance or day-to-day operations of ICANN, the U.S. government, through the DOC, retains a level of authority over the DNS via three separate contractual agreements. These are:

- the Joint Project Agreement/Memorandum of Understanding between DOC and ICANN, due to expire on September 30, 2009;

- the contract between IANA/ICANN and DOC to perform various technical functions such as allocating IP address blocks, editing the root zone file, and coordinating the assignment of unique protocol numbers; and
- the cooperative agreement between DOC and VeriSign to manage and maintain the official DNS root zone file.

Joint Project Agreement

The current Joint Project Agreement (JPA) between DOC and ICANN, an extension of the revised and amended MOU dating back to 1998, is scheduled to expire on September 30, 2009.[237] Under the JPA, ICANN agreed to "continue in its commitment to the private sector management of the Internet DNS, by promoting the security and stability of the global Internet, while maintaining, and promoting competition through its multi-stakeholder model."[238] Among the responsibilities ICANN agreed to be guided by are: ensuring the security and stability of the Internet; promoting transparency in its operation and decisions; promoting responsive and effective accountability mechanisms to ensure bottom-up participatory policy development processes; ensuring that competition, consumer interests, and Internet DNS stability and security issues are considered in TLD management decisions; facilitating effective consideration of advice from governments through the Government Advisory Council; and exhibiting corporate responsibility and an administrative structure that promotes good governance.

The JPA directed DOC to conduct a "mid-term review" of ICANN's continuing transition to the private sector. On October 30, 2007, DOC asked for public comments on ICANN's progress towards becoming a more stable organization with greater transparency and accountability in its procedures and decision making. On February 28, 2008, DOC/NTIA held a public meeting to hear the views of Internet stakeholders.[239] The ICANN Board stated that ICANN had met its responsibilities under the JPA, that the JPA should conclude during the months leading up to September 2009, and that DOC oversight and authority over ICANN under the JPA should be ended at that time.

Various Internet stakeholders disagreed as to whether DOC should maintain control over ICANN after the current JPA expires. Many U.S. industry and public interest groups argued that ICANN was not yet sufficiently transparent and accountable, that U.S. government oversight and authority (e.g. DOC acting as a "steward" or "backstop" to ICANN) was necessary to prevent undue control of the DNS by international or foreign governmental bodies, and that continued DOC oversight was needed until full privatization is warranted. On the other hand, many international entities and groups from countries outside the United States argued that ICANN had sufficiently met conditions for privatization, and that continued U.S. government control over an international organization was not appropriate. In the 110th Congress, Senator Snowe introduced S.Res. 564 which stated the sense of the Senate that although ICANN had made progress in achieving the goals of accountability and transparency as directed by the JPA, more progress was needed.[240]

On April 24, 2009, NTIA issued a Notice of Inquiry (NOI) seeking public comment on the upcoming expiration of the JPA between DOC and ICANN.[241] According to NTIA, the mid-term review showed that while some progress had been made, there remained key areas where further work was required to increase institutional confidence in ICANN. These areas included long-term stability, accountability, responsiveness, continued private sector leadership, stakeholder participation, increased contract compliance, and enhanced competition. Given that ICANN has stated publicly that, from its point of view, the JPA will conclude on September 30, 2009, NTIA asked for public comments regarding the progress of transition of the technical coordination and management of the DNS to the private sector, as well as the model of private sector leadership and bottom-up policy development which ICANN represents. Specifically, the NOI asked whether sufficient progress has been achieved for the transition to take place by September 30, 2009, and if not, what should be done.

On June 4, 2009, the House Committee on Energy and Commerce, Subcommittee on Communications, Technology, and the Internet, held a hearing examining the expiration of the JPA and other issues. Most Members of the Committee expressed the view that the JPA (or a similar agreement between DOC and ICANN) should be extended.

DOC Agreements with IANA and VeriSign

A contract between DOC and ICANN, which currently extends through September 30, 2011, authorizes the Internet Assigned Numbers Authority (IANA) to perform various technical functions such as allocating IP address blocks, editing the root zone file, and coordinating the assignment of unique protocol numbers. Additionally, a cooperative agreement between DOC and VeriSign (operator of the .com and .net registries) authorizes VeriSign to manage and maintain the official root zone file that is contained in the Internet's root servers that underlie the functioning of the DNS.[242]

By virtue of these legal agreements, the DOC has policy authority over the root zone file,[243] meaning that the U.S. government can approve or deny any changes or modifications made to the root zone file (changes, for example, such as adding a new top level domain). The June 30, 2005 U.S. government principles on the Internet's domain name system stated the intention to "preserve the security and stability" of the DNS, and asserted that "the United States is committed to taking no action that would have the potential to adversely impact the effective and efficient operation of the DNS and will therefore maintain its historic role in authorizing changes or modifications to the authoritative root zone file."[244]

The JPA is separate and distinct from the DOC legal agreements with ICANN and VeriSign. As such, the expiration of the JPA would not directly affect U.S. government authority over the DNS root zone file. Although ICANN has not advocated ending U.S. government authority over the root zone file, foreign governmental bodies have argued that it is inappropriate for the U.S. government to maintain exclusive authority over the DNS.
ICANN and the International Community

Because cyberspace and the Internet transcend national boundaries, and because the successful functioning of the DNS relies on participating entities worldwide, ICANN is by definition an international organization. Both the ICANN Board of Directors and the various constituency groups who influence and shape ICANN policy decisions are composed of members from all over the world. However, many in the international community, including foreign governments, have argued that it is inappropriate for the U.S. government to maintain its legacy authority and control over ICANN and the DNS, and have suggested that management of the DNS should be accountable to a higher intergovernmental body.

The United Nations (U.N.), at the December 2003 World Summit on the Information Society (WSIS), debated and agreed to study the issue of how to achieve greater international involvement in the governance of the Internet and the domain name system in particular. The study was conducted by the U.N.'s Working Group on Internet Governance (WGIG). On July 14, 2005, the WGIG released its report, stating that no single government should have a preeminent role in relation to international Internet governance. The report called for further internationalization of Internet governance, and proposed the creation of a new global forum for Internet stakeholders. Four possible models were put forth, including two involving the creation of new Internet governance bodies linked to the U.N. Under three of the four models, ICANN would either be supplanted or made accountable to a higher intergovernmental body. The report's conclusions were scheduled to be considered during the second phase of the WSIS held in Tunis in November 2005. U.S. officials stated their opposition to transferring control and administration of the domain name system from ICANN to any international body. Similarly, the 109th Congress expressed its support for maintaining U.S. control over ICANN (H.Con.Res. 268 and S.Res. 323).[245]

The European Union (EU) initially supported the U.S. position. However, during September 2005 preparatory meetings, the EU seemingly shifted its support towards an approach which favored an enhanced international role in governing the Internet. Conflict at the WSIS Tunis Summit over control of the domain name system was averted by the announcement, on November 15, 2005, of an Internet governance agreement between the United States, the EU, and over 100 other nations. Under this agreement, ICANN and the United States remained in control of the domain name system. A new international group under the auspices of the U.N. was formed—the Internet Governance Forum—which provides an ongoing forum for all stakeholders (both governments and nongovernmental groups) to discuss and debate Internet policy issues. The Internet Governance Forum does not have binding authority. It is slated to run through 2010, at which point the U.N. will consider whether to continue the body.

With the JPA between ICANN and DOC scheduled to expire on September 30, 2009, the international community is again suggesting various mechanisms for ensuring ICANN's accountability on an international level. On May 4, 2009, Viviane Reding, European Commissioner for Information Society and Media, released a statement stating that a "moment of truth will come on 30 September this year, when the current agreement between ICANN and the US Government expires," and that "in the long run, it is not defendable that the government department of only one country has oversight of an internet function which is used by hundreds of millions of people in countries all over the world."[246] Commissioner Reding proposed a fully privatized and fully independent ICANN that would be advised on selected issues by a "G-12 for Internet Governance," an informal group of twelve government representatives from around the world. Additionally, judicial review of ICANN decisions, if requested by aggrieved parties, would be provided by a small independent international tribunal.[247]

Adding New Generic Top Level Domains (gTLDs)

Top Level Domains (TLDs) are the suffixes that appear at the end of an address (after the "dot"). TLDs can be either a country code such as .us, .uk, or .jp, or a generic TLD (gTLD) such as .com, .org, or .gov. Prior to ICANN's establishment, there were eight gTLDs (.com, .org, .net, .gov, .mil, .edu, .int., and .arpa). In 2000 and 2004, ICANN held application rounds for new gTLDs; there are currently 21 gTLDs. Some are reserved or restricted to particular types of organizations (e.g. .museum, .gov, .travel) and others are open for registration by anyone (.com, .org, .info).[248] Applicants for new gTLDs are typically commercial and nonprofit organizations who seek to become ICANN-recognized registries that will establish and operate name servers for their TLD registry, as well as implement a domain name registration process for that particular TLD.

With the growth of the Internet and the accompanying growth in demand for domain names, debate has focused on whether and how to further expand the number of gTLDs. In October 2007, the Generic Names Supporting Organization (GNSO) approved a recommendation to initiate a process that could yield an indefinite number of new generic top-level domains. Although previous gTLD application rounds in 2000 and 2004 were competitions designed to award a limited number of gTLDs, the new process is intended to award gTLDs to any applicant that meets ICANN's set criteria and that withstands any objections (if any) raised by outside parties. The result could be an unlimited number of new gTLDs, depending on the volume of applications.

The ICANN Board of Directors approved the GNSO recommendations in June 2008, and in October 2008, ICANN published a draft applicant guide book, available for public comment, which detailed how new gTLDs would be made available to applying prospective registries. Among the major criticisms raised in the public comments were the magnitude of ICANN's suggested gTLD application and registry fees, and concerns over the impact of multiple new gTLDs on trademark holders who, many argued, would be compelled to assume high costs of addressing the possible proliferation of cybersquatters inhabiting an unlimited number of new gTLDs.

ICANN released a revised applicant guide book ("Second Draft Applicant Guidebook") in February 2009. The Second Draft Applicant Guidebook maintains the gTLD evaluation fee at $185,000, but reduces the yearly registry fee from (at a minimum) $75,000 to $25,000 plus $0.25 per transaction year for registries with more than 50,000 registrations. ICANN identified four particularly controversial and/or complex issues that "need more examination and discussion before they can be changed in a future draft guidebook."[249] These are: security and stability, malicious conduct, trademark protection, and the need for a demand/economic analysis that examines whether additional gTLDs will result in increased competition and consumer choice.

ICANN is currently studying and collecting further information and analysis on these issues. Regarding trademark protection, the ICANN board, on March 6, 2009, authorized the GNSO's Intellectual Property Constituency to form an Implementation Recommendation Team (IRT) to provide possible solutions to trademark issues raised by the implementation of new gTLDs.[250] ICANN has said that there will be a third draft version of the applicant guidebook, and that the new gTLD application round is anticipated to open in the first quarter of 2010.

ICANN and Cybersecurity

The security and stability of the Internet has always been a preeminent goal of DNS operation and management. One issue of recent concern is an intrinsic vulnerability in the DNS which allows malicious parties to distribute false DNS information. Under this scenario, Internet users could be unknowingly re-directed to fraudulent and deceptive websites established to collect passwords and sensitive account information.

A technology called DNS Security Extensions (DNSSEC) has been developed to mitigate those vulnerabilities. DNSSEC assures the validity of transmitted DNS addresses by digitally "signing" DNS data via electronic signature. "Signing the root" (deploying DNSSEC on the root zone) is a necessary first and critical step towards protecting against malicious attacks on the DNS.[251] On October 9, 2009, NTIA issued a Notice of Inquiry (NOI) seeking public comment on the deployment of DNSSEC into the Internet's DNS infrastructure, including the authoritative root zone.[252] On June 3, 2009, NTIA and the National Institute of Standards and Technology (NIST) announced they will work with ICANN and VeriSign to develop an interim approach for deploying DNS SEC in the root zone by the end of 2009.[253]

Meanwhile, section 8 of S. 773, the Cybersecurity Act of 2009, would require that any renewals or modifications made to DOC contracts regarding the operation of IANA be subject to review by a Cybersecurity Advisory Panel. S. 773 would also require NTIA to "develop a strategy to implement a secure domain name addressing system."

Privacy and the WHOIS Database

Any person or entity who registers a domain name is required to provide contact information (phone number, address, email) which is entered into a public online database (the "WHOIS" database). The scope and accessibility of WHOIS database information has been an issue of contention. Privacy advocates have argued that access to such information should be limited, while many businesses, intellectual property interests, law enforcement agencies, and the U.S. government have argued that complete and accurate WHOIS information should continue to be publicly accessible. Over the past several years, ICANN has debated this issue through its Generic Names Supporting Organization (GNSO), which is developing policy recommendations on what data should be publicly available through the WHOIS database. On April 12, 2006, the GNSO approved an official "working definition" for the purpose of the public display of WHOIS information. The GNSO supported a narrow technical definition favored by privacy advocates, registries, registrars, and non-commercial user constituencies, rather then a more expansive definition favored by intellectual property interests, business constituencies, Internet service providers, law enforcement agencies, and the Department of Commerce (through its participation in ICANN's Governmental Advisory Committee). At ICANN's June 2006 meeting, opponents of limiting access to WHOIS data continued urging ICANN to reconsider the working definition. On October 31, 2007, the GNSO voted to defer a decision on WHOIS database privacy and recommended more studies. The GNSO also rejected a proposal to allow Internet users the option of listing third party contact information rather than their own private data. It will now be up to the ICANN Board to decide whether or how to proceed.[254]

APPENDIX. CONGRESSIONAL HEARINGS ON THE DOMAIN NAME SYSTEM

Date	Congressional Committee	Topic
June 4, 2009	House Energy and Commerce	"Oversight of the Internet Corporation for Assigned Names and Numbers (ICANN)"
September 21, 2006	House Energy and Commerce	"ICANN Internet Governance: Is It Working?"
September 20, 2006	Senate Commerce, Science and Transportation	"Internet Governance: the Future of ICANN"
July 18, 2006	House Financial Services	"ICANN and the WHOIS Database: Providing Access to Protect Consumers from Phishing"
June 7, 2006	House Small Business	"Contracting the Internet: Does ICANN Create a Barrier to Small Business?"
September 30, 2004	Senate Commerce, Science and Transportation	"ICANN Oversight and Security of Internet Root Servers and the Domain Name System (DNS)"
May 6, 2004	House Energy and Commerce	"The 'Dot Kids' Internet Domain: Protecting Children Online"
July 31, 2003	Senate Commerce, Science and Transportation	"Internet Corporation for Assigned Names and Numbers (ICANN)"
September 4, 2003	House Judiciary	"Internet Domain Name Fraud – the U.S. Government's Role in Ensuring Public Access to Accurate WHOIS Data"
September 12, 2002	Senate Commerce, Science and Transportation	"Hearing on ICANN Governance"
June 12, 2002	Senate Commerce, Science and Transportation	"Dot Kids Implementation and Efficiency Act of 2002"
May 22, 2002	House Judiciary	"The Accuracy and Integrity of the WHOIS Database"
November 1, 2001	House Energy and Commerce	"Dot Kids Name Act of 2001"
July 12, 2001	House Judiciary	"The Whois Database: Privacy and Intellectual Property Issues"
March 22, 2001	House Judiciary	"ICANN, New gTLDs, and the Protection of Intellectual Property"
February 14, 2001	Senate Commerce, Science and Transportation	"Hearing on ICANN Governance"
February 8, 2001	House Energy and Commerce	"Is ICANN's New Generation of Internet Domain Name Selection Process Thwarting Competition?"
July 28, 1999	House Judiciary	"Internet Domain Names and Intellectual Property Rights"
July 22, 1999	Senate Judiciary	"Cybersquatting and Internet Consumer Protection"
July 22, 1999	House Energy and Commerce	"Domain Name System Privatization: Is ICANN Out of Control?"
October 7, 1998	House Science	"Transferring the Domain Name System to the Private Sector: Private Sector Implementation of the Administration's Internet 'White Paper'"
June 10, 1998	House Commerce	"Electronic Commerce: The Future of the Domain Name System"
March 31, 1998	House Science	"Domain Name System: Where Do We Go From Here?"
February 21, 1998	House Judiciary	"Internet Domain Name Trademark Protection"
November 5, 1997	House Judiciary	"Internet Domain Name Trademark Protection"
September 30, 1997	House Science	"Domain Name System (Part 2)"
September 25, 1997	House Science	"Domain Name System (Part 1)"

CONCLUDING OBSERVATIONS

Many of the technical, operational, and management decisions regarding the DNS can have significant impacts on Internet-related policy issues such as intellectual property, privacy, e-commerce, and cybersecurity. As such, decisions made by ICANN affect Internet stakeholders around the world. In transferring management of the DNS to the private sector, the key policy question has always been how to best ensure achievement of the White Paper principles: Internet stability and security, competition, private and bottom-up policymaking and coordination, and fair representation of the Internet community. What is the best process to ensure these goals, and how should various stakeholders—companies, institutions, individuals, governments—fit into this process?

ICANN has established governance processes which are intended to give access to Internet stakeholders into important decisions. With the impending expiration of the ICANN-DOC Joint Project Agreement on September 30, 2009, Congress and the Administration are examining whether those processes are sufficient to give the full range of Internet stakeholders meaningful input into ICANN decisions, and whether ICANN is sufficiently accountable to those Internet stakeholders.[255]

A related issue is whether the U.S. government's unique authority over the DNS root zone should continue indefinitely. Foreign governments have argued that it is inappropriate for the U.S. government to have exclusive authority over the worldwide DNS, and that technical coordination and management of the DNS should be accountable to international governmental entities. On the other hand, many U.S. officials argue that it is critical for the U.S. government to maintain authority over the DNS in order to guarantee the stability and security of the Internet.

Author Contact Information

Lennard G. Kruger
Specialist in Science and Technology Policy
lkruger@crs.loc.gov, 7-7070

End notes

[231] Management of Internet Names and Addresses, National Telecommunications and Information Administration, Department of Commerce, *Federal Register*, Vol. 63, No. 111, June 10, 1998, 31741.

[232] See http://www.ntia.doc.gov/ntiahome/domainname/USDNSprinciples_06302005.pdf.

[233] ICANN, 2008 *Annual Report*, December 31, 2008, p. 24, available at http://www.icann.org/ en/annualreport/ annual-report-2008-en.pdf.

[234] A list of ICANN-accredited registrars is available at http://www.icann.org/en/registries/agreements.htm.

[235] A list of current agreements between ICANN and registry operators is available at http://www.icann.org/en/ registries/ agreements.htm.

[236] ICANN, Draft FY10 Operating Plan and Budget, May 17, 2009, p. 47, available at http://www.icann.org/en/ financials/proposed-opplan-budget-v1-fy10-17may09-en.pdf.

[237] Joint Project Agreement between the U.S. Department of Commerce and the Internet Corporation for Assigned Names and Numbers, September 29, 2006, available at http://www.ntia.doc.gov/ntiahome/ domainname/ agreements/ jpa/ICANNJPA_09292006.htm.

[238] Affirmation of Responsibilities for ICANN's Private Sector Management, approved by the ICANN Board of Directors September 25, 2006, available at http://www.ntia.doc.gov/ntiahome/domainname/agreements/jpa/ICANNBoardResolution_09252006.htm.

[239] See http://www.ntia.doc.gov/ntiahome/domainname/jpamidtermreview.html.

[240] In the 110th Congress, S.Res. 564 was referred to the Committee on Commerce, Science, and Transportation. It did not advance to the Senate floor.

[241] Department of Commerce, National Telecommunications and Information Administration, "Assessment of the Transition of the Technical Coordination and Management of the Internet's Domain Name and Addressing System," 74 *Federal Register* 18688, April 24, 2009.

[242] "The root zone file defines the DNS. For all practical purposes, a top level domain (and, therefore, all of its lower- level domains) is in the DNS if and only if it is listed in the root zone file. Therefore, presence in the root determines which DNS domains are available on the Internet." National Research Council, Committee on Internet Navigation and the Domain Name System: Technical Alternatives and Policy Implications, Signposts on Cyberspace: The Domain Name System and Internet Navigation, National Academy Press, Washington DC, 2005, p. 97.

[243] Milton Mueller, *Political Oversight of ICANN: A Briefing for the WSIS Summit*, Internet Governance Project, November 1, 2005, p. 4.

[244] See http://www.ntia.doc.gov/ntiahome/domainname/USDNSprinciples_06302005.pdf.

[245] In the 109th Congress, H.Con.Res. 268 was passed unanimously by the House on November 16, 2005. S.Res. 323 was passed in the Senate by Unanimous Consent on November 18, 2005.

[246] Commissioner Reding's Weekly Videomessage Theme: "The Future of Internet Governance: Towards an Accountable ICANN," May 4, 2009, available at http://ec.europa.eu/commission_barroso/reding/video/text/message_20090504.pdf.

[247] Because ICANN is currently incorporated in the State of California, legal challenges to ICANN decisions are adjudicated in California state courts.

[248] The 21 current gTLDs are listed at http://www.iana.org/domains/root/db/#.

[249] ICANN, *New gTLD Draft Applicant Guidebook: Analysis of Public Comment*, February 18, 2009, p. 3, available at http://www.icann.org/en/topics/new-gtlds/agv1-analysis-public-comments-18feb09-en.pdf.

[250] See http://www.icann.org/en/announcements/announcement-26mar09-en.htm.

[251] Internet Corporation for Assigned Names and Numbers, "DNSSEC – What Is It and Why Is It Important?" October 9, 2008, available at http://icann.org/en/announcements/dnssec-qaa-09oct08-en.htm.

[252] Department of Commerce, National Telecommunications and Information Administration, "Enhancing the Security and Stability of the Internet's Domain Name and Addressing System," 73 *Federal Register* 59608, October 9, 2008.

[253] Department of Commerce, National Institute of Standards and Technology, *NIST News Release*, "Commerce Department to Work With ICANN and VeriSign to Enhance the Security and Stability of the Internet's Domain Name and Addressing System," June 3, 2009.

[254] See ICANN "Whois Services" page, available at http://www.icann.org/topics/whois-services/.

[255] ICANN has established internal accountability mechanisms (an Ombudsman, a Reconsideration Committee, and an independent review process) which are intended to address complaints and disputes over ICANN decisions. See http://www.icann.org/en/general/accountability_review.html.

In: Trends in Internet Research
Editor: B.G. Kutais

ISBN: 978-1-59454-140-7

Chapter 6

INTERNET TAXATION: ISSUES AND LEGISLATION[*]

Steven Maguire and Nonna A. Noto

ABSTRACT

Congress is involved in issues of state and local taxation of Internet transactions because commerce conducted by parties in different states over the Internet falls under the Commerce Clause of the Constitution. Currently, the "Internet Tax Moratorium" prohibits (1) new taxes on Internet access services and (2) multiple or discriminatory taxes on Internet commerce. The moratorium was created by the Internet Tax Freedom Act (ITFA) of 1998 (112 Stat. 2681) and has been extended twice. The original moratorium expired on October 21, 2001. Congress extended the moratorium through November 1, 2003, with the Internet Tax Nondiscrimination Act, P.L. 107-75. The moratorium was extended for an additional four years, through November 1, 2007, by the Internet Tax Nondiscrimination Act, P.L. 108-435. On October 31, 2007, P.L. 110-108, the Internet Tax Freedom Act Amendments Act of 2007 was passed extending the moratorium through November 1, 2014. Generally, taxes on Internet access that have continued in place since before October 1, 1998, are protected by a grandfather clause.

An issue previously raised in connection with the Internet tax moratorium concerned states streamlining their sales taxes in order to gain remote tax collection authority. In the 110th Congress, S. 34 and H.R. 3396 would grant states that comply with the Streamlined Sales and Use Tax Agreement the authority to require remote sellers to collect state and local taxes on interstate sales. Another related issue is whether and how to have Congress set the nexus standards under which a state is entitled to impose a business activity tax (BAT, e.g., corporate net income tax, franchise tax, business and occupation tax, gross receipts tax) on a company located outside the state, but with some business activities in the state. In the 110th Congress, S. 1726 and its twin H.R. 5267 would establish more-uniform standards — generally higher standards — for the level of business activity that would create nexus and thus state corporate income taxability. For more on state corporate income taxes, see CRS Report RL3 2297, *State Corporate Income Taxes: A Description and Analysis*, by Steven Maguire.

This report will be updated as legislative events warrant.

---

[*] This is an edited, reformatted and augmented version of a Congressional Research Service Publication, Order Code RL33261 Prepared for Members and Committees of Congress, July 7, 2009.

History

The Internet Tax Freedom Act (ITFA) was enacted on October 21, 1998, as Title XI of Division C of P.L. 105-277, the Omnibus Consolidated and Emergency Supplemental Appropriations Act, 1999.[256] The ITFA placed a three-year moratorium on the ability of state and local governments to (1) impose new taxes on Internet access or (2) impose any multiple or discriminatory taxes on electronic commerce. The act grandfathered the state and local access taxes that were "... generally imposed and actually enforced prior to October 1, 1998...."

This initial Internet tax moratorium expired on October 21, 2001. The Internet Tax Nondiscrimination Act, P.L. 107-75, enacted on November 28, 2001, provided for a two-year extension of the prior moratorium, through November 1, 2003. The moratorium was extended for an additional four years, through November 1, 2007, by the Internet Tax Nondiscrimination Act, P.L. 108-43 5, enacted on December 3, 2004. Taxes on Internet access that were in place before October 1, 1998, were protected by a grandfather clause. The 2004 (P.L. 108-435) extension also grandfathered pre-November 1, 2003, taxes (mostly on digital subscriber line or DSL services) through November 1, 2005, and excluded from the moratorium taxes on voice or similar service utilizing voice over Internet protocol (VoIP). These services were not as prevalent at the time the original moratorium was enacted. As part of compromise negotiations in the 108th Congress, the grandfathering protection for Internet access taxes in Wisconsin was limited to three years (through November 1, 2006) instead of four, and the ability of Texas municipalities to collect franchise fees from telecommunications providers that use public lands was protected. The 2004 act included several modifications and refinements to the original ITFA. Specifically, the 2004 act:

- Extended the Internet tax moratorium for four years, retroactively one year to November 1, 2003, and forward three years until November 1, 2007. The moratorium barred state and local governments from imposing any new taxes on Internet access or imposing any multiple or discriminatory taxes on electronic commerce.
- Clarified that the term "tax on Internet access" applies regardless of whether the tax is imposed on a provider or buyer of Internet access.
- Made explicit that a "tax on Internet access" does not include a tax levied on net income, capital stock, net worth, or property value.
- Provided that the terms "Internet access" and "Internet access service" do "not include telecommunications services, except to the extent such services are purchased, used, or sold by a provider of Internet access to provide Internet access." (This permits some portion of telecommunications services to be included under the tax moratorium.)
- Extended the grandfather protection from November 1, 2003, until November 1, 2007, for state and local governments which taxed Internet access prior to October 1, 1998. An exception was made for a state telecommunications service tax in Wisconsin, for which protection was extended only until November 1, 2006. Protection was extended only until November 1, 2005, for taxes on Internet access that were generally imposed and actually enforced as of November 1, 2003. This provision applies mainly to taxes on digital subscriber line (DSL) services.

Explicitly protected the Texas municipal access line fee. This provision is intended to protect the ability of Texas municipalities to collect franchise fees from telecommunications providers that use public lands.

Included a new accounting rule that charges for Internet access may be subject to taxation in cases where they are aggregated with charges for telecommunications services or other charges that are subject to taxation — unless the Internet access provider can reasonably identify the charges for Internet access.

Stated that nothing in the act prevents the collection of any charges for federal or state universal service programs (for telephone service), or for state or local 911 and E-9 11 (emergency call) services, nor does it affect any federal or state regulatory non-tax proceeding (such as FCC regulatory proceedings).

Clarified that the moratorium does not apply to taxes on Voice over Internet Protocol (VoIP) services. This section does not apply to services that are incidental to Internet access, such as voice-capable e-mail or instant messaging.

And provided for the GAO (Government Accountability Office) to study the effects of the Internet tax moratorium on the revenues of state and local governments and on the deployment and adoption of broadband technologies for Internet access throughout the United States, including under-served rural areas. The study was to compare deployment in states that tax broadband Internet access service with states that do not. The Comptroller General was to report the findings, conclusions, and any recommendations from the study to the Senate Committee on Commerce, Science, and Transportation and the House Committee on Energy and Commerce by November 1, 2005. The report was published in January 2006.[257]

ISSUES

The five main issues surrounding Internet taxation and e-commerce that Congress may address before the 2014 expiration are as follows:

whether or not to extend the moratorium on Internet access taxes and if so, temporarily or permanently;

whether, if the moratorium were to be extended, to continue to grant grandfather protection for states that imposed taxes on Internet access before the original moratorium was enacted;

how to better define Internet access and discriminatory taxes to the satisfaction of all stakeholders;

whether to grant states the authority to require remote sellers to collect use taxes if the states adopted a streamlined sales tax system; and

if congressional codification of guidelines is needed for establishing whether or not a business engaged in interstate commerce has nexus in a jurisdiction for purposes of business activity tax (BAT, e.g., corporate income tax, franchise tax, business license tax) liability.

These issues remain similar to those considered in 2004 and 2007, the two most recent times the Internet tax moratorium was temporarily extended. Growth in Internet technology and electronic commerce, however, may generate new policy questions before 2014.

The Moratorium: Permanent vs. Temporary Extension?

The intent of the Internet Tax Freedom Act (enacted in 1998) was to prevent state taxes on Internet access, to ensure that multiple jurisdictions could not tax the same electronic commerce transaction, and to ensure that commerce over the Internet would not be singled out for discriminatory tax treatment. Supporters of extending the moratorium contend that the Internet should continue to be protected from the administrative and financial burdens of taxation in order to further advance of Internet technology and associated economic activity.[258] Opponents of extending the moratorium contend that a federal moratorium infringes on the states' independent authority to levy taxes and, further, that Internet transactions and services should not be afforded preferential tax treatment.

Supporters of permanent extension of the moratorium maintain it would eliminate the need for Congress to revisit the issues surrounding Internet taxation when a temporary moratorium expires. Permanent extension presumably could also provide both the producers and consumers of Internet services greater certainty about state and local taxation of the Internet. Opponents, on the other hand, say a permanent extension would not address the underlying issue of federal restrictions on state taxation, nor would it clarify the definition of Internet access.

Opponents of a permanent extension of the moratorium point out that a temporary one would allow Congress to periodically review the conditions of the moratorium and the effect of the moratorium on the states. Reassessment could then be made in the context of developments in computer technology and business organization, as well as state and local government tax administration. A temporary extension could also provide more time for the states to further simplify their sales and use taxes. (See the discussion below on *Streamlined Sales Taxes and Remote Collection Authority*.)

Allowing the moratorium to sunset would permit states to tax Internet access, although, in practice, the trend has been for states to repeal their Internet access taxes. As Internet technology continues to change the telecommunications industry, however, state and local governments will likely modify how the industry is taxed. A sunset of the moratorium could induce states to address the taxation of telecommunications more broadly.

Grandfathering of Existing Access Taxes

The Internet Tax Freedom Act exempted from the moratorium taxes on Internet access that were "... generally imposed and actually enforced prior to October 1, 1998...." When ITFA legislation was being considered in the spring of 1998, 10 states and the District of Columbia were already applying their sales tax to Internet access services.[259] Subsequently, Connecticut, Iowa, Tennessee, and the District of Columbia eliminated their tax on Internet access, and South Carolina has not enforced the collection of its tax during the federal moratorium. These developments left six states imposing a sales tax (or equivalent tax) on Internet access as of January 2006: New Mexico, North Dakota, Ohio (on commercial use only), South Dakota, Texas (on monthly charges over $25), and Wisconsin.[260] In addition, Hawaii levies its general excise tax, New Hampshire its communications services tax (imposed on all two-way communications equipment), and Washington State its business and occupation tax (a gross receipts tax levied on business) on Internet access. The Congressional Budget Office believes that several *local* jurisdictions in Colorado, Ohio, South Dakota, Texas, Washington, and Wisconsin also are collecting taxes on Internet access.[261]

The grandfathering protection was continued when the ITFA moratorium was extended for two years in 2001 (through November 1, 2003). The act further extended the grandfathering protection for pre-October 1998 taxes through November 1, 2007. A second grandfathering issue arose in 2004 as states began to tax Internet access provided through digital subscriber lines (DSL), a high-speed telephone service. DSL is considered a telecommunication service and was exempt from the original moratorium and thus taxable. ITFA grandfathered pre-November 2003 taxes (mostly taxes on DSL service) through November 1, 2005. The last extension discontinued the grandfathering protection for grandfathered states that had repealed or stopped enforcing collection of the sales tax on Internet access services.[262]

In its cost estimates for H.R. 49 and S. 150 in the 108th Congress, the Congressional Budget Office (CBO) determined that eliminating the grandfathering protection for Internet access taxes would impose an intergovernmental mandate as defined in the Unfunded Mandates Reform Act (UMRA, 2 U.S.C. 1501-1571).[263] According to CBO, the prohibition of taxes on Internet access that were then collected in *up to* 10 states (in 2003, at the time of the CBO study, more states had Internet access taxes) and a few local jurisdictions in six states, would cost these jurisdictions approximately $80 million to $120 million per year. This estimate alone exceeded the UMRA threshold of $59 million in 2003, in the case of H.R. 49, and $64 million in 2007 (adjusted annually for inflation), in the case of S. 150. CBO noted that additional state and local revenues could be lost if more telecommunications services and information content were redefined as Internet access.

Definitions

As noted earlier, the ITFA tax moratorium prohibits new taxes on Internet access and multiple or discriminatory taxes on electronic commerce. The act's definitions of *Internet access* and of *discriminatory tax*, in particular, have been the source of some concern and legal uncertainty for state and local governments, providers of new-technology Internet access service, telecommunications companies offering bundled communications and information services, supporters of federal and state universal service programs, and companies with "dot.com" subsidiaries.

Taxation of Internet Access

The taxation of Internet access most commonly refers to the application of state and local sales and use taxes to the monthly charges that retail subscribers pay for access to the Internet. These payments may go to traditional dial-up Internet service providers (ISPs) or to the local telephone or cable TV company. According to the Federation of Tax Administrators, the tax may also take the form of a sales and use tax or excise tax levied specifically on telecommunications, information services, or data processing services, the definition of which encompasses "charges for Internet access." P.L. 108-43 5 clarified that a "tax on Internet access" applies regardless of whether the tax is imposed on a provider or buyer of Internet access.[264] P.L. 110-108 further refined the definition of Internet access to include "homepage, electronic mail and instant messaging" services.[265]

Telecommunications Industry Concerns

Telecommunications carriers were concerned that Internet access offered through primarily telecommunications technologies, such as DSL or wireless services, might not be treated as exempt from tax, while access offered over other technologies, such as cable modem, would be exempt. In an attempt to address these concerns, both P.L. 110-108 and P.L. 108-435 provided that all forms of telecommunications services used to provide Internet access would be exempt from state and local taxes under the moratorium.[266]

State and Local Government Concerns

Before enactment of P.L. 108- 435, state and local governments were concerned that the tax moratorium could be interpreted to go far beyond retail Internet access. Ultimately, P.L. 108-435 made explicit that the term "tax on Internet access" would not include a tax levied on net income, capital stock, net worth, or property value. It extended the grandfather protection for existing Internet access taxes until November 1, 2007, with the exception of Wisconsin, where protection ended on November 1, 2006. It explicitly protected the Texas municipal access line fee; this protects the ability of Texas municipalities to collect franchise fees from telecommunications providers that use public lands. P.L. 110-108 clarified further the types of taxes that were outside of the moratorium.

In addition, state and local governments were concerned that with the growth of Internet telephony (Voice over Internet Protocol, VoIP), there would be less traditional telephone service or plain old telephone service (POTS) remaining in the tax base. Currently, state and local taxes on voice telephone services produce $12 billion in annual revenues.[267] P.L. 108-435 and P.L. 110-108 both clarified that the tax moratorium does not apply to VoIP services, which may be taxed.[268]

Bundling of Services

The breadth of coverage in the first sentence of the definition of Internet access shown above gives rise to concern on the part of state and local revenue departments that the tax-protection of Internet access may extend to "bundled" products and services that might otherwise be taxable if purchased on their own. These could include data and information services, cable television, books, magazines, games, music, and video on demand, for example. These types of products and services can be offered online and sold as part of an Internet access service.[269]

P.L. 108-435 included a new accounting rule which addressed the bundling issue. Under this rule, Internet access service may be taxable if access fees are aggregated with fees for otherwise-taxable telecommunications services. If the Internet access provider can reasonably identify the charges for Internet access, then the Internet access, however, is not taxable.

Funding Universal Service

Some Members of Congress were concerned about protecting the financing source for the Universal Service Fund (USF).[270] The USF is administered by the Universal Service Administrative Company, an independent not-for-profit organization operating under the auspices of the Federal Communications Commission (FCC). The USF is financed by mandatory contributions from interstate telecommunications carriers.[271] A company's USF contribution is a percentage of its interstate and international end-user revenues.[272] Some states also levy charges on the intrastate retail revenues of telecommunications carriers for their state's universal service fund.[273]

Supporters of the universal service programs were concerned that efforts to protect Internet access and associated telecommunications services should not reduce the funding base for universal service. The moratorium does not prevent the federal government or the states from imposing or collecting the fees or charges on telecommunications that are used to finance the universal service program. Nor does it prevent states or local governments from collecting fees or charges to support 911 or E-9 11 (emergency) services. Nor does it affect any federal or state regulatory proceeding that is not related to taxation.

Multiple Taxes

The ban on multiple taxes prohibits more than one state, or more than one local jurisdiction at the same level of government (i.e., more than one county or one city), from imposing a tax on the same transaction, unless a credit is offered for taxes paid to another jurisdiction. However, the state, county, and city in which an electronic commerce transaction takes place could all levy their sales taxes on the transaction.

Discriminatory Taxes

In practice, the ban on discriminatory taxes on electronic commerce means that transactions arranged over the Internet are to be taxed in the same manner as mail-order or telephone sales. Under the current judicial interpretation of nexus as applied to mail-order sales, a state cannot require an out-of- state seller to collect a use tax from the customer unless the seller has a physical presence in the taxing state.[274] (A use tax is the companion tax to the sales tax, applicable to interstate sales.) Congress or the Supreme Court would need to act to grant or approve the states' ability to require out-of-state tax collection, whether the transaction was arranged over the Internet or by mail order, telephone, or other means.

The second part of the ITFA's definition of discriminatory tax lists conditions under which a remote seller's use of a computer server, an Internet access service, or online services does not establish nexus. These circumstances include the sole ability to access a site on a remote seller's out-of-state computer server; the display of a remote seller's information or content on the out-of-state computer server of a provider of Internet access service or online services; and processing of orders through the out-of-state computer server of a provider of Internet access service or online services. Some businesses have taken advantage of these nexus limits in the ITFA's definition of discriminatory tax to establish what are referred to as Internet kiosks or dot-com subsidiaries. The businesses claim that these Internet-based operations are free from sales and use tax collection requirements. Critics object that these methods of business organization are an abuse of the definition of discriminatory tax.

Streamlined Sales Taxes and Remote Collection Authority

In earlier Congresses, the debate surrounding legislation to extend the Internet tax moratorium was linked to the states' quest for sales and use tax collection authority. The issue continues to be whether Congress is willing to grant states the authority to require remote (out-of-state) sellers to collect use taxes on interstate sales conditioned on a simplification of state and local sales and use tax systems. Bills were introduced in conjunction with an extension of the moratorium that enumerated criteria for a simplified sales and use tax system, and procedures for Congress to grant tax collection authority. In contrast, in the 108th Congress and continuing into the 109th and 110th Congress, the sales tax issue has been pursued separately from the moratorium.

Remote Collection Issue

Under current law, a vendor with substantial nexus (usually defined as physical presence) in its customer's state collects the state (and local) sales tax on sales arranged over the Internet (or by telephone, mail order, or other means). In contrast, an out-of-state vendor without substantial nexus in the customer's state is not required to collect the sales tax.[275] Technically, the customer is required to remit a "use" tax to his or her state of residence.[276] In practice, however, use tax compliance by non-business purchasers is low. Because of this low compliance, many states have long wanted to require out-of-state vendors without physical presence in the respective states (referred to as remote sellers) to collect the use tax from the customer. This would apply to all interstate sales, whether arranged over the Internet or by mail-order catalog, telephone, or other means.

The Streamlined Sales and Use Tax Agreement (SSUTA)

Acknowledging administrative complexity as a major obstacle to remote collection authority, the states began a concerted effort to simplify state and local sales and use tax through the Streamlined Sales Tax Project (SSTP).[277] The project commenced in March 2000, midway through the initial ITFA moratorium (October 1998 - October 2001). As of February 27, 2008, 17 states were designated as "full" members for having approved a model interstate agreement to simplify their sales tax systems, known as the Streamlined Sales and Use Tax Agreement (SSUTA).[278] The agreement establishes uniform definitions for taxable goods and services and requires that a participating state and local government have only one statewide tax rate for each type of product. Another five states are "associate" members for partially complying with the SSUTA. Each state would retain the power to define which products are taxable and establish its tax rate.

In the 110th Congress, S. 34 (Enzi) and H.R. 3396 (Delahunt) would grant states that comply with the SSUTA the authority to require remote sellers to collect state and local use taxes on interstate sales.

Business Activity Tax (BAT) Nexus Standards

The possibility that states could be authorized to require remote vendors to collect sales and use taxes on interstate sales raised concerns that states would then attempt to impose income and other business taxes on those vendors. In response, some multistate businesses asked Congress to clarify nexus standards for state and local business activity taxes (BATs).[279] Past court decisions and the landmark P.L. 86-272, enacted in 1959 (15 U.S.C. 381 et seq.), clarified nexus by identifying those activities which would *not* establish nexus. Generally, soliciting the sale of tangible goods in a state for shipment by common carrier from locations outside the state would not be sufficient to trigger nexus.

Proponents of federally defined nexus standards contend that current federal law does not sufficiently define substantial nexus. The issue before Congress is whether to codify nexus rules for intangible property and services, not just tangible goods as provided for in P.L. 86-272. Currently, each state independently implements rules that establish nexus for economic activities that are not covered by P.L. 86-272. Although state rules are very similar for many services and activities, there is still significant variation among states on the threshold for establishing nexus. In theory, Congress could establish uniform federal standards for imposing state business activity taxes on out-of-state businesses.

Some representatives of state and local governments, however, are concerned that enacting federal nexus guidelines could restrict their ability to levy corporate income taxes or other BATs on business activities conducted in their state. For example, if Congress implemented thresholds at the midpoint level of all existing state nexus rules, by definition, many states would lose taxpayers that did not meet the new standard for substantial nexus. The states with the lowest nexus thresholds would fare the worst under such a scenario. Perhaps more importantly,"bright line" legislation would expand the definition of economic activity beyond tangible goods to include intangible goods and services.

The remote collection authority bills offered in earlier Congresses typically provided that out-of-state vendors that collected sales and use taxes would not then be subject to business activity taxes by virtue of their tax collection for the state.[280] In the 1 10th Congress, the BAT nexus issue had been kept separate from both the extension of the Internet tax moratorium and the sales tax simplification issue.

ACTION IN THE 110TH CONGRESS

Internet Tax Moratorium Legislation

On October 31, 2007, P.L. 110-108, the Internet Tax Freedom Act Amendments Act of 2007, was passed extending the moratorium through November 1, 2014. Generally, taxes on Internet access that have continued in place since before October 1, 1998, are protected by a grandfather clause.

Internet-Commerce-Related Legislation

SSUTA

In the Senate, S. 34 (Senator Enzi) and H.R. 3396 (Senator Delahunt) would grant states that comply with the Streamlined Sales and Use Tax Agreement the authority to require remote sellers to collect state and local taxes on interstate sales. H.R. 3396 has 10 cosponsors and S. 34 has three cosponsors.

BAT Nexus

A proposal to address state business activity taxation has also been introduced in the 110th Congress. S. 1726 (Senator Schumer and Senator Crapo) and its companion H.R. 5267 (Representative Boucher and Representative Goodlatte) would establish a physical presence standard for business activity taxes and expand the test to include intangible goods and services. More specifically, they would (1) amend P.L. 86-272 to extend to all sales (not just tangible personal property) and to other state and local business activity taxes (not just net income taxes) the protection from taxation on interstate commerce if the only activity within a state was soliciting orders for sales; (2) establish physical presence as the nexus standard for levying state and local business activity taxes on interstate commerce; and (3) generally require use of employees or property in a state for more than a combined 15 days per calendar year to establish nexus. In addition, the legislation would provide a de minimus standard for firms whose physical presence is "limited or transient."[281]

End Note

[256] Title XII was also part of S. 442, 105th Congress, the underlying ITFA legislation. Titles XI and XII, 112 Stat. 2681-719 through 728 (1998). Title XI is codified as the ITFA in 47 U.S.C. 151 note. Title XII is codified as 19 U.S.C. 2241 note.

[257] U.S. Government Accountability Office, *Internet Access Tax Moratorium: Revenue Impacts Will Vary by State*, GAO-06-273, Jan. 2006.

[258] U.S. Congress, Committee on Commerce, Science, and Transportation, *Internet Tax Non-Discrimination Act of 2003*, report to accompany S. 150, 1 08th Cong., 1st sess., S.Rept. 108- 155, (Washington: GPO, 2003), p. 1.

[259] National Conference of State Legislatures, "Which States Tax Internet Access?" March 25, 1998.

[260] Vertex, Inc., Tax Cybrary. Available at [http://www.vertexinc.com], visited July 7, 2008.

[261] Congressional Budget Office, "Cost Estimate for S. 150, the Internet Tax Nondiscrimination Act," Sept. 9, 2003. Contained in U.S. Congress, Senate, Committee on Commerce, Science, and Transportation, *Internet Tax Non-discrimination Act of 2003*, Report on S. 150, 108th Cong., 1st sess., Report 108-155, Sept. 29, 2003 (Washington: GPO, 2003), p. 7. Cost estimate also available at [http://www.cbo.gov].

[262] Sec. 6 of P.L. 110-108.

[263] Congressional Budget Office, "Cost Estimate for H.R. 49, Internet Tax Nondiscrimination Act," as ordered reported by the House Committee on the Judiciary on July 16, 2003, Washington, July 21, 2003; and "Cost Estimate for S. 150, the Internet Tax Nondiscrimination Act." Both available at [http://www.cbo.gov].

[264] A recent GAO (op. cit. Jan. 2006, p. 23) report concluded that ISP acquired services are not protected by the moratorium.

[265] See Section 4(2) of P.L. 110-108.

[266] For more information, see U.S. Congress, Senate Committee on Commerce, Science, and Transportation, *Internet Tax Non-discrimination Act of 2003*, Report on S. 150,1 08th Cong., 1st sess., S.Rept. 108-155, Sept. 29, 2003 (Washington: GPO, 2003).

[267] Michael Mazerov, "A Permanent Ban on Internet Access Taxation Risks Serious Erosion of State and Local Telephone Tax Revenue as Phone Calls Migrate to the Internet," Center on Budget and Policy Priorities, Washington, DC, Feb. 11, 2004, p. 1. Available at [http://www.cbpp.org/2-1 1-04sfp.pdf], visited July 7, 2008.

[268] For objections to a tax prohibition on VoIP, see Michael Mazerov, "Proposed 'Voice over Internet Protocol Regulatory Freedom Act' Threatens to Strip States and Localities of Billions of Dollars in Annual Tax Revenues," Center on Budget and Policy Priorities, Washington, DC, July 20, 2004. Available at [http://www.cbpp.org/7-20-04tax.pdf], visited July 7, 2008.

[269] Harley Duncan and Matt Tomalis, "On the Internet Tax Freedom Act: The Forgotten First Sentence, " *State Tax Notes*, March 29, 2004, pp. 1105-1108.

[270] The USF subsidizes telephone service to low-income consumers and to high-cost rural and insular areas. Through the E-rate or education-rate program instituted by the Telecommunications Act of 1996, the USF also subsidizes telecommunications discounts for schools and libraries. Also as a result of the 1996 act, the USF subsidizes communications links between rural health care providers and urban medical centers. For further information on the E-rate program, see CRS Report RL320 18, *The E-R ate Program: Universal Service Fund Telecommunications Discounts for Schools*, by Angele A. Gilroy.

[271] All telecommunications providers that furnish service between states must contribute to the USF. This includes long distance companies, local telephone companies, wireless telephone companies, paging companies, and payphone providers.

[272] The percentage, known as the contribution factor, is set quarterly, and varies depending on the financing needs of the universal service programs. The proposed contribution factor for the third quarter of 2008 is 0.114 or 11.4%. Federal Communications Commission, Contribution Factors and Quarterly Filings, available at [http://www.fcc.gov/omd/ contribution-factor.html], visited June 23, 2008.

[273] State charges are typically levied on the intrastate retail revenues of wireline carriers and, in some states, wireless carriers as well.

[274] For additional discussion, see CRS Report RS2 1537, *State Sales Taxation of Internet Transactions*, by John R. Luckey.

[275] In 1967 and again in 1992, the Supreme Court invited the Congress to take action on this issue. See the following decisions: *National Bellas Hess, Inc. v. Illinois Department of Revenue*, 386 U.S. 753 (1967) and Quill Corp. v. North Dakota, 504 U.S. 298 (1992).

[276] The use tax is the companion tax to the sales tax, created to ensure that cross-border transactions are not favored in the state tax code.

[277] For more on the Streamlined Sales and Use Tax Agreement, see CRS Report RL342 11, *State and Local Taxes and the Streamlined Sales and Use Tax Agreement*, by Steven Maguire.

[278] The states are: Arkansas, Indiana, Iowa, Kansas, Kentucky, Michigan, Minnesota, Nebraska, New Jersey, North Carolina, North Dakota, Oklahoma, Rhode Island, South Dakota, Vermont, West Virginia, and Wyoming. Available at: [http://www.streamlinedsalestax.org/Legislation _status/Index.html], visited June 30, 2008.

[279] Business activity taxes are commonly thought of as corporate income taxes, but may also include franchise taxes, business license taxes, business and occupation taxes, a tax on gross receipts, gross income or gross profits, value-added taxes, single business taxes, and capital stock taxes. They do not include taxes on transactions, like sales and use taxes or excise taxes. For more on state corporate income taxes, see CRS Report RL32297, *State Corporate Income Taxes: A Description and Analysis*, by Steven Maguire.

[280] For more on state BATs, see CRS Report RL32297, *State Corporate Income Taxes: A Description and Analysis*, by Steven Maguire.

[281] Sec. 3(b)(2).

In: Trends in Internet Research
Editor: B.G. Kutais
ISBN: 978-1-59454-140-7

Chapter 7

UNLAWFUL INTERNET GAMBLING ENFORCEMENT ACT AND ITS IMPLEMENTING REGULATIONS*

Charles Doyle[1] and Brian T. Yeh[2]

ABSTRACT

The Unlawful Internet Gambling Enforcement Act (UIGEA) seeks to cut off the flow of revenue to unlawful Internet gambling businesses. It outlaws receipt of checks, credit card charges, electronic funds transfers, and the like by such businesses. It also enlists the assistance of banks, credit card issuers and other payment system participants to help stem the flow. To that end, it authorizes the Treasury Department and the Federal Reserve System (the Agencies), in consultation with the Justice Department, to promulgate implementing regulations. Proposed regulations were announced with a comment period that ended on December 12, 2007, 72 *Fed. Reg.* 56680 (October 4, 2007). After taking into consideration the public comments on the proposed rule, the Agencies adopted a final rule implementing the provisions of the UIGEA, 73 *Fed. Reg.* 69382 (November 18, 2008); the rule is effective January 19, 2009, with a compliance date of December 1, 2009.

The final rule substantially resembles the proposed rule, with several modifications in response to public comments. It addresses the feasibility of identifying and interdicting the flow of illicit Internet gambling proceeds in five payment systems: card systems, money transmission systems, wire transfer systems, check collection systems, and the Automated Clearing House (ACH) system. It suggests that, except for financial institutions that deal directly with illegal Internet gambling operators, tracking the flow of revenue within the wire transfer, check collection, and ACH systems is not feasible at this point. It therefore exempts them from the regulations' requirements. It charges those with whom illegal Internet gambling operators may deal directly within those three systems, and participants in the card and money transmission systems, to adopt policies and procedures to enable them to identify the nature of their customers' business, to employ customer agreements barring tainted transactions, and to

---

* This is an edited, reformatted and augmented version of a Congressional Research Service Publication, Order Code RL33261 Prepared for Members and Committees of Congress, July 7, 2009.

[1] Charles Doyle, Senior Specialist in American Public Law cdoyle@crs.loc.gov, 7-6968

[2] Brian T. Yeh, Legislative Attorney, byeh@crs.loc.gov, 7-5182

establish and maintain remedial steps to deal with tainted transactions when they are identified. The final rule provides non-exclusive examples of reasonably designed policies and procedures to prevent restricted transactions. The rule also explains why the Agencies rejected a check-list-of-unlawful-Internet-gambling-operators approach, asserting that such a list of businesses would not be practical, efficient, or effective in preventing unlawful Internet gambling. Rather, the Agencies argued that flexible, risk-based due diligence procedures conducted by participants in the payment systems, in establishing and maintaining commercial customer relationships, is the most effective method to prevent or prohibit the restricted transactions.

Several bills have been introduced in the 111th Congress related to Internet gambling. H.R. 2266 (Reasonable Prudence in Regulation Act) would delay the implementation of the UIGEA regulations by one year, establishing an effective date of December 1, 2010. H.R. 2267 (Internet Gambling Regulation, Consumer Protection, and Enforcement Act) would establish a federal licensing program, administered by the Treasury Department, under which Internet gambling companies may lawfully operate and accept bets or wagers from individuals located in the United States. H.R. 2268 (Internet Gambling Regulation and Tax Enforcement Act of 2009) would establish a licensing fee regime within the Internal Revenue Code for Internet gambling operators.

BACKGROUND

Passage of the Unlawful Internet Gambling Enforcement Act (UIGEA) in 2006 as Title VIII of the SAFE Port Act[282] represented the culmination of legislative consideration that began with the recommendations of the National Gambling Commission.[283]

UIGEA prohibits gambling businesses from accepting checks, credit cards charges, electronic transfers, and similar payments in connection with illegal Internet gambling.[284] It exempts lawful intrastate and intratribal Internet gambling operations that feature age and location verification requirements imposed as a matter of law.[285] It leaves in place questions as to the extent to which the Interstate Horseracing Act curtails the reach of other federal laws,[286] an issue that was at the center of World Trade Organization (WTO) litigation.[287] It instructs the Secretary of the Treasury and the Board of Governors of the Federal Reserve, in consultation with the Attorney General, to issue implementing regulations within 270 days of passage.[288]

As a consequence of UIGEA and Department of Justice enforcement efforts, NETeller, which reportedly processed more than $10 billion in gambling proceeds between U.S. customers and offshore Internet gambling business from 1999 to 2007, entered into a deferred prosecution agreement under which it agreed to discontinue U.S. operations, cooperate with investigators, and to pay the U.S. $136 million in sanctions and to return an additional $96 million to U.S. customers.[289] Several offshore Internet gambling companies have apparently sought similar agreements.[290] A number of large banking institutions, which underwrote the initial public offers for offshore Internet gambling companies on the London stock exchange, have been the targets of grand jury subpoenas as well.[291]

REGULATIONS IMPLEMENTING UIGEA

UIGEA calls for regulations that require "each designated payment system, and all participants therein, to identify and block or otherwise prevent or prohibit restricted transactions through the establishment of policies and procedures" reasonably calculated to have that result, 31 U.S.C. 5364(a). On October 4, 2007, the Board of Governors of the Federal Reserve System and the Treasury Department (the Agencies) issued proposed regulations implementing UIGEA, 72 *Fed. Reg.* 56680. The proposal invited commentators to suggest alternatives and critiques before the close of the comment period on December 12, 2007. The proposal offered to exempt substantial activities in those payment systems in which tracking is not possible now and in which it may ultimately not be feasible. It also noted that the two Agencies felt that they have no authority to compel payment system participants to serve lawful Internet gambling operators.[292] After taking into consideration the public comments on the proposed rule and consulting with the Department of Justice (as required by the UIGEA), the Agencies adopted a final rule implementing the provisions of the UIGEA, 73 *Fed. Reg.* 69382 (November 18, 2008); the rule is effective January 19, 2009, with a compliance date of December 1, 2009.

Designated Payment Systems & Due Diligence

The final rule identifies five relevant payment systems that could be used in connection with, or to facilitate, the "restricted transactions" used for Internet gambling: Automated Clearing House System (ACH), card systems, check collection systems, money transmitting business, and wire transfer systems, new 31 C.F.R. §132.3. The rule defines a "restricted transaction" to mean any transactions or transmittals involving any credit, funds, instrument, or proceeds that the UIGEA prohibits any person engaged in the business of betting or wagering from knowingly accepting, in connection with the participation of another person in unlawful Internet gambling, new 31 C.F.R. §132.2(y). However, the rule does *not* provide a regulatory definition of the term "unlawful Internet gambling," and instead uses the UIGEA's definition, which relies on underlying federal or state gambling laws.[293]

While the Agencies expect that card systems will find that using a merchant and transaction coding system is "the method of choice" to identify and block restricted transactions, the Agencies felt that the most efficient way for other designated payment systems to comply with the UIGEA is through "adequate due diligence by participants when opening accounts for commercial customers to reduce the risk that a commercial customer will introduce restricted transactions into the payment system in the first place," 73 *Fed. Reg.* 69394 (November 18, 2008).

The rule directs participants in the designated systems, unless exempted, to "establish and implement written policies and procedures reasonably designed to identify and block or otherwise prevent or prohibit restricted transactions," new 31 C.F.R. §132.5(a), and then provides non-exclusive examples of reasonably compliant policies and procedures for each system, new 31 C.F.R. § 132.6. Participants may comply by adopting the policies and procedures of their payments system or by adopting their own, new 31 C.F.R. §§132.5(b), 132.6(a). Participants that establish and implement procedures for due diligence of their commercial customer accounts or commercial customer relationships will be considered in compliance with the regulation if the procedures include the following steps, new 31 C.F.R. § 132.6(b):

1. At the establishment of the account or relationship, the participant conducts due diligence of a commercial customer and its activities commensurate with the participant's judgment of the risk of restricted transactions presented by the customer's business.
2. Based on its due diligence, the participant makes a determination regarding the risk the commercial customer presents of engaging in an Internet gambling business. Such a determination may take one of the two courses set forth below:

   a. The participant determines that the commercial customer presents a minimal risk of engaging in an Internet gambling business (such as commercial customers that are directly supervised by a federal functional regulator,[294] or an agency, department, or division of the federal government or a state government), or
   b. The participant cannot determine that the commercial customer presents a minimal risk of engaging in an Internet gambling business, in which case it must obtain a certification from the commercial customer that it does not engage in an Internet gambling business. If the commercial customer does engage in an Internet gambling business, the participant must obtain: (1) documentation that provides evidence of the customer's legal authority to engage in the Internet gambling business and a written commitment by the commercial customer to notify the participant of any changes in its legal authority to engage in its Internet gambling business, and (2) a third-party certification that the commercial customer's systems for engaging in the Internet gambling business are reasonably designed to ensure that the commercial customer's Internet gambling business will remain within the licensed or otherwise lawful limits, including with respect to age and location verification.

3. The participant notifies all of its commercial customers that restricted transactions are prohibited from being processed through the account or relationship, "through a term in the commercial customer agreement, a simple notice sent to the customer, or through some other method, "73 Fed. Reg. 69393 (November 18, 2008).

Non-Exclusive Examples of Compliant Policies and Procedures

Of the five payment systems, a "card system" as understood by the regulations is one that settles transactions involving credit card, debit card, pre-paid card, or stored value product and in which the cards "are issued or authorized by the operator of the system and used to purchase goods or services or to obtain a cash advance," new 31 C.F.R. § 132.2(f). Merchant codes are a standard feature of the system which permits the system to identify particular types of businesses, 71 *Fed. Reg.* 56684 (October 4, 2007). There are no card system exemptions from the regulations' requirements. Examples of reasonably compliant policies and procedures feature due diligence and prophylactic procedural components. The standards involve screening merchants to determine the nature of their business, a clause prohibiting restricted transactions within the merchant agreement, as well as maintaining and monitoring a business coding system to identify and block restricted transactions, new 31 C.F.R. § 132.6(d).

"Money transmitting businesses" are entities such as Western Union and PayPal that are in the business of transmitting funds, 71 *Fed. Reg.* 56684 (October 4, 2007). They too are without exemption from the UIGEA implementing regulations. Examples of acceptable policies and procedures for money transmitting businesses feature procedures to identify the nature of a subscriber's business, subscriber agreements to avoid restricted transactions, procedures to check for suspicious payment patterns, and an outline of remedial actions (access denial, account termination)[295] to be taken when restricted transactions are found, new 31 C.F.R. §132.6(f).

The regulations contain exemptions in varying degrees for the other payment systems. In essence, because of the difficulties of identifying tainted transactions, they limit requirements to those who may deal directly with the unlawful Internet gambling businesses. In the case of "check collection systems," the coded information available to the system with respect to a particular check is limited information identifying the bank and account upon which the check is drawn, and the number and amount of the check, 72 *Fed. Reg.* 56687 (October 4, 2007). Information identifying the payee is not coded and a "requirement to analyze each check with respect to the payee would substantially ... reduce the efficiency of the check collection system," 72 *Fed. Reg.* 56687 (October 4, 2007). Consequently, the final rule exempts all participants in a particular check collection through a check collection system except for "the first U.S. institution to which a check is transferred, in this case the institution receiving the check deposit from the gambling business,"72 *Fed. Reg.* 56687 (October 4, 2007)—namely, the depositary bank, new 31 C.F.R. §132.4(b).

Banks in which a payee deposits a check are covered by the regulations as are banks which receive a check for collection from a foreign bank. The rule offers examples for both circumstances. In the case of a check received from a foreign bank, examples of a depositary bank's reasonably compliant policies and procedures are procedures to inform the foreign banking office after the depositary bank has actual knowledge[296] that the checks are restricted transactions (such actual knowledge being obtained through notification by a government entity such as law enforcement or a regulatory agency), new 31 C.F.R. § 132.6(e)(2). In the purely domestic cases, examples of reasonably compliant policies and procedures would include (1) due diligence in establishing and maintaining customer relations sufficient to identify the nature of a customer's business, and to provide for a prohibition on tainted transactions in the customer agreement, and (2) remedial action (refuse to deposit a check; close an account) should a tainted transaction be unearthed, new 31 C.F.R. §132.6(e)(1).

"Wire transfer systems" come in two forms. One involves a large volume transactions between banks; the second, customer-initiated transfers from one bank to another, 72 *Fed. Reg.* 56685 (October 4, 2007). Like the check collection systems, under current practices only the recipient bank is in a realistic position to determine the nature of the payee's business. The Agencies sought public comments on whether additional safeguards should be required of the initiating bank in such cases, 72 *Fed. Reg.* 56687 (October 4, 2007), but ultimately decided to exempt all but the bank receiving the transfer, new 31 C.F.R. § 132.4(d).

Banks that receive a wire transfer (the beneficiary's bank) are covered by the regulations, and examples of reasonably compliant policies and practices resemble those provided for check collection system participants: know your customer, have a no-tainted transaction customer agreement clause, and have a remedial procedure (transfer denied; account closed) when tainted transactions surface, new 31 C.F.R. § 132.6(g).

The "Automated Clearing House System" (ACH) is a system for settling batched electronic entries for financial institutions. The entries may be recurring credit transfers such as payroll direct deposit payments or recurring debit transfers such as mortgage payments, 72 *Fed. Reg.* 56683 (October 4, 2007). The entries may also include one time individual credit or debit transfers, *Id.* Banks periodically package credit and debit transfers and send them to a ACH system operator who sorts them out and assigns them to the banks in which the accounts to be credited or debited are found, *Id.* Participants are identified not according to whether they are transferring credits or debits but according which institution initiated the transfer, i.e. originating depository financial institutions (ODFI) and receiving depository financial institutions (RDFI), *Id.*

The final rule exempts all participants processing a particular transaction through an ACH system, except for the RFDI in an ACH credit transaction, the ODFI in an ACH debit transaction, and the receiving gateway operator that receives instructions for an ACH debit transaction directly from a foreign sender, new 31 C.F.R. § 132.4(a). These entities are not exempt under the theory that in any tainted transaction they will be in the best position to assess the nature of the business of the beneficiary of the transfer and to identify and block transfers to unlawful Internet gambling operators, 72 *Fed. Reg.* 56686 (October 4, 2007). The ACH system operator, ODFIs in a credit transaction and RDFIs in a debit transaction are exempt from the regulations, however, *Id.*

The examples of ACH system reasonably compliant policies and procedures are comparable to those for check collection and wire transfer systems: in purely domestic cases, know your customer, have a no-tainted transaction customer agreement clause, have a remedial procedure (disallow origination of ACH debit transactions; account closed) when tainted transactions surface; in the case of receiving transfers from overseas, know your foreign gateway operator, have a no-tainted transaction agreement, have a remedial procedure (ACH services denied; termination of cross-border relationship) when tainted transactions surface, new 31 C.F.R. § 132.6(c). The Agencies explained that U.S. participants processing *outbound* cross-border credit transactions (ACH credits and wire transfers) are exempted "because there are no reasonably practical steps that a U.S. participant could take to prevent their consumer customers from sending restricted transactions cross-border," 73 *Fed. Reg.* 69389 (November 18, 2008). The Agencies explained that there is insufficient information to allow U.S. participants to identify and block restricted transactions in cross-border ACH credit transactions and sending wire transfers abroad, *Id.*

Unlawful Internet Gambling Operators Watch List

In the proposed regulations, the Agencies had explained why they did not follow a list-of-unlawful-Internet-gamblers approach similar to that used to deny drug dealers and terrorists access to American financial services (such as those administered by the Office of Foreign Assets Control (OFAC)), 72 *Fed. Reg.* 56690 (October 4, 2007).

The OFAC system is a product of the International Economic Emergency Powers Act (IEEPA) which grants the President extraordinary powers to deal with foreign threats to the national security, foreign policy or economy of the United States.[297] The Presidents have exercised their powers under IEEPA to bar financial dealings with various identified drug dealers and terrorists among others.[298] OFAC maintains an online list of the dealers and terrorists subject to the freeze.[299] It might be thought that assembling a list of known unlawful Internet gambling operators and their fiscal accomplices might work just as well.

After considering the public comments on this issue, the Agencies concluded that maintaining such a list would be a time-consuming effort for which they lack the expertise, and they also questioned its effectiveness, 73 *Fed. Reg.* 69384 (November 18, 2008). The Agencies provided several reasons to support their position that the watch list would be inefficient and ineffective in preventing unlawful activity:

- Because the UIGEA does not precisely define what activities constitute unlawful Internet gambling, but rather refers to activities that are illegal under various federal or state gambling laws, creating such a list would require the Agencies to interpret those laws in a way that might "set up conflicts or confusion with interpretations by the entities that actually enforce those laws."
- The payment transactions may not necessarily be made payable to the business's listed name.
- The list might become quickly outdated to the extent that Internet gambling businesses could quickly change their payments information to evade the law.

LEGISLATION IN THE 111TH CONGRESS

Several bills have been introduced in the 111th Congress that would liberalize federal online gambling laws.

Reasonable Prudence in Regulation Act

Introduced by Representative Frank, the Chairman of the House Financial Services Committee, the Reasonable Prudence in Regulation Act (H.R. 2266) would delay the date for compliance with the UIGEA regulations by one year, until December 1, 2010.

Internet Gambling Regulation, Consumer Protection, and Enforcement Act

Another bill introduced by Representative Frank, the Internet Gambling Regulation, Consumer Protection, and Enforcement Act (H.R. 2267), would establish a federal licensing regime under which Internet gambling operators may lawfully accept bets or wagers from individuals located in the United States. The Secretary of the Treasury would have full regulatory authority over the Internet gambling licensing program, including the power to approve, deny, renew, or revoke licenses to operate an Internet gambling facility. In addition, H.R. 2267 would establish specific minimum standards for Internet gambling licensees to satisfy, including the following:[300]

1. Establishing safeguards to verify that the customer placing a bet or wager is of legal age as defined by the law of the state or tribal area in which the individual is located at the time the bet or wager is placed.
2. Requiring mechanisms that verify that the customer placing a bet or wager is physically located in a jurisdiction that permits Internet gambling.
3. Ensuring the collection of all taxes relating to Internet gambling from customers and from any licensee.
4. Maintaining safeguards to combat fraud, money laundering, and the financing of terrorism.
5. Maintaining safeguards to protect the customer's privacy and security.
6. Establishing safeguards to combat compulsive Internet gambling.

Indian tribes and states may opt-out of the Internet gambling regime if they provide notice to the Secretary of the Treasury before the end of the 90-day period after enactment of the Internet Gambling Regulation, Consumer Protection, and Enforcement Act.[301] Therefore, customers located within Indian tribes and states that elected to opt-out would be prohibited from engaging in Internet gambling activities, and licensees would be responsible for blocking access to those customers. Finally, the bill contains a clause that expressly states that H.R. 2267 does not provide any authorization for an Internet gambling facility to knowingly accept bets or wagers on sporting events in violation of federal law.[302]

Internet Gambling Regulation and Tax Enforcement Act of 2009

Representative McDermott introduced a related bill to Representative Frank's licensing legislation, the Internet Gambling Regulation and Tax Enforcement Act of 2009 (H.R. 2268). This bill would establish a licensing fee regime within the Internal Revenue Code for Internet gambling operators. In support of the legislation, Representative McDermott cited an April 2009 study conducted by the accounting firm PricewaterhouseCoopers that estimated that regulating Internet gambling could generate up to $48.6 billion (excluding online sports gambling) or $62.7 billion (including online sports gambling) in federal revenues over a 10-year period.[303] H.R. 2268 would require each licensee to pay a monthly Internet gambling license fee in an amount equal to 2% of all funds deposited by customers during that month.[304] In addition, customers would be required to pay income taxes on their Internet gambling winnings.[305]

Legislation in the 110th Congress

In the 110th Congress, Representatives Frank and McDermott had introduced legislation similar to their bills in the 111th Congress. The 110th Congress also considered legislation, the Skill Game Protection Act (H.R. 2610), that would have removed from Wire Act[306] and UIGEA coverage games such as poker, which enthusiasts consider games of skill.[307] Finally, the Payments System Protection Act of 2008 (H.R. 6870), introduced by Representative Frank, would have prohibited the Agencies from proposing, prescribing, or implementing any regulation called for under the UIGEA, including the proposed regulations, except to the extent that such regulation pertains to unlawful Internet sports gambling. Furthermore, the bill would have required the Agencies to develop and implement regulations that include a definition of "unlawful Internet gambling" and require the Secretary of the Treasury to compile and maintain a list of unlawful Internet gambling businesses; however, such regulations would not have been effective if they "require any person to block or refuse to honor any transaction, or prohibit the acceptance of any product or service of such person, other than in connection with a business on the list maintained by the Secretary."

End Notes

[282] P.L. 109-347, 120 Stat. 1952 (31 U.S.C. 5361-5367) (2006).

[283] National Gambling Impact Study Commission, *Final Report* at 5-12 (1999). Earlier related CRS Reports include CRS Report RS22418, *Internet Gambling: Two Approaches in the 109th Congress*, from which some of this report is drawn, and CRS Report RS2 1487, *Internet Gambling: A Sketch of Legislative Proposals in the 108th and 109th Congresses*, which includes a more extensive discussion of the legislation's evolution.

[284] 31 U.S.C. 5363.

[285] 31 U.S.C. 5362.

[286] 31 U.S.C. 5362(10)(D)(iii). The Justice Department and certain members of the horse racing industry disagree over the extent to which the Horseracing Act amends the coverage of the Wire Act that outlaws the interstate transmission by wire of certain information related to gambling. UIGEA denies that its provisions are intended to resolve the dispute.

[287] *See e.g., Don't Bet on the United States's Internet Gambling Laws: The Tension Between Internet Gambling Legislation and World Trade Organization Commitments*, 2007 COLUMBIA BUSINESS LAW REVIEW 439. In the WTO dispute, Caribbean nation Antigua and Barbuda ("Antigua") argued that the United States discriminates against foreign Internet gambling operators while permitting domestic, online gambling on horse racing, in violation of U.S. market access commitments under the General Agreement on Trade in Services treaty. Antigua won its case before the WTO, and on December 21, 2007, a WTO arbitration report determined that Antigua had suffered $21 million in damages annually. The WTO arbitrator ruled that Antigua may request authorization to suspend a maximum $21 million annually in obligations owed to the United States under the WTO Agreement on Trade-Related Aspects of Intellectual Property Rights. (In other words, Antigua could infringe the rights of U.S. holders of copyrights, trademarks, and patents, up to $21 million a year.) Decision by the Arbitrator, Recourse to Arbitration by the United States for Arbitration under Article 22.6 of the DSU, United States—Measures Affecting the Cross-Border Supply of Gambling and Betting Services, WT/DS285/ARB (December 21, 2007). For more information on this case, see CRS Report RL32014, WTO *Dispute Settlement: Status of U.S. Compliance in Pending Cases*, by Jeanne J. Grimmett.

[288] 31 U.S.C. 5364.

[289] "Neteller to Pay Dollars 136m Gambling Penalty," *Financial Times USA* at 16 (July 19, 2007).

[290] *Id.*; "Sportingbet Cuts Deal," *Express on Sunday* at 7 (August 5, 2007) ("Sportingbet is now following the lead of rivals PartyGaming and 888 Holdings which started talks with the United States Attorney's Office ... in a bid to remove the threat of any criminal proceedings ... "); Eric Pfanner, "A New Chance for Online Gambling in the U.S.," *New York Times* (April 27, 2009) ("This month, PartyGaming agreed to a $105 million settlement with the U.S. attorney's office in New York, involving the period before 2006, when it acknowledged that its activities had been 'contrary to certain U.S. laws.' In turn, the U.S. authorities agreed not to prosecute the company, which is listed on the London Stock Exchange, or its executives.").

[291] Andrew Ross Sorkin and Stephanie Saul, "Gambling Subpoenas on Wall St," *New York Times*, at C1 (January 22, 2007).

[292] "Some payment system operators have indicated that, for business reasons, they have decided to avoid processing any gambling transactions, even if lawful, because among other things, they believe that these transactions are not sufficiently profitable to warrant the higher risk they believe these transactions pose." The Agencies do not believe UIGEA authorizes them to countermand such a decision, *72 Fed. Reg.* 56688 (October 4, 2007).

[293] "Unlawful Internet gambling means to place, receive, or otherwise knowingly transmit a bet or wager by any means which involves the use, at least in part, of the Internet where such bet or wager is unlawful under any applicable Federal or State law in the State or Tribal lands in which the bet or wager is initiated, received, or otherwise made. The term does not include placing, receiving, or otherwise transmitting a bet or wager that is excluded from the definition of this term by the Act as an intrastate transaction or an intra-tribal

transaction, and does not include any activity that is allowed under the Interstate Horseracing Act of 1978." 31 C.F.R. § 132.2(bb).

[294] The term "federal functional regulator" means—the Board of Governors of the Federal Reserve System; the Office of the Comptroller of the Currency; the Board of Directors of the Federal Deposit Insurance Corporation; (D) the Director of the Office of Thrift Supervision; (E) the National Credit Union Administration Board; and (F) the Securities and Exchange Commission. 15 U.S.C. §6809.

[295] However, "[a]s the examples in the rule are non-exclusive, a system or participant may choose to include fines in its policies and procedures where appropriate." 73 *Fed. Reg.* 69393 (November 18, 2008).

[296] "Actual knowledge" is defined by the regulation to mean, with respect to a transaction or commercial customer, "when a particular fact with respect to that transaction or commercial customer is known by or brought to the attention of (1) an individual in the organization responsible for the organization's compliance function with respect to that transaction or commercial customer, or (2) an officer of the organization." 31 C.F.R. § 132.2(a).

[297] 50 U.S.C. 1701-1707.

[298] *See e.g.*, E.O. 12978, Blocking Assets and Prohibiting Transactions With Significant Narcotics Traffickers, 60 *Fed. Reg.* 54579 (October 21, 1995); E.O. 13219, Blocking Property of Persons Who Threaten International Stabilization Efforts in the Western Balkans, 66 *Fed. Reg.* 34777 (June 26, 2001).

[299] 31 C.F.R. ch.V, App.A (July 1, 2006), available on November 1, 2007 at http://www.treasury.gov/offices/enforcement/ofac/sdn/t1 1sdn.pdf.

[300] H.R. 2267, §2, adding new 31 U.S.C. § 5383(g).

[301] *Id.*, adding new 31 U.S.C. § 5386. Although the bill's Indian tribe opt-out provision requires Indian tribes' principal chief or other chief executive officer to inform the Secretary of the Treasury of the decision to opt-out from allowing individuals in their jurisdiction to participate in Internet gambling, the bill's state opt-out provision requires the governor of a state to inform the "Director" of such opt-out. Yet the term "Director" is nowhere defined in the legislation. The reference to "Director" may well be an unintentional carry-over from Representative Frank's bill in the 110th Congress, H.R. 2046, which would have empowered the Director of the Financial Crimes Enforcement Network to oversee and operate the Internet gambling licensing program that would have been established under that bill.

[302] H.R. 2267, §2, adding new 31 U.S.C. § 5387. Under existing federal law, it is unlawful for a governmental entity or a private person to sponsor, operate, advertise, promote, license, or authorize a lottery, sweepstakes, or other betting, gambling, or wagering scheme based, directly or indirectly, on one or more competitive games in which amateur or professional athletes participate, with certain limited exceptions (parimutuel animal racing or jai-alai games). 28 U.S.C. § 3702. However, the UIGEA's definition of "bet or wager" explicitly does not include participation in any fantasy or simulation sports games, 31 U.S.C. § 5362(1)(E)(ix).

[303] Press Release, *Rep. McDermott Introduces Internet Gaming Tax Legislation Companion Bill to Rep. Frank's Legislation to License and Regulate Online Gaming*, May 6, 2009 (referring to PricewaterhouseCoopers, *Estimate of Federal Revenue Effect of Proposal to Regulate and Tax Online Gambling* (April 24, 2009), *available at* http://www.safeandsecureig.org/media/pwc09.pdf).

[304] H.R. 2268, §2(a), adding new 26 U.S.C. § 4491(a).

[305] *Id.*, §4(d), adding new 26 U.S.C. § 861(a)(9).

[306] 18 U.S.C. 1084 ("Whoever being engaged in the business of betting or wagering knowingly uses a wire communication facility for the transmission in interstate or foreign commerce of bets or wagers or information assisting in the placing of bets or wagers on any sporting event or contest, or for the transmission of a wire communication which entitles the recipient to receive money or credit as a result of bets or wagers, or for information assisting in the placing of bets or wagers, shall be fined under this title or imprisoned not more than two years, or both.").

[307] Apparently with games like poker in mind, when defining the bets and wagers within its reach, UIGEA uses the phrase "a game subject to chance," when speaking of prohibited speculation upon contests, sporting events, and games, 31 U.S.C. 5362(1)(A), rather than the phrase "opportunity to win is predominantly subject to chance," which it uses when speaking of prohibited speculation on lotteries, 31 U.S.C. 5362(1)(B).

In: Trends in Internet Research
Editor: B.G. Kutais

ISBN: 978-1-59454-140-7

Chapter 8

INTERNET SEARCH ENGINES: COPYRIGHT'S "FAIR USE" IN REPRODUCTION AND PUBLIC DISPLAY RIGHTS*

Robin Jeweler[1] and Brian T. Yeh[2]

ABSTRACT

Hyperlinking, in-line linking, caching, framing, thumbnails. Terms that describe Internet functionality pose interpretative challenges for the courts as they determine how these activities relate to a copyright holder's traditional right to control reproduction, display, and distribution of protected works. At issue is whether basic operation of the Internet, in some cases, constitutes or facilitates copyright infringement. If so, is the activity a "fair use" protected by the Copyright Act? These issues frequently implicate search engines, which scan the web to allow users to find content for uses, both legitimate and illegitimate.

In 2003, the Ninth Circuit Court of Appeals decided *Kelly v. Arriba Soft Corp.*, holding that a search engine's online display of "thumbnail" images was a fair use of copyright protected work. More recently, a U.S. district court considered an Internet search engine's caching, linking, and the display of thumbnails in a context other than that approved in *Kelly*. In *Field v. Google*, the district court found that Google's system of displaying cached images did not infringe the content owner's copyright. And in *Perfect 10 v. Amazon.com Inc.*, the Ninth Circuit revisited and expanded upon its holding in *Kelly*, finding that a search engine's use of thumbnail images and practice of in-line linking, framing, and caching were not infringing. But it left open the question of possible secondary liability for contributory copyright infringement and possible immunity under the Digital Millennium Copyright Act.

Taken together, these cases indicate a willingness by the courts to acknowledge the social utility of online indexing, and factor it into fair use analysis; to adapt copyright law

---

* This is an edited, reformatted and augmented version of a Congressional Research Service Publication, Order Code RL33810 Prepared for Members and Committees of Congress, January 28, 2008.

[1] Robin Jeweler, Legislative Attorney rjeweler@crs.loc.gov, 7-7893

[2] Brian T. Yeh, Legislative Attorney, byeh@crs.loc.gov, 7-5182

to the core functionality and purpose of Internet, even when that means requiring content owners to affirmatively act, such as by the use of meta-tags; and to consider and balance conflicts between useful functions, such as online indexing and caching, against emerging, viable new markets for content owners.

INTRODUCTION

Hyperlinking, in-line linking, caching, framing, thumbnails. Terms that describe Internet functionality pose interpretative challenges for the courts as they determine how these activities relate to a copyright holder's traditional right to control reproduction, display, and distribution of protected works. At issue is whether basic operation of the Internet, in some cases, constitutes or facilitates copyright infringement. If so, is the activity is a "fair use" protected by the Copyright Act? These issues frequently implicate search engines, which scan the web to allow users to find posted content. Both the posted content and the end-use thereof may be legitimate or infringing.

In 2003, the Ninth Circuit Court of Appeals decided *Kelly v. Arriba Soft Corp.*, which held that a search engine's online display of protected "thumbnail" images was a fair use of copyright protected work. More recently, courts have considered an Internet search engine's caching, linking, and the display of thumbnails in a context other than that approved in Kelly. In Field v. Google, a U.S. district court found that Google's system of displaying cached images did not infringe the content owner's copyright. And in *Perfect 10 v. Amazon.com Inc.*, the Ninth Circuit reconsidered issues relating to a search engine's practice using thumbnail images, in-line linking, and framing, finding the uses to be noninfringing. They are discussed below.

KELLY V. ARRIBA SOFT CORP.: THUMBNAIL IMAGES

Kelly v. Arriba Soft Corp.[308] is a significant Internet copyright case arising from the Ninth Circuit Court of Appeals. There, the court addressed the interface between the public's fair use rights and two of a copyright holder's exclusive rights—those of reproduction and public display.

Factual and Procedural Background

In *Kelly*, the defendant Arriba operated a "visual search engine" that allowed users to search for and retrieve images from the Internet. To provide this functionality, Arriba developed a computer program that would "crawl" the Internet searching for images to index. It would then download full-sized copies of those images onto Arriba's server and generate lower resolution thumbnails. Once the thumbnails were created, the program deleted the full-sized originals from the server.

Arriba altered its display format several times. In response to a search query, the search engine produced a "Results" page, which listed of a number of reduced, "thumbnail" images. When a user would double-click these images, a full-sized version of the image would appear.

From January 1999 to June 1999, the full-sized images were produced by "in-line linking," a process that retrieved the full-sized image from the original website and displayed it on the Arriba Web page. From July 1999 until sometime after August 2000, the results page contained thumbnails accompanied by a "Source" link and a "Details" link. The "Details" link produced a separate screen containing the thumbnail image and a link to the originating site. Clicking the "Source" link would produce two new windows on top of the Arriba page. The window in the forefront contained the full-sized image, imported directly from the originating website. Underneath that was another window displaying the originating Web page. This technique is known as framing, where an image from a second website is viewed within a frame that is pulled into the primary site's Web page. Currently, when a user clicks on the thumbnail, the user is sent to the originating site via an "out line" link (a link that directs the user from the linking-site to the linked-to site).[309]

Arriba's crawler copied 35 of Kelly's copyrighted photographs into the Arriba database. Kelly sued Arriba for copyright infringement, complaining of Arriba's thumbnails, as well as its in-line and framing links. The district court ruled that Arriba's use of both the thumbnails and the full- sized images was a fair use.[310] Kelly appealed to the Ninth Circuit Court of Appeals.

The Ninth Circuit's Decision

On appeal, the Ninth Circuit affirmed the district court's finding that the reproduction of images to create the thumbnails and their display by Arriba's search engine was a fair use. But it reversed the lower court holding that Arriba's in-line display of the larger image was a fair use as well .[311]

Thumbnails. An owner of a copyright has the exclusive right to reproduce copies of the work.[312] To establish a claim of copyright infringement by reproduction, the plaintiff must show ownership of the copyright and copying by the defendant. There was "no dispute that Kelly owned the copyright to the images and that Arriba copied those images. Therefore," the court ruled, "Kelly established a prima facie case of copyright infringement."[313]

However, a claim of copyright infringement is subject to certain statutory exceptions, including the fair use exception.[314] This exception "permits courts to avoid rigid application of the copyright statute when, on occasion, it would stifle the very creativity which that statute is designed to foster."[315]

To determine whether Arriba's use of Kelly's images was a fair use, the court weighed four statutorily-prescribed factors: (1) the purpose and character of the use, including whether such use is of a commercial nature or is for nonprofit educational purposes;[316] (2) the nature of the copyrighted work; (3) the amount and substantiality of the portion used in relation to the copyrighted work as a whole; and (4) the effect of the use upon the potential market for or value of the copyrighted work.[317]

Applying the first factor, the court noted that the "more transformative the new work, the less important the other factors, including commercialism, become"[318] and held that the thumbnails were transformative because they were "much smaller, lower-resolution images that served an entirely different function than Kelly's original images."[319] Furthermore, it would be unlikely "that anyone would use Arriba's thumbnails for illustrative or aesthetic purposes because enlarging them sacrifices their clarity," the court found.[320] Thus, the first fair use factor weighed in favor of Arriba.

The court held that the second factor, the nature of the copyrighted work, weighed slightly in favor of Kelly because the photographs were creative in nature.[321] The third factor, the amount and substantiality of the portion used, was deemed not to weigh in either party's favor, even though Arriba copied the entire image.[322]

Finally, the court held that the fourth factor, the effect of the use on the potential market for or value of the copyrighted work, weighed in favor of Arriba. The fourth factor required the court to consider "not only the extent of market harm caused by the particular actions of the alleged infringer, but also whether unrestricted and widespread conduct of the sort engaged in by the defendant ... would result in a substantially adverse impact on the potential market for the original."[323] The court found that Arriba's creation and use of the thumbnails would not harm the market for or value of Kelly's images.[324] Accordingly, on balance, the court found that the display of the thumbnails was a fair use.

Field v. Google: Caching

In *Field v. Google*,[325] a U.S. district court considered a claim for copyright infringement against the Internet search engine, Google. Field sought statutory damages and injunctive relief against Google for permitting Internet users to access copies of images temporarily stored on its online repository, or cache. In the course of granting summary judgment for Google, the court explained the caching process:

> There are billions of Web pages accessible on the Internet. It would be impossible for Google to locate and index or catalog them manually. Accordingly, Google, like other search engines, uses an automated program (called the "Googlebot") to continuously crawl across the Internet, to locate and analyze available Web pages, and to catalog those Web pages into Google's searchable Web index.
>
> As part of this process, Google makes and analyzes a copy of each Web page that it finds, and stores the HTML code from those pages in a temporary repository called a cache. Once Google indexes and stores a Web page in the cache, it can include that page, as appropriate, in the search results it displays to users in response to their queries.
>
> When Google displays Web pages in its search results, the first item appearing in each result is the title of a Web page which, if clicked by the user, will take the user to the online location of that page. The title is followed by a short "snippet" from the Web page in smaller font. Following the snippet, Google typically provides the full URL for the page. Then, in the same smaller font, Google often displays another link labeled "Cached."
>
> When clicked, the "Cached" link directs an Internet user to the archival copy of a Web page stored in Google's system cache, rather than to the original Web site for that page. By clicking on the "Cached" link for a page, a user can view the

"snapshot" of that page, as it appeared the last time the site was visited and analyzed by the Googlebot.[326]

The court emphasized that there are numerous, industry-wide mechanisms, such as "meta-tags," for website owners to use communicate with Internet search engines. Owners can instruct crawlers, or robots, *not* to analyze or display a site in its web index. Owners posting on the Internet can use a Google-specific "no-archive" meta-tag to instruct the search engine not to provide cached links to a website. In view of these well-established means for communicating with Internet search engines, the court concluded that the plaintiff "decided to manufacture a claim for copyright infringement against Google in the hopes of making money from Google's standard practice."[327]

Despite its acknowledgment of the plaintiff's rather dubious motives, the court nevertheless discussed the merits of the copyright infringement claims. Specifically, the plaintiff did *not* claim that Google committed infringement when the Googlebot made initial copies of Field's copyrighted Web pages and stored them in its cache. Rather, the alleged infringing activity occurred when a Google user clicked on a cached link to the Web page and downloaded a copy of those pages from Google's computers.

Assuming, for the purposes of summary judgment, that Google's display of cached links to Field's work did constitute direct copyright infringement, the court considered four defenses raised by Google, and found in its favor on all counts.

Implied License. First, the court found that the plaintiff had granted Google an implied, nonexclusive license to display the work because "[c]onsent to use the copyrighted work need not be manifested verbally and may be inferred based on silence where the copyright holder knows of the use and encourages it."[328] Field's failure to use meta-tags to instruct the search engine not to cache could reasonably be interpreted as a grant of a license for that use.

Estoppel. The court invoked the facts supporting its finding of an implied license to support the equitable argument that Field was precluded from asserting a copyright claim. The court reiterated that Field could have prevented the caching, did not do so, and allowed Google to detrimentally rely on the absence of meta-tags. Had Google known the defendant's objection to displaying cached versions of its website, it would not have done so.

Fair Use. In a detailed analysis, the court concluded that Google's cache satisfies the statutory criteria for a fair use:

Purpose and character of use. The search engine's use of the protected material is transformative. Rather than serving an artistic function, its display of the images served an archival function, allowing users to access content when the original page is inaccessible.

Nature of the copyrighted works. Even assuming the copyrighted images are creative, Field published his works on the Internet, making them available to world for free; he added code to his site to ensure that all search engines would include his website in their search listings.

Amount and substantiality of the use. The court found that Google's display of entire Web pages in its cached links serves multiple transformative and socially valuable purposes. It cited the U.S. Supreme Court's decision in *Sony Corp. v. Universal Studios, Inc.*[329] and *Kelly, supra,* as examples where copying of an entire work is a fair use.

The effect of the use upon the potential market for or value of the copyrighted work. Although the plaintiff distributed his images on the Internet for free, he argued that Google's activity undercut licensing fees that he could potentially develop by selling access to cached links to his website. The court found that there was no evidence of an existing or developing market for licensing search engines the right to allow access to Web pages through cached links.

Good Faith. In addition to the statutory criteria of 17 U.S.C. § 107, the court considered equitable factors and found the Google operates in good faith because it honors industry-wide protocols to refrain from caching where so instructed. Conversely, the plaintiff deliberately ignored the protocols available to him in order to establish a claim for copyright infringement.

The Digital Millennium Copyright Act (DMCA). Finally, the court held that Google is protected by the safe harbor provision of the DMCA, which states that "[a] service provider shall not be liable for monetary relief ... for infringement of copyright by reason of the intermediate and temporary storage of material on a system or network controlled or operated by or for the service provider[.]"[330]

Perfect 10 v. Amazon.com: In-line Linking and Thumbnail Images

Procedural Background. More recently, in *Perfect 10 v. Amazon.com*, the Ninth Circuit revisited and expanded upon several of the issues that it had considered earlier in Kelly. Perfect 10, a company that markets and sells copyrighted images of nude models, filed actions to enjoin Google and Amazon.com from infringing its copyrighted photographs. Specifically, it sought to prevent Google's display of thumbnail images on its Image Search function, and to prevent both Google and Amazon from linking to third-party websites that provided full-sized, infringing versions of the images.

The district court found that in-line linking and framing were permissible, non-infringing uses of protected content. Therefore, it did not enjoin Google from linking to third-party websites that display full-sized infringing versions of the images, holding that Perfect 10 was not likely to prevail on its claim that Google violated its display or distribution rights by linking to these images. But the district court did enter a preliminary injunction against Google for its creation and public display of the thumbnail versions of Perfect 10's images. In a separate action, the court declined to preliminarily enjoin Amazon.com from giving users access to similar information provided to Amazon.com by Google.

The court of appeals affirmed the district court's holding with respect to the permissibility of in- line linking and framing. But it reversed the holding with respect to the use of thumbnail images, finding the use to be fair despite the potential of the thumbnails to encroach upon a potential commercial market for their use. It left open the questions of possible liability for contributory copyright infringement and/or immunity therefor under the DMCA, remanding the case to the district court for appropriate findings. These decisions are examined below.[331]

Perfect 10 v. Google in U.S. District Court

In *Perfect 10 v. Google,*[332] a U.S. district court considered the issue of thumbnails in a different context from that of *Kelly*. Perfect 10 (P10) publishes an adult magazine and operates a subscription website that features copyrighted photographs of nude models. Its proprietary website is not available to public search. Other websites, however, display, without permission, images and content from P10. Google, in response to image search inquiries, displayed thumbnail copies of P10's photos and linked to the third-party websites, which hosted and served the full- sized, infringing images. P10 filed suit against Google, claiming, among other things, direct, contributory, and vicarious copyright infringement.

As framed by the district court, the issues before it pitted IP rights against "the dazzling capacity of internet technology to assemble, organize, store, access, and display intellectual property 'content'[.] ...[The] issue, in a nutshell, is: does a search engine infringe copyrighted images when it displays them on an 'image search' function in the form of 'thumbnails' but not infringe when, through in-line linking, it displays copyrighted images served by another website?"[333]

For the reasons discussed below, the district court found that Google's in-line linking to and framing of infringing full-size images posted on third-party websites was not infringing, but that its display of thumbnail images was likely to be considered infringing.[334]

Linking and Framing. With respect to in-line linking and framing of full-size images from third- party websites, the court considered, not whether the activity was infringing, but a more preliminary question. Is linking or framing a "display" for copyright purposes? If it does not come within the ambit of the copyright holder's exclusive rights, it is not necessary to reach the question of copyright infringement.

Linking is a basic function of the Internet. The term "hyperlinking" is used to describe text or images, that when clicked by a user, transport him to a different webpage. "In-line linking" is somewhat different. It refers to the process whereby a webpage incorporates by reference content stored on and served by another website.

The parties before the court offered two theories for considering whether in-line linking is a display: the "server" test advocated by Google and the "incorporation" test advocated by P10. The server test defines a display as the "act of *serving* content over the web—*i.e.*, physically sending ones and zeroes over the internet to the user's browser."[335] The "incorporation" test would adopt a visual perspective wherein a display occurs from the act of incorporating content into a webpage that is pulled up by the browser. P10 argued that the webpage that incorporates the content through in-line linking causes the "appearance" of copyrighted content and is therefore "displaying" it for copyright purposes, regardless of where it is stored.

Reviewing precedent, the court acknowledged that there is substantial authority to the effect that traditional hyperlinking does *not* support claims of direct copyright infringement because there is no copying or display involved.[336] But there is little discussion of in-line linking.[337]

The court adopted the "server" test and held that a site that in-line links to another does not itself "display" the content for copyright purposes. Among the reasons given for its determination is that the server test is more technologically appropriate and better reflects the reality of how content travels over the Internet. Further it viewed the server test as liability "neutral." Application of the test doesn't invite infringing activities by search engines, nor does it preclude all liability. It would, more narrowly, "preclude search engines from being held directly liable for in-line linking and/or framing infringing content stored on third-party websites."[338] The direct infringers were the websites that "stole" P 10's full-size images and posted them on the Internet. Finally, the court reasoned, that

> [T]he server test maintains, however uneasily, the delicate balance for which copyright law strives—*i.e.*, between encouraging the creation of creative works and encouraging the dissemination of information. Merely to index the web so that users can more readily find the information they seek should not constitute direct infringement, but to host and serve infringing content may directly violate the rights of copyright holders."[339]

Thumbnail Images. Applying the server test to the thumbnail images, it was clear that Google did display them. Google acknowledged that it copied and stored them on its own servers. The issue then became, like that in *Kelly*, whether Google's use of P 10's images as thumbnails was a fair use. Analyzing statutory fair use criteria, the court concluded that Google's use of the thumbnails was *not* a fair use:

Purpose and character of use. Google's use of the thumbnails was a commercial use; it derived commercial benefit in the form of increased user traffic and advertising revenue. In *Kelly*, the court of appeals acknowledged that Arriba's use of thumbnails was commercial, yet concluded that search results were more "incidental and less exploitative" than other traditional commercial uses. Here, the commercial nature of Google's use was distinguishable because Google derived specific revenue from an ad sharing program with the third-party websites that hosted the infringing images.

P10 had entered into a licensing agreement with others for the sale and distribution of its reduced- size images for download to and use on cell phones. A significant factor supporting a finding of fair use is a court's determination that the use is transformative, discussed *supra*. Although the court found that Google's use of thumbnails to simplify and expedite access to information was transformative, it found it to be "consumptive" as well, *i.e.*, the use merely supersedes the object of the original instead of adding a further purpose or different character. Google's thumbnails superceded, or usurped, the market for the sale of reduced-size images, because cell phone users could download and save the images directly from Google.

Nature of the copyrighted works. Use of published works, including images, are more likely to qualify as a fair use because the first appearance of the creative expression has already occurred.

Amount and substantiality of the use. As in *Kelly*, the court found that Google used no more of the image than necessary to achieve the objective of providing effective image-search capability.

The effect of the use upon the potential market for or value of the copyrighted work. While Google's use of thumbnails did *not* harm the market for copyrighted full-size images, it *did* cause harm to the *potential* market for sales of P10's reduced-size images to cell phone users.

The court also considered and rejected P10's allegation that Google was guilty of contributory and vicarious copyright infringement liability.

Perfect 10 v. Amazon.com in the Ninth Circuit Court of Appeals

Linking and Framing. In tacitly adopting the "server" test and affirming the district court's finding that linking and framing did not violate the copyright holder's rights of display and reproduction, the court of appeals made several observations. It considered P10's contention that when Google frames a full-size image, it gives the "impression" that it is showing the image. The court acknowledged that linking and framing may cause some computer users to believe they are viewing a Google Web page when, in fact, Google, through HTML instructions, has directed the user's browser to the website publisher's computer that stores the image. But the Copyright Act, unlike the Trademark Act, does not protect a copyright holder against acts that may cause consumer confusion.[340] The same logic obtains with respect to the display of cached webpages. Even if the cache copies are no longer available on the third-party's website, it is the website publisher's computer, not Google's, that stores and displays the infringing cached image.

Burden of Proof in Establishing the Fair Use Defense. Before reviewing the district court's conclusion regarding Google's fair use defense, the appellate court first dealt with the question of which party bears the burden of proving an affirmative defense, such as fair use, on a motion for a preliminary injunction in a copyright infringement case. The Ninth Circuit Court of Appeals had not previously, conclusively ruled on this issue.[341] The appellate court disagreed with the district court's holding that P10 had the burden of demonstrating its likely success in overcoming the fair use defense raised by Google. The court of appeals ruled that "[a]t trial, the defendant in an infringement action bears the burden of proving fair use."[342] Thus, once Perfect 10 had shown a likelihood of success on the merits, the burden should have shifted to Google to show that its affirmative defense of fair use will succeed. The appellate court explained that the district court was in error for placing the burden, with respect to the fair use defense, on the party seeking a preliminary injunction in a copyright infringement case.[343]

Thumbnail Images. The district court was also in error regarding its determination that Google's display of thumbnail images was not a fair use. In reversing the lower court's decision on fair use, the court of appeals reconsidered the weight to be accorded to the statutory factors. It differed with the district court's analysis regarding character of use and market impact.

Purpose and character of use. The court laid major emphasis, and weight, on the transformative nature of a search engine's display as an electronic reference tool:

> Although an image may have been created originally to serve an entertainment, aesthetic, or informative function, a search engine transforms the image into a pointer directing a user to a source of information. ... [A] search engine provides social benefit by incorporating an original work into a new work, namely, an electronic reference tool.... In other words, a search engine puts images "in a different context" so that they are "transformed into a new creation."[344]

The court considered the judicial rule that "parody" is a fair use, and concluded that "[i]ndeed, a search engine may be more transformative than a parody because a search engine provides an entirely new use for the original work, while a parody typically has the same entertainment purpose as the original work."[345]

The fact that Google profited from its AdSense advertising program and that P 10's market for the sale of thumbnail images could be superceded by the Google display did not outweigh the public interest value of the transformative use, in the court's opinion. It noted the absence of evidence that downloads of thumbnails for mobile phone use actually occurred. Hence, the court's analysis of thumbnails from *Kelly* was controlling:

> Accordingly, we disagree with the district court's conclusion that because Google's use of the thumbnails could supersede Perfect 10's cell phone download use and because the use was more commercial than Arriba's, this fair use factor weighed "slightly" in favor of Perfect 10. Instead, we conclude that the transformative nature of Google's use is more significant than any incidental superseding use or the minor commercial aspects of Google's search engine and website. Therefore, the district court erred in determining this factor weighed in favor of Perfect 10.[346]

Effect of use on the market. Similarly, with respect to P10's market for the sale of its full-sized images, the court rejected the argument that market harm may be presumed if the intended use of an image is for commercial gain. Market harm to a copyright holder will not be "readily inferred" when an arguably infringing use is otherwise transformative. And, since the "potential harm" to the market for the sale of thumbnails was hypothetical, the court concluded that the significant transformative use outweighed the unproven use of Google's thumbnails for cell phone downloads. It vacated the district court's preliminary injunction regarding Google's use of thumbnails.

Likewise, the copying function related to caching of full-sized images performed automatically is a transformative, and, ultimately, a fair use, so long as the cache copies no more than necessary to assist the Internet user and the copying has no more than a minimal effect on the owner's right, while having a considerable public benefit.[347]

Secondary Liability. The court of appeals opinion devotes considerable attention to the question of Google's possible liability for secondary copyright infringement, that is, contributory and/or vicarious infringement. It was uncontested that third-party websites were posting infringing copies of P10's images. The court rejected the assertion that Google's automatic caching of copies of full-sized images from third-party sites was direct infringement. But it reversed the district court's determination that P10 was not likely to succeed with a claim for secondary liability against Google, and remanded the case for reconsideration in light of its opinion.

As defined by the Supreme Court, "[o]ne infringes contributorily by intentionally inducing or encouraging direct infringement, and infringes vicariously by profiting from direct infringement while declining to exercise a right to stop or limit it."[348] As applied by the Ninth Circuit, "a computer system operator can be held contributorily liable if it 'has actual knowledge that specific infringing material is available using its system,' and can 'take simple measures to prevent further damage' to copyrighted works, yet continues to provide access to infringing works."[349]

The court of appeals first considered whether Google intentionally encouraged infringement. The district court held that Google did not materially contribute to infringing conduct because it did not undertake any substantial promotional or advertising efforts to encourage visits to infringing websites, nor provide significant revenues to the infringing websites.[350] But the court of appeals disagreed, reasoning:

> There is no dispute that Google substantially assists websites to distribute their infringing copies to a worldwide market and assists a worldwide audience of users to access infringing materials. We cannot discount the effect of such a service on copyright owners, even though Google's assistance is available to all websites, not just infringing ones. Applying our test, Google could be held contributorily liable if it had knowledge that infringing Perfect 10 images were available using its search engine, could take simple measures to prevent further damage to Perfect 10's copyrighted works, and failed to take such steps.[351]

With respect to vicarious infringement, a plaintiff must establish that the defendant "exercises the requisite control over the direct infringer and that the defendant derives a direct financial benefit from the direct infringement."[352] The court found that P10 did not demonstrate that Google has the legal right to stop or limit direct infringement by third-party websites.

Because the district court determined that P10 was unlikely to succeed on its contributory and vicarious liability claims, it did not reach Google's arguments that it qualified for immunity from liability under the DMCA, 17 U.S.C. § 512. The district court was directed to consider whether Google was entitled to the limitations on liability provided by title II of the DMCA on remand.

CONCLUSION

It is no coincidence that search engines are frequently-named defendants in online copyright infringement litigation. Their role in Internet connectivity is vital. The infringement liability implications of that role are arguably more complex than a preliminary determination whether an individual website is posting infringing content.

In the DMCA, Congress amended the Copyright Act to create a safe harbor for the Internet service provider that operates as a "passive conduit" for transmission and exchange of third-party offerings. As the sophistication of Internet mass-offerings grow, from text and images to broader audiovisual formats, the function of the search engines is likely to increase in scope and sophistication as well. A valuable component is the actual search and indexing function which enables Internet users to post and find content. Most prominent search engines are, however, commercial, profit-making entities who benefit from traffic generated by their search capabilities. Providing search capability creates and satisfies an important market, but what impact does it have on emerging ones?

As the courts apply traditional copyright principles to the Internet, they must factor in its functionality and architecture. In *Kelly*, the Ninth Circuit grappled with the concept of displaying thumbnail images as a search tool. It found the use to be highly transformative, socially valuable, and "fair," but reserved judgment on the questions of in-line linking and framing. In *Field*, the district court considered caching, finding it to be fair as well. Of great significance to the court was the fact that content owners can control the ability of search engines to search and/or cache their websites. In *Perfect 10*, the Ninth Circuit considered thumbnail displays in a different context: namely, where a search engine displays thumbnails of infringing images and derives advertising revenue that is more closely linked to the posting. Although plaintiff had persuaded the lower court that the thumbnails, though transformative of the full-size images, could or would undermine a developing market for reduced-size images, the court of appeals reaffirmed the fair use analysis derived from *Kelly*. And, it took up where *Kelly* left off, holding that in-line linking and framing were not displays for copyright purposes. But the court left open the possibility that a search engine's actual conduct with respect to infringing content could be proven to be contributory infringement.

Taken together, these cases indicate a willingness by the courts to acknowledge the social utility of online indexing, and factor it into fair use analysis; to adapt copyright law to the core functionality and purpose of Internet, even when that means requiring content owners to act affirmatively, such as by the use of meta-tags; and to weigh and balance conflicts between useful functions, such as online indexing and caching, against emerging, viable new markets for content owners.

End Note

[308] 336 F.3d 811 (9th Cir. 2003).

[309] Arriba Soft subsequently changed its name to "Ditto.com".

[310] Kelly v. Arriba Soft Corp., 77 F. Supp. 2d 1116 (C.D. Cal. 1999).

[311] An earlier decision, subsequently withdrawn by the Ninth Circuit Court of Appeals and often referred to in judicial opinions as *Kelly I*, held that the in-line display of the larger image of Kelly's work was *not* a fair use and was therefore infringing. *Kelly v.* Arriba Soft Corp, 280 F.3d 934 (9th Cir. 2002). In its revised opinion, referred to as *Kelly II*, discussed above, the court determined that the issue of in-line linking had not been adequately raised by the parties and should not have been decided by the district court.

[312] *See* 17 U.S.C. §106.

[313] *Kelly*, 336 F.3d at 817.

[314] 17 U.S.C. §107.

[315] Dr. Seuss Enters., L.P. v. Penguin Books USA, Inc., 109 F.3d 1394, 1399 (9th Cir. 1997).

[316] The Supreme Court has held that "the central purpose of this investigation is to see ... whether the new work merely supersede[s] the objects of the original creation, or instead adds something new, with a further purpose or different character, altering the first with new expression, meaning, or message; it asks, in other words, whether and to what extent the new work is transformative." Campbell v. Acuff-Rose Music, Inc., 510 U.S. 569, 579 (1994).

[317] 17 U.S.C. § 107.

[318] *Kelly*, 330 F.3d at 818 n. 14, *citing Campbell*, 510 U.S. at 579.

[319] *Kelly*, 330 F.3d at 818. While Kelly's images were artistic works used for illustrative purposes and to portray scenes from the American West in an aesthetic manner, Arriba's use of Kelly's images in the thumbnails was unrelated to any aesthetic purpose. Arriba's search engine functions as a tool to help index and improve access to images on the Internet and their related websites.

[320] *Id.* at 819.
[321] *Id.* at 820.
[322] While wholesale copying does not preclude fair use per se, copying an entire work militates against a finding of fair use. However, the extent of permissible copying varies with the purpose and character of the use. "If the secondary user only copies as much as is necessary for his or her intended use, then this factor will not weigh against him or her." *Id.* at 821. Applying this principle, the court found that if Arriba only copied part of the image, it would be more difficult to identify it, thereby reducing the usefulness of the visual search engine. Therefore, the court concluded, it was reasonable to copy the entire image.
[323] *Id.* at 821, *citing Campbell*, 510 U.S. at 590. *See also*, 3 M. Nimmer & D. Nimmer, NIMMER ON COPYRIGHT § 13.05[A][4], at 13-102.61 (1993).
[324] *Kelly*, 330 F.3d at 821. The court emphasized that "Arriba's use of Kelly's images would not harm Kelly's ability to sell or license his full-sized images. Arriba does not sell or license its thumbnails to other parties. Anyone who downloaded the thumbnails would not be successful selling the full-sized images because of the low-resolution of the thumbnails. There would be no way to view, create, or sell a clear, full-sized image without going to Kelly's websites." *Id.* at 821-822.
[325] 412 F. Supp.2d 1106 (D. Nev. 2006).
[326] *Id.* at 1110-1111 (references and footnotes omitted).
[327] *Id.* at 1113.
[328] *Id.* at 1116.
[329] 464 U.S. 417 (1984)(holding that in-home recording, *i.e.*,"time-shifting" of free broadcast tv is a fair use).
[330] 17 U.S.C. § 512(b).
[331] Although Google and Amazon.com were separately named defendants in actions that were subsequently consolidated, the issues examined and the majority of the courts' analyses focus on the issues as they relate to Google, as does this report.
[332] 416 F. Supp.2d 828 (C.D.Ca.. 2006), *aff'd in part, rev'd in part sub nom* Perfect 10 v. Amazon.com, 508 F.3d 1146 (9th Cir. 2007).
[333] 416 F. Supp. at 831.
[334] Because the action before the court was a motion for a preliminary injunction, the court cast its findings as "probabilities of success" on the various claims.
[335] *Id.* at 839.
[336] *Id.* at 842.
[337] The Ninth Circuit found it to be copyright infringement in its subsequently withdrawn opinion in *Kelly I. See* footnote 4 *supra*.
[338] *Id.* at 844.
[339] *Id.* (emphasis in original). Conversely, "[t]o adopt the incorporation test would cause a tremendous chilling effect on the core functionality of the web—its capacity to link, a vital feature of the internet that makes it accessible, creative, and valuable." *Id.* at 840.
[340] Perfect 10, Inc. v. Amazon.com, Inc., 508 F.3d 1146, 1161 (9th Cir. 2007).
[341] The appellate court had previously used qualified language in addressing this issue, thereby not reaching a definite conclusion. *See* A&M Records v. Napster, Inc., 239 F.3d 1004, 1014 n.3 (9th Cir. 2001) ("We conclude that *even if* plaintiffs bear the burden of establishing that they would likely prevail against Napster's affirmative defenses at the preliminary injunction stage, the record supports the district court's conclusion that Napster users do not engage in fair use of the copyrighted materials.") (emphasis added).
[342] *Perfect 10,* 508 F.3d at 1158, *citing* Campbell v. Acuff-Rose Music, Inc., 510 U.S. 569, 590 (1994).
[343] An earlier decision, Perfect 10, Inc. v. Amazon.com, Inc., 487 F.3d 701 (9th Cir. 2007), had upheld the district court's choice of the plaintiff to bear the burden of establishing fair use for purposes of a preliminary injunction motion. However, that opinion was amended seven months later, 508 F.3d 1146, with the appellate court reversing itself and instead deciding to place the burden on the defendant.
[344] *Perfect 10*, 508 F.3d at 1 165(citations omitted).
[345] *Id.*
[346] *Id.* at 1167 (citations omitted).
[347] *Id.* at 1169-70.
[348] *Id.* at 1170, citing Metro-Goldwyn-Mayer Studios Inc. v. Grokster, Ltd.,545 U.S. 913, 930 (2005) (internal citations and footnotes omitted).
[349] *Id.* at 1172 (citations omitted).
[350] 416 F.Supp.2d at 854-56.
[351] *Perfect* 10, 508 F.3d at 1172.
[352] *Id.* at 1173.

In: Trends in Internet Research
Editor: B.G. Kutais

ISBN: 978-1-59454-140-7

Chapter 9

CONSTITUTIONALITY OF REQUIRING SEXUALLY EXPLICIT MATERIAL ON THE INTERNET TO BE UNDER A SEPARATE DOMAIN NAME*

Henry Cohen

ABSTRACT

It has been proposed that there be a domain on the Internet exclusively for websites that contain sexually explicit material; it might be labeled ".xxx" to complement the current ".com," ".org," and others. Some propose making use of a ".xxx" domain voluntary, and a June 26, 2008, decision by the Internet Corporation for Assigned Names and Numbers (ICAAN) to allow a virtually unlimited number of top-level domain names may make the voluntary use of ".xxx" possible in 2009. Others propose that Congress make use of ".xxx" mandatory for websites that contain sexually explicit material. This proposal raises the question whether a mandatory separate domain would violate the First Amendment, and this report focuses on that question.

It is unclear whether making a ".xxx" domain mandatory would violate the First Amendment. Whether it would be constitutional might depend upon whether a court viewed it as a content-based restriction on speech or as analogous to the zoning of adult theaters, or even as a mere disclosure requirement that did not raise a significant First Amendment issue. If a court viewed it as a content-based restriction on speech, then it would be constitutional only if the court found that it served a compelling governmental interest by the least restrictive means. Other factors that could affect its constitutionality might be whether it imposed criminal penalties and whether it were limited to websites that are predominantly pornographic.

---

* This is an edited, reformatted and augmented version of a Congressional Research Service Publication, Order Code RL33224 Prepared for Members and Committees of Congress, Updated July 14, 2008.

A VOLUNTARY ".XXX" DOMAIN

It has been proposed that there be a domain on the Internet exclusively for Websites that contain sexually explicit material; it might be labeled ".xxx" to complement the current ".com," ".org," and others. Some propose making use of a ".xxx" domain voluntary, but others propose that Congress make it mandatory. The latter proposal raises the question whether a mandatory separate domain would violate the First Amendment, and this report focuses on that question.

Congress has already provided for a ".kids" domain: the Dot Kids Implementation and Efficiency Act of 2002 directs the National Telecommunication and Information Administration (NTIA), which is an agency in the Department of Commerce, to establish a "new domain" "that provides access only to material that is suitable for minors and not harmful to minors."[353] The URL for the domain is [http://www.kids.us], and that site lists 20 websites that use the domain.[354]

An article reports that chairman and president of ICM Registry Inc., "Stuart Lawley, a Florida entrepreneur, [is] trying to establish a pornography-only '.xxx' domain. In such a realm, Lawley could restrict porn marketing to adults only, protect users' privacy, limit span and collect fees from Web masters. The .xxx proposal was finally slated for approval in August [2005] by the Internet Corporation for Assigned Names and Numbers (Icann), but because of a flurry of protest,"[355] was deferred, and, on May 10, 2006, ICAAN voted against the establishment of a ".xxx" domain. Another article explains that the reason that the proposal was put off is that "the Commerce Department sought more time to hear objections [and] ICANN cannot move forward without Commerce Department approval."[356]

On January 6, 2007, the Associated Press reported that ICAAN had revived the proposal and opened it for public comment, but, on March 30, 2007, ICAAN rejected the proposal.[357]

On June 26, 2008, ICAAN approved a plan that would allow a virtually unlimited number of top-level domains names. The plan could disallow a name for only a few reasons, such as that it is confusingly similar to an existing name or is "contrary to generally accepted legal norms relating to morality and public order that are recognized under international principles of law."[358] It remains to be seen whether, under this plan, ICAAN would approve an application to use a ".xxx" domain. Before the plan takes effect, ICAAN must approve a final version of it; this is expected to occur in early 2009.[359]

Some opponents of pornography support the proposal for a voluntary ".xxx" domain and some oppose it; likewise, some in the pornography business support the proposal and some oppose it. Both the above-mentioned articles comment on the support and opposition to the proposal:

- The proposal has had its share of critics. Some of them claim that a .xxx domain would provide legitimacy to the pornography industry. Supporters claim that a .xxx domain would make it easier for people to filter out content they do not want.
- The Family Research Council warns that it [the proposal] will simply breed more smut. But Senator Joe Lieberman supports a virtual red-light district because he says it would make the job of filtering out porn easier.
- Meanwhile, some pornographers, apparently drawn by the promise of catchier and more trustworthy U.R.L.'s, have gotten behind Lawley. Other skin-peddlers, echoing

the A.C.L.U., see the establishment of a voluntary porn zone as the first step toward the deportation of their industry to a distant corner of the Web, where their sites could easily be blocked by skittish Internet service providers, credit card companies and even governments.[360]

Finally, some opponents of pornography oppose the proposal for a voluntary ".xxx" domain because "sites would be free to keep their current '.com' address in effect making porn more easily accessible by creating yet another channel to house it."[361]

CONSTITUTIONALITY OF A MANDATORY ".XXX" DOMAIN

Two bills have been introduced to create a mandatory ".xxx" domain for material that is "harmful to minors," as the bills would define the term. They are S. 2426, 109th Congress, which was introduced by Senator Baucus, and S. 2137, 107th Congress, which was introduced by Senator Landrieu. Both bills direct the Secretary of Commerce, acting through the National Telecommunications and Information Administration, to establish the new domain.

The rest of this report will consider the constitutionality of a mandatory ".xxx" domain, without focusing on these bills or any other particular proposal. It does not matter for constitutional purposes specifically how the bill would define the material that it would require to be in the ".xxx" domain; we will assume merely that such material would include sexually explicit material that is protected by the First Amendment. And all sexually explicit material is generally protected by the First Amendment, unless it constitutes obscenity, or child pornography that is produced with an actual minor.[362]

Content-Based Discrimination

To require that websites with sexually explicit material be under a separate domain name would be to treat such material differently from other speech, and therefore could be viewed as discriminating against speech on the basis of its content. The Supreme Court has said that "[i]t is rare that a regulation restricting speech because of its content will ever be permissible."[363] As a general rule, the Supreme Court will uphold a content-based speech regulation only if it satisfies "strict scrutiny," which means only if it is necessary "to promote a compelling interest" and is "the least restrictive means to further the articulated interest."[364] By contrast, if a regulation of speech is "*justified* without reference to the content of the speech," then the Supreme Court considers it "content-neutral" and will uphold it if it "is designed to serve a substantial governmental interest and allows for reasonable alternative avenues of communication."[365] In other words, if a regulation of speech has a purpose other than to protect people from harm that the speech itself might cause, then it stands a better chance of being found constitutional.

One might argue that, although requiring sexually explicit material to be under a separate domain name would discriminate against speech on the basis of its content, that would not be the purpose of the requirement, and the requirement could be *justified* without reference to the content of the speech it would regulate. Its purpose would arguably be to facilitate parents' or librarians' use of filters when children access the Internet. It would accomplish this by dividing websites into two categories — those with sexually explicit material and those without it. This could be viewed as analogous to requiring "adult" movie theaters to locate in areas that are zoned for them. In *City of Renton v. Playtime Theaters, Inc.*, the Supreme Court upheld such zoning on the theory that it "is not aimed at the *content* of the films shown at 'adult motion picture theaters,' but rather at the *secondary effects* of such theaters on the surrounding community."[366] "The ordinance by its terms is designed to prevent crime, protect the city's retail trade, maintain property values, and generally 'protec[t] and preserv[e] the quality of [the city's] neighborhoods, commercial districts, and the quality of urban life,' not to suppress the expression of unpopular views."[367]

Analogously, one might argue, to restrict sexually explicit material to a separate domain name arguably would "zone" certain websites not because of the content of their speech but to lessen the "secondary effect" of minors' viewing those websites without parental approval. In effect, the proposal, like a zoning ordinance, would seek to isolate certain material into particular "neighborhoods" in cyberspace, and assist parents in preventing their children from visiting those "neighborhoods."

A possibly fatal flaw with this analogy, however, is that, in *Renton*, the secondary effects that the zoning ordinance sought to prevent — crime, lowered property values, and a deterioration in the quality of urban life — were not effects of viewing the regulated speech itself. The ".xxx" proposal, by contrast, would apparently attempt to protect minors from the effects of viewing the regulated speech itself, and these effects therefore are arguably not "secondary" in the sense that the Supreme Court meant in *Renton*. The ".xxx" proposal, from this view, would impose a burden on speech because Congress deems it harmful, and that is not a sufficient basis on which the government may regulate speech in a manner that affects adults, unless the regulation satisfies strict scrutiny.[368] In *Ashcroft v. Free Speech Coalition*, for example, the Supreme Court struck down a federal statute that banned "virtual" child pornography and other child pornography produced without the use of an actual minor, despite various harms that the government claimed that viewing such pornography could cause, such as "whet[ting] the appetites of pedophiles and encourag[ing] them to engage in illegal conduct."[369] The Supreme Court has stated: "We have made clear that the lesser scrutiny afforded regulations targeting the secondary effects of crime or declining property values has no application to content- based regulations targeting the primary effects of protected speech. The statute now before us burdens speech because of its content; it must receive strict scrutiny."[370]

Thus, a court might view the ".xxx" proposal either as a content-based regulation, which is constitutional only if it satisfies strict scrutiny by advancing a compelling governmental interest by the least restrictive means; or as a content-neutral regulation, which is constitutional if it advances a substantial governmental interest and allows for reasonable alternative avenues of communication. We will apply these two tests to the ".xxx" proposal, in the sections below titled "Strict scrutiny" and "Content-neutral scrutiny." First, however, we will explain why the ".xxx" proposal would even raise a free speech issue, in light of the fact that it would not censor speech.

Compelled Speech

The ".xxx" proposal could be viewed as, in effect, compelling speech on the part of websites with sexually explicit material. It would compel them to identify themselves, through use of a separate domain name, as containing such material. In general, it is as unconstitutional for the government to compel speech as it is for it to censor speech, except in the commercial context.[371] In *Riley v. National Federation of the Blind of North Carolina, Inc.*, a North Carolina statute required professional fundraisers for charities to disclose to potential donors the gross percentage of revenues retained in prior charitable solicitations. The Supreme Court held this unconstitutional, writing

> There is certainly some difference between compelled speech and compelled silence, but in the context of protected speech, the difference is without constitutional significance, for the First Amendment guarantees "freedom of speech," a term necessarily comprising the decision of both what to say and what *not* to say.[372]

In *Meese v. Keene*, however, the Court upheld compelled disclosure in a noncommercial context.[373] This case involved a provision of the Foreign Agents Registration Act of 1938, which requires that, when an agent of a foreign principal seeks to disseminate foreign "political propaganda," he must label such material with certain information, including his identity, the principal's identity, and the fact that he has registered with the Department of Justice. The material need not state that it is "political propaganda," but one agent objected to the statute's designating material by that term, which he considered pejorative. The agent wished to exhibit, without the required labels, three Canadian films on nuclear war and acid rain that the Justice Department had determined were "political propaganda."

In *Meese v. Keene*, the Supreme Court upheld the statute's use of the term, essentially because it considered the term not necessarily pejorative. On the subject of compelled disclosure, the Court wrote:

> Congress did not prohibit, edit, or restrain the distribution of advocacy materials. . . . To the contrary, Congress simply required the disseminators of such material to make additional disclosures that would better enable the public to evaluate the import of the propaganda.[374]

One might infer from this that compelled disclosure, in a noncommercial context, gives rise to no serious First Amendment issue, and nothing in the Court's opinion would seem to refute this inference. Thus, it seems impossible to reconcile this opinion with the Court's holding a year later in *Riley* (which did not mention *Meese v. Keene*) that, in a noncommercial context, there is no difference of constitutional significance between compelled speech and compelled silence.

In *Meese v. Keene*, furthermore, the Court did not mention earlier cases in which it had struck down laws compelling speech in a noncommercial context. For example, in *Wooley v. Maynard*, the Court struck down a New Hampshire statute requiring motorists to leave visible on their license plates the motto "Live Free or Die"[375]; in *West Virginia State Board of Education v. Barnette*, the Court held that a state may not require children to pledge allegiance to the United States[376]; and, *in Miami Herald Publishing Co. v. Tornillo*, the Court struck down a Florida statute that required newspapers to grant political candidates equal space to reply to the newspapers' criticism and attacks on their record.[377]

In any event, if one views the ".xxx" proposal as discriminating on the basis of content, then one could cite most of the compelled speech cases for the proposition that the ".xxx" proposal would be unconstitutional unless it can pass strict scrutiny. But one could cite *Meese v. Keene* (adapting the above quotation from it) to argue that the ".xxx" proposal would be constitutional because it would "not prohibit, edit, or restrain the distribution of [sexually explicit material]. . . . To the contrary, Congress [would] simply require[ ] the disseminators of such material to make additional disclosures that would better enable the public to evaluate the [content] of the [website]."

Strict Scrutiny

If the ".xxx" proposal were viewed as content-based, and not as constitutional simply by virtue of its similarity to the statute upheld in Meese v. Keene, then, as noted, it would be subject to "strict scrutiny," which means that it would be constitutional only if it is necessary "to promote a compelling interest," and is "the least restrictive means to further the articulated interest."[378]

Though the Supreme Court may be becoming less absolute in viewing the protection of all minors, regardless of age, from all sexual material, to be a compelling interest,[379] it has never struck down, on the ground that it did not further a compelling governmental interest, a statute aimed at denying minors access to sexual material. Rather, the Court tends to assume the existence of a compelling governmental interest in denying minors access to pornography and move on to the "least restrictive means" part of the strict scrutiny test, upholding or striking down the statute on that issue. In striking down the part of the Communications Decency Act of 1996 that banned from the Internet all "indecent" material that was accessible to minors, the Court wrote:

> In order to deny minors access to potentially harmful speech, the CDA effectively suppresses a large amount of speech that adults have a constitutional right to receive and to address to one another. That burden on adult speech is unacceptable if less restrictive alternatives would be at least as effective in achieving the legitimate purpose that the statute was enacted to serve.[380]

The ".xxx" proposal would not suppress speech, but would only compel it to be under a separate domain name. But are there less restrictive means by which to accomplish the ".xxx" proposal's goal? We will consider two alternative means.

One alternative might be to make use of the separate domain name voluntary. The question with respect to this alternative would be whether there would be an incentive for sexually explicit websites to use a separate domain name voluntarily — an incentive sufficient to induce enough of them to use a separate domain name so as to make the proposal as effective as it would be if it compelled them to use a separate domain name. An incentive, arguably, is that, just as the proposal would make it easier to block websites that use a separate domain name, it might make it easier to locate websites that use a separate domain name.

In addition, one might argue, a statute could effectively make use of a separate domain name mandatory only for websites based in the United States, as the U.S. government does not generally have authority over foreign websites. Therefore, a statute that mandated use of a separate domain name would not cover all websites with sexually explicit material, and this would appear to strengthen the case that voluntary use of a separate domain name would be as effective as mandatory use.[381]

A second alternative to the proposal might be one that already exists: the Dot Kids Implementation and Efficiency Act of 2002, mentioned at the beginning of this report. This statute may enable parents who wish to do so to block out all websites *not* under the "dot kids" domain name. If parents used a filter to prevent their children from gaining access to any website that does not use the "dot kids" domain, then they would be denying their children access to much material on the Internet that is not sexually explicit. If one deems a purpose of both the "Dot Kids" statute and the ".xxx" proposal to be not only to deny children access to sexually explicit material, but *not* to deny them access to non-sexually explicit material, then the "Dot Kids" Act might be viewed as less effective than the ".xxx" proposal, and therefore as not an adequate alternative to the latter. But, in another respect, the "Dot Kids" statute could be more effective because it could enable parents to block foreign as well as domestic websites; in that respect it might be viewed as an adequate alternative to the ".xxx" proposal.

Content-Neutral Scrutiny

If a court were to find the ".xxx" proposal to be analogous to the zoning of "adult" theaters that the Supreme Court has upheld, then it would ask whether the proposal is designed to serve a substantial governmental interest and allows for reasonable alternative avenues of communication. Because it appears that a court would likely find the proposal to serve a "compelling" interest, a court would ipso facto likely find the proposal to meet the less rigorous test of serving a "substantial" interest. And, because the proposal would not prevent anyone from posting protected speech, but would merely require them to post some speech under a separate domain name, it apparently could not even be said to reduce their avenues of communication except insofar as Internet users chose to block websites that used the separate domain name. Though the proposal would presumably facilitate such blocking, it would not require it, and therefore would seem likely to be found constitutional if this less-than-strict-scrutiny test were applied.

Criminal Penalties

A factor that might make a difference to the ".xxx" proposal's constitutionality is whether it imposed criminal penalties; if it did, that might tip the balance toward making it unconstitutional. In *Reno v. American Civil Liberties Union*, the Supreme Court, in striking down the Communications Decency Act of 1996, was apparently influenced by the fact that the statute would have imposed criminal penalties, including imprisonment.[382] It distinguished *Federal Communications Commission v. Pacifica Foundation*, in which it had upheld the ban on "indecent" material on broadcast media, in part on the ground that the radio station that had broadcast George Carlin's "Filthy Words" monologue had been penalized with only a Federal Communications Commission declaratory order.[383] "[T]he Commission's declaratory order," the Court in Reno wrote, "was not punitive; we expressly refused to decide whether the indecent broadcast 'would justify a criminal prosecution.'"[384]

Breadth of the Requirement

Another factor that might make a difference to the ".xxx" proposal's constitutionality is whether it applied only to websites that contained predominantly pornographic material, or it applied to any posting of material that might be deemed pornographic, even on websites that did not contain predominantly pornographic material. The latter approach would seem more problematic from a constitutional standpoint because it would deter any website not under the ".xxx" domain name from posting material that might be deemed pornographic, even if the website posted it for other than pornographic purposes, and even if the website contained material that was predominantly, for example, of a literary, artistic, or medical nature that would not attract children.

But even a proposal that applied only to websites that contained predominately pornographic material might be unconstitutional if it defined too vaguely the websites that it would require to use the ".xxx" domain. The constitutional problem with an overly vague definition is that it might deter a website that did not use the ".xxx" domain from posting sexually explicit material for its literary, artistic, or medical content. It might be deterred for fear that the material could be construed as pornographic and the website sanctioned. A vague law violates due process because it fails to "give the person of ordinary intelligence a reasonable opportunity to know what is prohibited, so that he may act accordingly.... [P]erhaps the most important factor affecting the clarity that the Constitution demands of a law is whether it threatens to inhibit the exercise of constitutionally protected rights. If, for example, the law interferes with the right of free speech or of association, a more stringent vagueness test should apply."[385]

Conclusion

If a court were to apply "strict scrutiny" to the ".xxx" proposal, then it appears difficult to predict whether it would be constitutional. Although it seems likely that the Supreme Court would find that it serves a compelling governmental interest, it is not certain whether it would find that it would be the least restrictive means to serve that interest. If a court were to apply "content-neutral scrutiny," or if the Court were to follow its reasoning in *Meese v. Keene*, then it seems likely that it would find the ".xxx" proposal to be constitutional.

End Notes

[353] P.L. 107-3 17 (2002), 47 U.S.C. § 941.
[354] [http://www.kids.us/sitelist.html?catALL].
[355] Jascha Hoffman, "Porn Suffix, The" (sic), *New York Times Magazine* (December 11, 2005).

[356] Eric J. Sinrod, "Time For A .xxx Internet Domain?" [http://writ.news.findlaw.com/ commentary/2005 1 229 _sinrod.html].
[357] Associated Press, "Plan Would Create '.xxx' Web Porn Domain," *New York Times* (January 6, 2007); Thomas Crampton, "Agency Rejects .xxx Suffixes for Sex-Related Sites on Internet," *New York Times* (March 31, 2007).
[358] ICANN Generic Names Supporting Organisation, Final Report, Introduction of New Generic Top-Level Domains, 8 August 2007. [http://gnso.icann.org/issues/new-gtlds/pdp¬dec05-fr-parta-08aug07.htm#_Toc35657637].
[359] "Biggest Expansion in gTLDs Approved for Implementation" (June 26, 2008). [http://www.icann.org/en/announcements/announcement-4-26jun08-en.htm].
[360] Hoffman, *supra*, note 3.
[361] Brian Bergstein, "Asia gets domain, .xxx delayed," *Miami Herald* (December 6, 2005).
[362] See CRS Report 98-670, *Obscenity, Child Pornography, and Indecency: Recent Developments and Pending Issues*, by Henry Cohen.
[363] United States v. Playboy Entertainment Group, Inc., 529 U.S. 801, 818 (2000).
[364] Sable Communications of California, Inc. v. Federal Communications Commission, 492 U.S. 115, 126 (1989).
[365] Renton v. Playtime Theatres, Inc., 475 U.S. 41, 48, 50 (1986) (emphasis in original).
[366] *Id.* at 47 (emphasis in original).
[367] *Id.* at 48.
[368] If sexually explicit speech is regulated in a manner that affects only minors, then it is more likely to be constitutional. In *Ginsberg v. New York*, 390 U.S. 629, 634 (1968), for example, the Supreme Court upheld a state statute that prohibited the sale to minors of what the Court called "'girlie' picture magazines." When, however, the government has restricted adults' access to speech, even with the purpose of protecting minors, the Court has held that "the Government may not 'reduc[e] the adult population . . . to . . . only what is fit for children.'" See, e.g., Reno v. American Civil Liberties Union, 521 U.S. 844, 875 (1997), in which the Court struck down the part of the Communications Decency Act of 1996 that prohibited "indecent" material on the Internet.
[369] 535 U.S. 234, 253 (2002).
[370] *Playboy, supra* note 11, 529 U.S. at 815 (citations omitted). *See also*, Reno v. American Civil Liberties Union, 521 U.S. 844, 867-868 (1997) (rejecting the government's claim that prohibiting "indecent" material on the Internet "constitutes a sort of 'cyberzoning'" aimed at "'secondary' effects"), and separate opinion by Justice O'Connor in *Reno*, 529 U.S. at 888 ("a 'zoning' law is valid only if adults are still able to obtain the regulated speech").
[371] Compelling commercial speech (i.e., disclosures in commercial advertisements and on product labels) is generally constitutional because the Supreme Court has held that "an advertiser's rights are reasonably protected as long as disclosure requirements are reasonably related to the State's interest in preventing deception of consumers. . . . The right of a commercial speaker not to divulge accurate information regarding his services is not . . . a fundamental right." Zauderer v. Office of Disciplinary Counsel, 471 U.S. 626, 651, 652 n.14 (1985).
[372] 487 U.S. 781, 796-797 (1988) (italics in original).
[373] 481 U.S. 465 (1987).
[374] *Id.* at 480.
[375] 430 U.S. 705 (1977).
[376] 319 U.S. 624 (1943).
[377] 418 U.S. 241 (1974).
[378] *Sable, supra*, note 12.
[379] *See*, THE CONSTITUTION OF THE UNITED STATES OF AMERICA: ANALYSIS AND INTERPRETATION (2004), at 1233, n.1 146 (n.1 174 in the Web version at [http://www.crs.gov/products/conan/Amendment0 1/topic_3_1 2_1 2.html]).
[380] *Reno, supra* note 16, 521 U.S. at 874.
[381] This was one of the reasons that the Supreme Court upheld a preliminary injunction against enforcement of the Child Online Protection Act. *See*, Ashcroft v. American Civil Liberties Union, 542 U.S. 656, 667 (2004) ("The District Court noted in its factfindings that one witness estimated that 40% of harmful-to-minors content comes from overseas").
[382] *Reno, supra*, note 16, 521 U.S. at 867.
[383] 438 U.S. 726 (1978).
[384] *Reno, supra* note 16, 521 U.S. at 867.
[385] Hoffman Estates v. Flipside, Hoffman Estates, 455 U.S. 489, 497-499 (1982).

In: Trends in Internet Research
Editor: B.G. Kutais

ISBN: 978-1-59454-140-7

Chapter 10

PROTECTION OF CHILDREN ONLINE: FEDERAL AND STATE LAWS ADDRESSING CYBERSTALKING, CYBERHARASSMENT, AND CYBERBULLYING*

Alison M. Smith[1]

ABSTRACT

While Congress, under the Commerce Clause, has authority to regulate the Internet, Internet "harassment" presents new challenges for legislators in terms of defining and prosecuting such activity. Definitions for these terms vary based upon jurisdiction. Internet harassment usually encompasses "cyberstalking," "cyberharassment," and/or "cyberbullying." If one were to categorize these offenses based on danger or greatest potential harm, cyberstalking would be the most dangerous, followed by cyberharassment and then cyberbullying. Generally, cyberstalking includes a credible threat of harm, while the other two do not. Cyberharassment and/or cyberbullying may cause embarrassment, annoyance, or humiliation to the victim. Some individuals use the terms cyberharassment and cyberbullying interchangeably, while others reserve the term cyberbullying to describe harassment between minors, usually within the school context.

While laws that address cyberstalking exist at both the federal and state levels, the question of how to handle situations that do not involve a credible threat of harm against minors has drawn congressional interest. Recent high-profile cases involving teen suicides illustrate the harmful effects of Internet harassment on young people. To address the problem, H.R. 1966 was introduced in the 111th Congress. This bill would amend title 18 of the United States Code by making cyberbullying a federal crime with a punishment of up to two years of imprisonment and/or a fine.

Legislators have traditionally enacted laws prohibiting child pornography, child luring, and child sexual exploitation. However, Internet harassment potentially causes emotional harm to its victims as opposed to the physical harm inflicted by the aforementioned activities. In addressing these concerns, legislators strive to maintain a balance between enacting statutes broad enough to cover undesirable behavior, while

---

* This is an edited, reformatted and augmented version of a Congressional Research Service Publication, Order Code RL34651 Prepared for Members and Committees of Congress, April 15, 2009.

[1] Alison M. Smith, Legislative Attorney amsmith@crs.loc.gov, 7-6054

simultaneously narrow enough to prevent infringement upon an individual's right to express oneself under the First Amendment.

The First Amendment protects certain forms of speech, but this protection is limited within the school environment. While school administrators have more flexibility in disciplining children whose speech disrupts the learning environment, this flexibility does not cover all forms of Internet harassment. As Internet harassment is a relatively new phenomenon, courts are just beginning to determine the constitutionality and scope of these school policies and statutes. This report discusses Internet crimes, such as cyberbullying, cyberharassment, and cyberstalking, along with the limitations of such laws in the current environment. It will be updated as events warrant.

INTRODUCTION

Federal and state laws have always played a role in protecting minors from criminal victimization. For example, Congress has enacted laws dealing with child pornography, child luring, and child sexual exploitation. However, given its immediacy, anonymity, and accessibility, the Internet offers a forum, through social networking sites,[386] for harassment and other social ills committed against minors. The Internet's nuances present new challenges for federal and state legislators and law enforcement personnel responsible for defining and prosecuting criminal use. This is especially true with the relatively new crime of Internet "harassment." The term Internet harassment usually encompasses "cyberstalking," "cyberharassment," and/or "cyberbullying." These activities, when committed against minors, may cause emotional harm. Recent high-profile cases involving teen suicides demonstrate the potentially severe consequences of this emotional harm. As such, legislators are faced with determining how to handle the problem.

Various laws, not specific to minors, govern traditional crimes such as stalking and harassment, which generally include a threat of harm. These laws generally criminalize unlawful conduct that fails to rise to the level of assault or battery.[387] Recognizing that the Internet can be used to stalk or harass individuals, Congress and some states have amended "traditional" stalking and harassment statutes to include Internet activity. However, these statutes are generally inapplicable in situations in which minors suffer emotional harm due to embarrassment or humiliation. When, if ever, should criminal sanctions be imposed for these incidents? Should legislators amend traditional stalking and harassment statutes to cover these situations? Or should legislators create new crimes covering such activity? Should such activity conducted by a neighbor, for example, be prosecuted on the federal level because the Internet was used? Or should prosecution of such activity remain at the state level? These are just some of the questions legislators may consider in addressing the problem of Internet harassment of children. While these policy considerations are noteworthy, this report focuses on the applicable constitutional constraints legislators may consider in drafting legislation in this area.

BACKGROUND

Congressional Authority to Legislate Internet Activities

Generally, states assert jurisdiction over law enforcement authority within their borders. However, Congress may legislate in the state law enforcement arena under certain constitutionally permissible circumstances. For example, Article I, Section 8, Clause 4 of the United States Constitution authorizes Congress to "regulate Commerce with foreign Nations, and among the several States." There are three categories of activities subject to congressional regulation under the Commerce Clause. Congress may regulate the use of the channels of interstate commerce,[388] or persons or things in interstate commerce, although a threat may come only from intrastate activities.[389] Finally, Congress may regulate those activities having a substantial relation to interstate commerce (i.e., those activities that substantially affect interstate commerce).[390] As the Internet is an instrumentality of interstate commerce, Congress has the power to enact appropriate legislation. Pursuant to this authority, Congress has enacted laws designed to protect children.

Selected Federal Internet Laws

Congress has enacted several statutes designed to address protection of children on the Internet. These statutes run the gamut from establishing new crimes (i.e., use of interstate facilities to transmit information about a minor)[391] to expanding the scope of existing crimes (i.e., child luring). In addition, Congress has enacted laws designed to curtail both the downloading of inappropriate content by children and the uploading of impermissible personal information from children.[392]

Child Online Privacy Protection Act (COPPA)/Child Online Protection Act (COPA)/Children's Internet Protection Act (CIPA)

The Child Online Privacy Protection Act (COPPA)[393] is directed to the protection of children less than 13 years of age from operators of commercial websites or online services.[394] COPPA mandates several requirements for sites that either direct their services to children under the age of 13 or have actual knowledge that their general audience site is collecting information from such children.[395] The act applies to individually identifiable information about children, and requires, among other things, that sites post a clear notice of their data collection practices on their home pages and on every page where information is requested.[396]

Another federal statute, the Child Online Protection Act (COPA),[397] restricts access by minors to materials commercially distributed that are harmful to minors.[398] However, COPA has never taken effect because a federal district court issued a preliminary injunction against its enforcement pending trial. The injunction was affirmed on appeal by the Supreme Court, which, on June 29, 2004, remanded the case for trial.[399] On March 22, 2007, a federal district court found COPA unconstitutional and issued a permanent injunction against its enforcement.[400] On July 22, 2008, the Third Circuit Court of Appeals upheld the 2007 decision.[401]

Finally, the narrowest statute, the Children's Internet Protection Act (CIPA),[402] applies only to public libraries and schools and mandates that they employ software filters to restrict access by minors to inappropriate material.[403] CIPA has withstood challenge to its constitutionality.[404]

Use of Interstate Facilities to Transmit Information About a Minor

18 U.S.C. § 2425 prohibits the use of a facility of interstate commerce, such as a computer connected to the Internet, to transmit information about a minor under the age of 16 for criminal sexual purposes. Individuals convicted under this statute face a punishment of a fine and/or maximum imprisonment of five years.

Child Luring

In addition to the aforementioned protections, federal and state legislators have enacted several criminal provisions designed to punish Internet users who hurt minors physically. Some laws that traditionally protect children, such as those used to combat child pornography[405] and luring, have been expanded to apply to situations where an individual uses the Internet to facilitate the crimes. For example, "child luring" consists of an adult knowingly and intentionally inducing a child, by means of a computer, to engage in sexual intercourse or sexual conduct.[406] A majority of states have laws that specifically prohibit electronic luring or solicitation of minors by computer for the purpose of inducing them to engage in illegal sexual conduct.[407] On the federal level, child luring is covered by 18 U.S.C. § 2422(b), which prohibits the use of any facility or means of interstate commerce to knowingly persuade, induce, entice, or coerce a minor to engage in criminal sexual activity or prostitution, or to attempt to do so.[408] Violators of 18 U.S.C. § 2422(b) face a punishment of a fine and a minimum imprisonment of 10 years or life.

INTERNET HARASSMENT

Internet harassment is a new phenomenon that presents a challenge for law enforcement, legislators, educators, and parents. The term Internet harassment lacks a uniform definition but usually encompasses cyberstalking, cyberharassment, and/or cyberbullying. It is worth noting that most cyberstalking and/or cyberharassment statutes cover both adult and minor victims. If one were to categorize these activities based on danger or greatest potential harm, cyberstalking would be the most dangerous, followed by cyberharassment and then cyberbullying. Generally, cyberstalking includes a credible threat of harm, while the other two do not. Cyberharassment and/or cyberbullying may cause embarrassment, annoyance, or humiliation to the victim. Some individuals use the terms cyberharassment and cyberbullying interchangeably, while others reserve the term cyberbullying to describe harassment between minors, usually within the school context.

In a criminal context, these activities are predicated on a perpetrator's desire to inflict emotional harm, usually in the form of humiliation or embarrassment. Legislators are faced with several questions in tackling this problem as it pertains to minors. When, if ever, should individuals be criminally liable for causing humiliation or embarrassment to another? Should new laws be created to cover such action? Or, is it sufficient to amend existing laws?

Cyberstalking

Cyberstalking refers to the use of Internet, e-mail, or other electronic communications to stalk another person.[409] A cyberstalker may send repeated, threatening, or harassing messages. Or a cyberstalker can urge other Internet users into harassing or threatening a victim by utilizing Internet bulletin boards or chat rooms. For example, a cyberstalker may post a controversial or enticing message on a board under the victim's name, address, phone number, or e-mail address, resulting in the victim receiving subsequent unwanted responses. Each message, whether from the actual cyberstalker or others, may have the intended effect on the victim, even though the cyberstalker's effort tends to be minimal. Due to the lack of direct contact between the cyberstalker and the victim, it is sometimes difficult for law enforcement to identify, locate, arrest and subsequently prosecute the offender.

The anonymity of the Internet also provides new opportunities for cyberstalkers. A cyberstalker's true identity can be concealed by using different Internet service providers (ISPs) and/or by adopting multiple screen names. Anonymity leaves the cyberstalker in a somewhat advantageous position. Unbeknownst to the target, the perpetrator could be in another state, around the corner, or in the next cubicle at work. The perpetrator could be a former friend or lover, a total stranger met in a chat room, or simply a teenager playing a practical joke.

State and local law enforcement agencies are sometimes hampered by jurisdictional limitations. A cyberstalker located in a different city or state than the victim may present more of a challenge for local authorities investigating an incident. Even if a law enforcement agency is willing to pursue a case across state lines, it may be difficult to obtain assistance from out-of-state agencies when conduct has been limited to harassing e-mail messages without the occurrence of actual violence.

Several states have laws that explicitly include electronic forms of communication within stalking or harassment laws.[410] For example, California legislators amended the state stalking law to expressly include stalking via the Internet.[411] Under California law, a person commits stalking if he or she "willfully, maliciously, and repeatedly follows or harasses another person and ... makes a credible threat with the intent to place that person in reasonable fear for his or her safety, or the safety of his or her immediate family." The term "credible threat" includes threats that are (1) "performed through the use of an electronic communication device, (2) implied by a pattern of conduct or a combination of verbal, written, or electronically communicated statements."[412] provides a list of states that have enacted cyberstalking statutes.

Federal laws designed to combat cyberstalking exist. For example, 18 U.S.C. § 2261A prohibits an individual from using "the mail, any interactive computer service, or any facility of interstate or foreign commerce to engage in a course of conduct that causes substantial emotional distress to that person or places that person in reasonable fear of ... death." However, this statute is inapplicable in situations where both the victim and perpetrator are in the same state or tribal jurisdiction.[413] While this law was amended in 2006 to include "interactive computer service," courts have not addressed the term's scope and applicability to the Internet or instances of cyberstalking that cause "substantial emotional distress."[414]

In addition, 18 U.S.C. § 875 makes it a crime, punishable by up to five years' imprisonment, to transmit any communication in interstate or foreign commerce containing a threat to injure another person. Section 875(c) generally applies to any communication actually transmitted in interstate or foreign commerce.[415] This statute has been used primarily against threats conveyed via telephone.[416] However, the law has been expanded to prosecute cyberstalkers. For example, in *United States v. Kammersell,*[417] the court found that the term "transmits in interstate commerce," as it applied to the offense of making threatening communication, encompassed the alleged conduct of sending a threatening message via the Internet, despite the fact that the defendant and victim resided in the same state. The message had been sent from the defendant's computer in Riverdale, Utah, processed through the ISP 's message server in Virginia, and then transferred to the victim's computer in downtown Ogden, Utah, a few miles from the defendant's computer.

Thus, 18 U.S.C. § 875 has been expanded to cover threats transmitted via the Internet. However, a threat must be one that a reasonable person would take as a serious expression of an intention to inflict bodily harm and would perceive such expression as communicated to effect some change or achieve some goal through intimidation.[418] In *United States v. Alkhavaz,*[419] the court found that electronic mail messages between the defendant and another individual, expressing sexual interest in violence against third-party women and girls, did not constitute "communications containing a threat." Instead, the court concluded the communications were "attempts to foster a friendship based on shared sexual fantasies."[420]

One could argue that one of the limitations of 18 U.S.C. § 875(c) is its inapplicability to a situation where an individual engages in a pattern of conduct intended to "harass" or "annoy" another (absent some threat). Also, it is unclear whether this statute would apply to a situation in which a person harasses another by posting messages on a "public" bulletin board or in a chat room, encouraging others to harass or annoy the individual. It would appear that in some of these situations, a defendant may be prosecuted under the federal telephone harassment statute, 47 U.S.C. § 223.[421]

Cyberharassment

While cyberstalking laws exist at both the federal and state levels, they are generally inapplicable in situations referred to as cyberharassment and/or cyberbullying, depending upon the jurisdiction.[422]

Federal Telephone Harassment Statute[423]

nder federal law, some instances of cyberharassment may be prosecuted under 47 U.S.C. § 223, which carries a punishment of a fine and/or imprisonment.[424] One provision of this statute makes it a crime, punishable by up to two years in prison, to use a telephone or telecommunications device[425] to "annoy, abuse, harass, or threaten" any person at a dialed number.[426] In 2006, Congress expanded the definition of "telecommunications device" to include e-mail communications. However, the statute still requires that a perpetrator remain anonymous.[427] Although this statute covers both threats and harassment, it applies only to direct communication between a perpetrator and a victim. As such, it would be inapplicable in a situation where a person harasses another person by posting messages on a "public" bulletin board or in a chat room encouraging others to "harass" or "annoy" another individual. In addition, it is worth noting that although the statute has been found constitutional, that determination was made before the statute was amended. In *United States v. Bowker,*[428] the defendant made more than 100 anonymous phone calls to a television news reporter during a seven-month period. Many calls were threatening and sexual in nature.[429] The *Bowker* court reasoned that § 223(a)(1)(C) was not overbroad because

> [T]he focus of the telephone harassment statute is not simply annoying telephonic communications. It also prohibits abusive, threatening or harassing communications. Thus, the thrust of the statute is to prohibit communications intended to instill fear in the victim, not to provoke a discussion about political issues of the day.[430]

The court noted that while § 223(a)(1)(C) could have unconstitutional applications, that fact does not warrant facial invalidation.[431] The court concluded that Bowker's speech was not constitutionally protected because he called his victim "predominately, if not exclusively, for the purpose of invading her privacy and communicating express and implied threats of bodily harm."[432] Courts have yet to address this statute as it applies to Internet "harassment."

State Cyberharassment Statutes

Examples of cyberharassment include sending threatening or harassing e-mail messages and instant messages to another individual, posting highly offensive and/or hurtful blog entries about certain individuals, or creating entire Web pages for the sole purpose of tormenting and humiliating another individual. Generally, cyberharassment differs from cyberstalking in that a credible threat is not involved. Cyberharassment statutes vary by jurisdiction. Some are incorporated in general harassment statutes, while others are separate statutes. For example, the Iowa harassment statute provides that

[a] person commits harassment when, with intent to intimidate, annoy, or alarm another person, the person does any of the following:

> (1) Communicates with another by telephone, telegraph, writing or via electronic communication without a legitimate purpose and in a manner likely to cause the other person annoyance or harm ...[433]

Virginia's "harassment by computer" statute states:

> If any person, with the intent to coerce, intimidate, or harass any person, shall use a computer or computer network to communicate obscene, vulgar, profane, lewd, lascivious, or indecent language, or make any suggestion or proposal of an obscene nature, or threaten any illegal or immoral act, he shall be guilty of a Class 1 misdemeanor.[434]

Table 1 provides a list of states that have cyberharassment statutes.
Table 3 provides the statutory language addressing cyberharassment.

Cyberbullying

Although the Internet is a relatively new medium, it is being used for an old purpose—harassment of others. Children experiment online with different personas, and may be nastier in the Internet's anonymous atmosphere than they would be in person. In addition, targeted mockery can be far more painful when it is public, permanent, and written than when muttered in passing in a school hallway. Creating defamatory or sexually explicit depictions of students and school personnel on websites are two types of student Internet speech that may constitute cyberbullying.[435]

Cyberbullying generally refers to harassment occurring among school-aged children through the use of the Internet.[436] Recent incidents of teen suicides appear to illustrate the harm that may be caused by cyberbullying. According to media accounts, classmates sent Vermont teenager Ryan Patrick Halligan several instant messages questioning his sexuality. In addition, the teen was threatened, taunted, and incessantly insulted online. Ultimately, Halligan committed suicide.[437] Responding in part to the suicide, Vermont's state legislature passed an "anti-cyberbullying" law in 2004.[438] The statute requires schools to create disciplinary policies encompassing both on- and off-campus (limited to school-sponsored activities) bullying among school children.[439] The statute provides a broad definition of "bullying" that may be interpreted to include Internet misbehavior.

Several other states have passed legislation requiring or authorizing school districts to adopt cyberbullying policies. For example, in Arkansas, cyberbullying was added to the schools' anti-bullying policies and included in provisions for school officials to punish students for some off-campus activities "if the electronic act is directed specifically at students or school personnel and is maliciously intended for the purpose of disrupting school and has a high likelihood of succeeding in that purpose."[440] However, it should be noted that some of these policies are limited in their application.[441] For example, in Washington, the school district harassment prevention policies are applicable only to actions that take place "while on school grounds and during the day." In other words, some of these policies would not cover bullies from other districts or other states. In addition, adults who "harass" or "cyberbully" minors would not be covered in most instances.

In another teen suicide, the issue of an adult engaging in cyberbullying activities has caused some individuals to use the terms cyberharassment and cyberbullying interchangeably. On May 15, 2008, a federal grand jury indicted a Missouri woman for her alleged role in a MySpace hoax against a minor. The indictment alleged that the defendant created a false identity on the social network MySpace to obtain information from Megan Meier, a teenager. The indictment further alleged that this information was used to "torment, harass, humiliate, and embarrass" the juvenile. The false identity was that of a 16-year-old boy named "Josh Evans." Communications allegedly ensued between Megan and "Josh" for some time. According to media accounts, Megan took her life after receiving a cruel message from "Josh."[442] State prosecutors declined to prosecute this "harassment" activity,[443] noting that the woman's intent did not cross a threshold into criminal activity based on state laws governing stalking, harassment, and child endangerment.[444]

It is important to note that the federal government did not charge the Missouri woman with harassment of Meier. Rather, the government's legal theory was based on the Computer Fraud and Abuse Act,[445] specifically 18 U.S.C. § 1030(a)(2)(C) and (c)(2)(B)(2), which makes it a felony punishable by up to five years of imprisonment if one "intentionally accesses a computer without authorization ..., and thereby obtains ... information from any protected computer[446] if the conduct involved an interstate ... communication" and "the offense was committed in furtherance of any ... tortious act [in this case intentional infliction of emotional distress] in violation of the ... laws ... of any State." Prosecutors alleged that the defendant violated MySpace's terms of use[447] by using a fictitious name, thereby giving her no authority to access MySpace.[448]

To address the problem of cyberbullying, H.R. 1966 was introduced on April 9, 2009, during the 111th Congress.[449] This bill would amend title 18 of the United States Code by making cyberbullying a federal crime with a punishment of up to two years of imprisonment and/or a fine. Specifically, section 3 of H.R. 1966 states that:

> (a) Whoever transmits in interstate or foreign commerce any communication, with the intent to coerce, intimidate, harass, or cause substantial emotional distress to a person, using electronic means to support severe, repeated, and hostile behavior, shall be fined under this title or imprisoned not more than two years, or both.[450]

Constitutional Concerns and Considerations

There are constitutional principles that limit the authority of all governmental entities (federal, state, and local) to enact cyberharassment and/or cyberbullying statutes, namely the First and Fourteenth Amendments.

First Amendment: Freedom of Speech

True Threats

The First Amendment declares that "Congress shall make no law ... abridging the freedom of speech." The Fourteenth Amendment's due process clause imposes the same restriction upon the states,[451] many of whose constitutions have a comparable limitation on state legislative action.[452] Although the First Amendment guarantees free speech, the right is not absolute. Governments impose limitations on many types of speech, including fighting words,[453] false statements of fact,[454] and obscene speech.[455] Moreover, courts distinguish between constitutionally protected speech and other less socially valuable categories of speech.[456] Other examples of unprotected speech include speech that incites others to engage in lawless behavior,[457] constitutes true threats,[458] or is protected by intellectual property laws.[459] The U.S. Supreme Court has decided several cases that provide the framework in which states must act to protect the constitutionality of cyberharassment and/or cyberbullying statutes.

The Court has cited three reasons why threats of violence may be outside the First Amendment's protection: "protecting individuals from the fear of violence, from the disruption that fear engenders, and from the possibility that the threatened violence will occur."[460] However, in *Watts v. United States*,[461] the Court held that only "true threats" are outside the amendment's scope. In *Watts*, the defendant attended a political rally and made the statement, "I have already received my draft classification ... I am not going. If they ever make me carry a rifle the first man I want to get in my sights is [President] L.B.J."[462] The defendant was arrested and charged with violating 18 U.S.C. § 87 1(a) for "knowingly and willfully ... [making a] threat to take the life of or to inflict bodily harm upon the President of the United States." The defendant challenged his jury conviction.

The U.S. Supreme Court reversed, holding that, although the federal statute was not unconstitutionally overbroad, the defendant's statement was protected because it was not a "true threat." The Court found that the content of Watts's statement, the context in which the statement was made, and the audience's reaction[463] to the statement were all supportive of Watts's claim that he engaged in protected "political hyperbole."[464] The Court recognized that "true threats" should not be afforded First Amendment protection, and stated, "What is a threat must be distinguished from what is constitutionally protected speech."[465]

Watts did not establish a bright-line test for distinguishing a true threat from protected speech. As such, lower courts have created varying tests for determining whether speech rises to the level of a true threat.[466] The primary federal cases dealing with threat speech have arisen under 18 U.S.C. § 875, which imposes criminal sanctions on anyone who "transmits in interstate or foreign commerce any communication containing any threat to kidnap any person or any threat to injure the person of another," and 18 U.S.C. § 876, which prohibits threats against the President. The main point of contention among the circuits is whether the focus of a "true threat" test should be on the speaker or the listener. Some circuits evaluate the existence of a threat by determining whether the speaker should reasonably have foreseen his words to be threatening,[467] while others rest the determination on whether a reasonable recipient would be threatened by the statement.[468]

For example, in *Planned Parenthood v. American Coalition of Life Activists*,[469] the 9th Circuit Court of Appeals upheld a damage award in favor of four physicians and two health clinics that had provided medical services, including abortions, to women. The plaintiffs sued under the Freedom of Access to Clinic Entrances (FACE),[470] a federal statute that gives aggrieved persons a right of action against whomever by "threat of force ... intentionally ... intimidates any person because the person is or has been ... providing reproductive health services." The defendants had published "WANTED," "unWANTED," and "GUILTY" posters with the names, photographs, addresses, and other personal information of abortion doctors, three of whom were subsequently murdered by abortion opponents. The defendants also operated a "Nuremberg Files" website that listed approximately 200 people under the label "ABORTIONIST," with the legend: "Black font (working); Greyed-out Name (wounded); Strikethrough (fatality)."[471] The posters and website contained no language that literally constituted a threat, but, the court found, "they connote something they do not literally say," namely "You're Wanted or You're Guilty; You'll be shot or killed,"[472] and the defendants knew that the posters had caused abortion doctors to "quit out of fear for their lives."[473] In reaching its decision, the court concluded that a "true threat" is "a statement which, in the entire context and under all the circumstances, a reasonable person would foresee be interpreted by those to whom the statement is communicated as a serious expression of intent to inflict bodily harm upon that person."[474]

Based upon the aforementioned constitutional framework, it is likely that cyberstalking, cyberharassment, and/or cyberbullying statutes may be deemed constitutionally deficient if the situation does not rise to the level of a "true threat" under most circumstances. This analysis may be different depending on whether the challenged language is contained in a state statute or school policy.

Freedom of Speech Within the School Context

School officials are using cyberharassment and cyberbullying policies to take disciplinary action against students, including suspensions and expulsions. When students and/or parents have challenged schools' disciplinary response to students' "offensive" expression, courts have relied on Supreme Court precedent.[475] While students generally retain the protections of the First Amendment, these protections may not always mirror the constitutional protections afforded in other contexts. For example, in *Tinker v. Des Moines Independent Community School District*,[476] the Court held that student expression may be regulated only if it would substantially disrupt school operations or interfere with the rights of others.[477] In *Tinker*, students wore black armbands to school to protest the United States' involvement in Vietnam, despite knowledge that such action was in violation of school policy. The students were asked to remove the armbands, and upon their refusal were suspended until they came to school without the armbands. Thereafter, the students filed a complaint seeking to enjoin the school district from disciplining them. The district court dismissed the complaint, concluding that the school's policy against armbands was reasonable to prevent disturbance of school discipline. On appeal, the U.S. Supreme Court stated that the wearing of armbands for the purpose of expressing different viewpoints is the type of symbolic act within the protection of the First Amendment. Specifically, the Court ruled that "First Amendment rights, applied in light of the special characteristics of the school environment, are available to teachers and students. It can hardly be argued that either students or teachers shed their constitutional rights to freedom of expression at the schoolhouse gate."[478]

The Court subsequently refined the *Tinker* rationale as it applies to verbal expression or "pure speech." In *Bethel School District 403 v. Fraser*,[479] the Court ruled that school officials had the authority to discipline a student for violating school rules by delivering a lewd speech at a school assembly. In *Fraser*, a high school student gave a nominating speech on a classmate's behalf during an official school-wide assembly for student government elections. In this speech, the student used sexual innuendos. Reaction to the speech was mixed; some students yelled and simulated sexual acts, while other students and teachers were offended. The student was suspended for three days and prohibited from speaking at graduation. In deciding this case, the Court shifted focus from the students' rights articulated in *Tinker*, but instead emphasized the school's duty to inculcate habits and manners of civility and teach students the boundaries of socially appropriate behavior.[480] In addition, the Court noted the importance of protecting minors from vulgar, lewd, or indecent language.[481] As such, the Court concluded that the nomination speech had a disruptive effect on the education process, and that it was up to school officials to determine what manner of speech in the classroom or in school assembly is appropriate.[482]

While it is undisputed that the First Amendment does not protect "offensive" speech while on school grounds, courts are less clear when the speech occurs off school premises. For example, in *J.S. v. Bethlehem Area School District*,[483] an 8th grader created a website that contained derogatory remarks regarding a math teacher and a principal.[484] Most of the website was devoted to ridiculing the math teacher, comparing her to Adolph Hitler and making fun of her physical appearance.[485] In addition, the site contained a solicitation for contributions to pay for a "hit man."[486] School officials subsequently expelled the student, citing the extreme emotional distress suffered by the math teacher and the disruption the web site caused at the school.[487] The student argued that his website was protected speech.

In reviewing the case, the Pennsylvania Supreme Court decided two issues: (1) whether the student's speech constituted a true threat; and (2) whether the *Tinker* and *Fraser* standards permit a school district to discipline a student for off-campus speech. In addressing the "true threat" issue, the court determined that, although the website was in extremely poor taste, it was not a "true threat." Specifically, the court stated that "[w]e believe that the [w]ebsite, taken as a whole, was a sophomoric, crude, highly offensive and perhaps misguided attempt at humor or parody. However, it did not reflect a serious expression of intent to inflict harm," as the site focused primarily on the teacher's physical appearance, utilizing cartoons, hand drawings, and a reference to Adolph Hitler.[488]

The court then addressed whether First Amendment jurisprudence permitted the school to discipline a student for off-campus speech. It dismissed the argument that the website was off- campus speech beyond the school's jurisdiction. Specifically, the court stated that "[w]e find there is a sufficient nexus between the [w]ebsite and the school campus to consider the speech as occurring on-campus."[489] The court made this determination because the student had accessed the site at school, showed it to a fellow student, and informed other students about the site.[490]The court then reasoned that school officials could punish the student under the *Tinker* or *Fraser* standard[491]—under the *Fraser* standard because the speech on the website was vulgar and highly offensive,[492] and under the *Tinker* standard inasmuch as the website caused a substantial disruption of school activities.[493]

Similarly, in *Wisniewski v. Board of Ed.*,[494] the court affirmed the school district's suspension of an 8th grade student who had disseminated to friends an instant message icon showing a pistol firing a bullet at his English teacher, accompanied by the words, "Kill Mr. Van der Molen."[495] The student created the icon a couple of weeks after his class had been informed of a zero-tolerance policy regarding threats. The student also sent messages with the "objectionable" icon to approximately 15 other students, but not to any school personnel. Another student informed and provided the English teacher with a copy of the icon. The English teacher forwarded the information to the high school and middle school principals, as well as to law enforcement personnel. The student accepted responsibility for the icon's creation and was subsequently suspended for five days. The student was allowed to return to school pending a superintendent's hearing. The English teacher requested and was allowed a class reassignment. A police investigator as well as a psychologist determined that the student intended the icon to be a joke and not a threat toward the English teacher. However, a hearing officer found the determination unpersuasive and irrelevant. She concluded that the student had engaged "in the act of sending a threatening message to his buddies, the subject of which was a teacher."[496] In addition, she concluded that his action had disrupted school operations by "requiring special attention from school officials, replacement of the threatened teacher, and interviewing pupils during class time."[497] The student was subsequently suspended for a semester.

The student's parents filed suit against the school board and the superintendent, seeking damages under 42 U.S.C. § 1983, claiming that the student's icon was protected speech under the First Amendment and not a true threat. The district court dismissed the claim. The appellate court declined to address whether the icon was a true threat. Instead, the court applied the *Tinker* standard and concluded that even though the icon's creation and transmission had occurred off campus, it was reasonably foreseeable that school officials would find out about the icon and that it would "materially and substantially disrupt the work and discipline of the school."[498] Thus, the appellate court concluded that the First Amendment claim had been properly dismissed.[499]

However, in *Beussink v. Woodland R-IV School District*,[500] a U.S. district court held that the plaintiff had demonstrated the likelihood of success of his First Amendment claim. In this case, a high school student was suspended for the contents of a website that contained vulgar criticism directed toward school officials.[501] The student had created the website at home on his personal computer without using school facilities or resources. However, one of the student's friends became angry with him, accessed the website at school and showed it to the school's computer science teacher. The teacher informed the principal about the site. Immediately after viewing the site, the principal suspended the student. Due to the school's policy regarding absenteeism, the suspension resulted in the student failing all his classes.[502] In reviewing the student's suspension, the court determined that the evidence presented did not establish that Beussink had been disciplined because of the fear of disruption or interference with school discipline, but rather because the principal had been upset by the website's content. Thus, the court concluded that the web site did not materially and substantially interfere with school discipline, as *Tinker* requires.[503] As such, the court granted a preliminary injunction against the school district.

In *Lays hock v. Hermitage School District,*[504] the court held that a student's speech right had been violated when the school district failed to demonstrate a nexus between the student's parody of the principal and a substantial disruption of the school environment. The student created the "parody profile" of his principal on MySpace by using his grandmother's home computer. This parody profile displayed the principal's picture, which Layshock had copied from the school's website. The template for the profile allowed users to fill in background information and include answers to specific questions. The student answered the questions with what were alleged to be objectionable answers. For example, in response to a question regarding alcohol use, the profile read "big keg behind my desk." The profile also referred to the principal as a "big steroid freak" and reflected that the principal was "too drunk to remember" his birthday.[505] The principal subsequently discovered another parody profile created by another student. Apparently, there were at least three parody profiles.

Evidence was presented that indicated that other students had viewed Layshock's parody profile during school hours. In an attempt to curtail the creation of parody profiles, the school officials sought to block students' access to MySpace. The principal contacted MySpace directly, and succeeded in having the profiles disabled.[506] Students joked and talked about the parody profiles while in school. Teachers interviewed students to determine the profiles' creator or creators. When asked, Layshock admitted to creating one profile. Layshock was informed that he was being considered for disciplinary action for "Disruption of the normal school process: Disrespect: Harassment of a school administrator via a computer/internet with remarks that have demeaning implications: Gross misbehavior: Obscene, vulgar and profane language."[507] At a subsequent hearing, the student received a 10-day out-of-school suspension. Additional discipline included banning him from attending or participating in any events sponsored by the school district, and prohibiting him from participating in the high school graduation ceremony.

The court concluded that there were several gaps in the causation link between the student's off-campus conduct and any material and substantial disruption of school operations. The school district failed to demonstrate which parody profile caused the alleged disruption, as there were three other profiles available on MySpace during the same time frame. In addition, the court noted that the school district had failed to demonstrate that the alleged disruption was due to Layshock's parody and not the administrators' reactions. Furthermore, the court determined that the actual disruption had been rather minimal, as "no classes were cancelled, no widespread disorder occurred, there was no violence or student disciplinary action." As such, the court concluded that the school administrator lacked the authority to punish Layshock for his off-campus creation of the parody profile.

Fourteenth Amendment: Due Process

Another constitutional constraint on legislators and school administrators when drafting legislation or school policies aimed at curtailing "cyberharassment" and/or "cyberbullying" is the Fourteenth Amendment. Its provisions are as follows:

> All persons born or naturalized in the United States and subject to the jurisdiction thereof, are citizens of the United States and of the State wherein they reside. No State shall make or enforce any law which shall abridge the privileges or immunities of citizens of the United States; nor shall any State deprive any person of life, liberty, or property, without due process of law; nor deny to any person within its jurisdiction the equal protection of the laws.

The Fourteenth Amendment's due process clause includes two distinct aspects: substantive due process[508] and procedural due process. Procedural due process, based on principles of "fundamental fairness," addresses which legal procedures are required to be followed in state proceedings. Relevant issues include notice, opportunity for hearing, confrontation and cross- examination, discovery, basis of decision, and availability of counsel.

Criminal statutes that lack sufficient definiteness or specificity may be held "void for vagueness." Under this doctrine, a governmental regulation or statute may be declared void if it fails to give a person adequate warning that his or her conduct is prohibited or if it fails to set out adequate standards to prevent arbitrary and/or discriminatory enforcement.[509] In *Grayned v. City of Rockford*,[510] the U.S. Supreme Court stated that

> [v]ague laws offend several important values. First, because we assume that man is free to steer between lawful and unlawful conduct, we insist that laws give the person of ordinary intelligence a reasonable opportunity to know what is prohibited, so that he may act accordingly. Vague laws may trap the innocent by not providing fair warnings. Second, if arbitrary and discriminatory enforcement is to be prevented, laws must provide explicit standards for those who apply them. A vague law impermissibly delegates basic policy matters to policemen, judges, and juries for resolution on an ad hoc and subjective basis, with the attendant dangers of arbitrary and discriminatory applications.[511]

A statute may be so vague or threatening to constitutionally protected activity that it can be pronounced facially unconstitutional. For example, in *Papachristou v. City of Jacksonville*,[512] a unanimous Court struck down as facially invalid a vagrancy ordinance that punished

> dissolute persons who go about begging, ... common night walkers, ... common railers and brawlers, persons wandering or strolling around from place to place without any lawful purpose or object, habitual loafers, ... persons neglecting all lawful business and habitually spending their time by frequenting houses of ill fame,

gaming houses, or places where alcoholic beverages are sold or served, persons able to work but habitually living upon the earnings of their wives or minor children.[513]

The Court found the statute facially invalid, as it failed to provide fair notice or require specific intent to commit an unlawful act. The Court concluded that the statute permitted arbitrary and erratic arrests and convictions, provided police officers too much discretion, and criminalized activities that are normally innocent.[514]

A Texas appellate court applied the aforementioned principles in finding a state harassment statute unconstitutional. In *Karenev v. Texas*,[515] the Court of Appeals of Texas held that a state harassment statute that criminalized the sending of repeated "electronic communications in a manner reasonably likely to harass, annoy, alarm, abuse, torment, embarrass, or offend another" was unconstitutionally vague, and thus the statute was void. As such, the appellate court reversed the court's judgment and rendered judgment of acquittal. In this case, the defendant, after moving out of the marital residence, sent his estranged wife (Elena) a series of e-mail messages, all written in Bulgarian.[516] In some of these messages, as translated, the defendant predicted his wife's future and stated that "he would raise their child, Elena's mother would be paralyzed, and Elena would be in either a mental hospital or prison."[517] In another e-mail, the defendant called Elena "not even a regular slut ..., something much scarier," "a pathological li[ar], a dirty whore, a filthy thief, a rotten user, a sick nymphomaniac, a mental case, and a devil's work."[518] He also told her, "It is about time to pay for all of your filthy deeds which you have committed during your pathetic life!"[519] At trial, the defendant testified that during his travels to Bulgaria he had run into fortunetellers who asked him to relay the messages to Elena regarding her future. Presumably, these were fortunetellers Elena had relied on previously. A jury subsequently convicted the defendant on one count of harassment. The defendant challenged the constitutionality of the harassment statute.

The statute, as previously noted, stated in part that a person commits harassment "if with intent to harass, annoy, alarm, abuse, torment, or embarrass another he sends repeated electronic communications in a manner reasonably likely to harass, annoy, alarm, abuse, torment, embarrass, or offend another."[520] The court, relying on precedent,[521] found that the portions of the harassment statute establishing as an offense the sending of electronic communications that "annoy or alarm" are unconstitutionally vague. Also, the court noted that the terms "harass," "abuse," "torment," and "embarrass" are "susceptible to uncertainties of meaning."[522] In addition, the court determined that the statute fails to "establish a clear standard for whose sensibilities must be offended."[523]

The aforementioned principles are also applicable in the school setting. For example, in *Flaherty v. Keystone Oaks School District*,[524] the court held that the breadth of student handbook policies pertaining to discipline and technology were overreaching, thus violating students' free speech rights. In addition, the court held that the policies were unconstitutionally vague in definition and as applied. In this case, the student was disciplined for posting Internet messages on a message board devoted to high school volleyball in western Pennsylvania. The site was not sponsored or affiliated with the school district. One of the messages stated that one of the opposing players' mothers was a "bad teacher."[525] When school administrators were informed of the postings, the student faced disciplinary action.

In granting summary judgment, the court found the school policies overbroad for several reasons. First, the polices were not referred to or incorporated in the student handbook. In addition, the policy "authorizes discipline where a student's expression that is abusive, offending, harassing, or inappropriate, interferes with the educational program of the schools." The court concluded that the policy did not comply with the *Tinker* requirement that such discipline should be reserved for those circumstances that cause a substantial disruption to school operations.[526]

The court noted that even if it did not find the policy overbroad, it would find the student handbook policies unconstitutionally vague, as the terms "abuse, offend, harassment, and inappropriate" were not defined in any significant manner. In addition, the court found the policies not only vague in definition but also in application. The court noted that school personnel had varying interpretations of the policies. As such, the court concluded that the policies were vague enough to result in arbitrary enforcement. Therefore, the court concluded that the student handbook policies did not provide the student with adequate warning of proscribed conduct.

Conclusion

With the proliferation of potential uses and abuses of the Internet, the crime of Internet harassment presents challenges for law enforcement personnel, legislators, educators, and parents. These challenges are exacerbated by a lack of uniformity in defining the terms cyberharassment and cyberbullying. In addition, jurisdictional limits and the anonymity of the Internet sometimes make it difficult for law enforcement personnel to identify, locate, arrest, and prosecute alleged offenders. While states generally assert jurisdiction over law enforcement authority within their borders, Congress may legislate, pursuant to the Commerce Clause, Internet activities. Or Congress may elect to adopt a wait-and-see approach, monitoring state Internet harassment-related activities and the types of behavior prosecuted.

Legislators and school administrators continue to grapple with ways of combating cyberbullying, in light of recent high-profile teen suicides, while maintaining the free flow of information and opinion on the Internet. As Internet harassment may cause its victims emotional harm as opposed to physical harm, legislators must determine what level, if any, of harassment should be criminalized. While traditional harassment statutes may provide some guidance in drafting legislation and/or school policies, it is important to differentiate between the one-to-one communication of a telephone or e-mail communication and the one-to-many communication of a posting on a public website.

In drafting legislation or school policies, legislators and school administrators must consider the constitutional constraints of the First and Fourteenth Amendments. Statutes and school policies must be narrow enough not to infringe upon protected speech. In addition, such restrictions must provide adequate notice of what activities constitute Internet harassment. While school administrators arguably have more leeway in adopting Internet harassment policies, they are still generally limited to restricting speech that substantially or materially disrupts the educational process. To facilitate this goal, it may be desirable for legislation and school policies to include definitions for all relevant terms such as "annoy," "harass," "repeated communication," "alarm," or "torment," as these may be too vague or subjective, which may lead to an inordinate amount of prosecutorial discretion.

Table 1. Cyberharassment Statutes

State	Citation	Penalty
Alabama	Ala. Code § 13A-11-8	Misdemeanor
Alaska	Alaska Stat. § 1161.120	Misdemeanor
Arizona	Ariz. Rev. Stat. § 13-2921	Misdemeanor
Arkansas	Ark. Code § 5-41-108	Misdemeanor
California	Cal. Penal Code §§ 422 and 653(m)	Misdemeanor
Colorado	Colo. Rev. Stat. § 18-9-111	Misdemeanor
Connecticut	Conn. Gen. Stat. § 53A-182-83	1st Degree: Felony; 2nd Degree: Misdemeanor
Delaware	Del. Code 11 § 1311	Misdemeanor
Florida	Fla. Stat. § 784.048	Misdemeanor or Felony
Georgia		
Hawaii	Hawaii Rev. Stat. § 711-1106	Misdemeanor
Idaho		
Illinois	Ill. Comp. Stat. 720 § 135 1-2	Misdemeanor
Indiana	Ind. Code § 35-45-2-2	Misdemeanor
Iowa	Iowa Code § 708.7	
Kansas		
Kentucky		
Louisiana		
Maine		
Maryland	Md. Code § 3-3-805	Misdemeanor
Massachusetts	Mass. Gen. Laws § 265-43A	Felony
Michigan	Mich. Comp. Laws § 750.411s	Felony
Minnesota	Minn. Stat. § 609.749	Misdemeanor or Felony (if aggravated or repeated)
Mississippi	Miss. Code § 97-29-45	Misdemeanor
Missouri	V.A.M.S. § 565.090	Misdemeanor or Felony (if repeat offender or an adult over 21 against a minor 17 years or younger)
Montana	MCA § 45-8-213	Misdemeanor
Nebraska		
Nevada		
New Hampshire	N.H. Rev. Stat. § 644-4	Misdemeanor
New Jersey	N.J.S. § 2C 33-4	Misdemeanor
New Mexico		
New York	N.Y. Penal Law § 240.30	Misdemeanor
North Carolina	N.C.G.S.A. § 14-196.3	Misdemeanor
North Dakota		
Ohio	Ohio Rev. Code § 2917.21A	Misdemeanor
Oklahoma	Okla. Stat. 21 § 1172	Misdemeanor
Oregon	Or. Rev. Stat. § 166.065	Misdemeanor
Pennsylvania	Pa. Cons. Stat. 18 § 5504	Misdemeanor
Rhode Island		

Table 1. (Continued)

South Carolina	S.C. Code § 16-3-700(a)2	Misdemeanor
South Dakota	S.D. Cod. Laws § 49-31-31	Misdemeanor
Tennessee	Tenn. Code § 39-17-308	Misdemeanor
Texas	Tx.Penal Code § 42.07[a]	Misdemeanor
Utah	Utah code § 76-9-201	Misdemeanor
Vermont	13 V.S.A. § 1027	Misdemeanor
Virginia	Va. Code 18.2 § 152.7.1	Misdemeanor
Washington	Wash. Rev. Code § 9A.46.020	Misdemeanor
West Virginia	W. Va. Code § 61-3C-14A	Misdemeanor
Wisconsin	Wis. Stat. § 947.0125	Misdemeanor
Wyoming		

a. Provision ruled unconstitutional by Court of Appeals of Texas April 3, 2008, *Karenev v. Texas*, 2008 WL 902799.

Table 2. Cyberstalking Statutes

State	**Citation**	**Penalty**
Alabama		
Alaska	Alaska Stat. § 11.41.260	Misdemeanor (Felony if victim under 16)
Arizona		
Arkansas		
California	Cal. Penal Code § 646.9	Misdemeanor
Colorado	Colo. Rev. Stat. § 18-9-111	Felony
Connecticut		
Delaware		
Florida	Fla. Stat. § 784.048	Misdemeanor or Felony
Georgia	Georgia Code § 16-5-90	Misdemeanor
Hawaii		
Idaho	I.C. § 18-7906	Misdemeanor (Felony if victim under 16)
Illinois	Ill. Comp. Stat. 720 § 5-12-7.5	Felony
Indiana		
Iowa		
Kansas		
Kentucky		
Louisiana	La. Rev. Stat. § 14-40.3	Misdemeanor
Maine		
Maryland		
Massachusetts	Mass. Gen. Laws § 265 43	Felony
Michigan	Mich. Comp. Laws § 750.411(h)	Misdemeanor (Felony if victim under 18 and Defendant is 5 years older)
Minnesota	Minn. Stat. § 609.749	Misdemeanor (Felony if aggravated or repeated)
Mississippi	Miss. Code § 97-45-15	Felony

Table 2. (Continued)

State	Citation	Penalty
Missouri	V.A.M.S. § 565.225	Misdemeanor (Felony if aggravated)
Montana	MCA § 45-5-220	Misdemeanor
Nebraska		
Nevada		
New Hampshire		
New Jersey	N.J.S. § 2C 12 10	
New Mexico		
New York		
North Carolina	N.C.G.S.A. 14-§ 196.3	Misdemeanor
North Dakota		
Ohio	Ohio Rev. Code § 2903.211	Misdemeanor (Felony under some circumstances)
Oklahoma	Okla. Stat. 21-§ 1173	Misdemeanor
Oregon	Or. Rev. Stat. § 163.730-732	Misdemeanor
Pennsylvania	Pa. Cons. Stat. 18 § 5504	Misdemeanor
Rhode Island	R.I. Gen. Laws § 11-52-4.2	Misdemeanor (Felony on 2nd offense)
South Carolina	S.C. Code § 16 3 1700	Felony
South Dakota	S.D. Cod. Laws § 22-19A-1	Misdemeanor
Tennessee	T.C.A. § 39-17-315	Misdemeanor (Felony if victim under 18)
Texas		
Utah		
Vermont		
Virginia		
Washington	Wash. Rev. Code §§ 9A.46.110 and 9.61.260	Misdemeanor (Felony if threaten to kill)
West Virginia		
Wisconsin		
Wyoming	Wyo. Stat. § 6-2-506	Misdemeanor

Table 3. Cyberharassment Statutory Language, by State

State	Citation	Selected Statutory Language
Alabama	Ala. Code § 13A-11-8(b)(1)	**Harassing Communications:** with intent to harass or alarm; communiates anonymously or otherwise by telephone, telegraph, mail, or any other form of written or electronic communication, in a manner likely to harass or cause alarm.
Alaska	Alaska Stat. § 11.61.120	**Harassment in the 2nd Degree:** with intent to harass or annoy the other person: makes an obscene electronic communication, or a telephone call or electronic communication that threatens physical injury or sexual contact.
Arizona	Ariz. Rev. Stat. § 13-2921	**Harassment:** with intent to harass or with knowledge that harassing the other person; anonymously or otherwise communicates or causes a communication with another person by verbal, electronic, mechanical, telegraphic, telephonic or written means in a manner that harasses.

Table 3. (Continued)

State	Citation	Selected Statutory Language
Arkansas	Ark. Code § 5-41-108	**Unlawful Computerized Communications:** with the purpose to frighten, intimidate, threaten, abuse, or harass another, the person sends a message: (1) by electronic mail or other computerized communication system, and in that message threatens to cause physical injury, to any person or damage to the property of any person; (2) by electronic mail or other computerized communication system with the reasonable expectation that the other person will receive the message and in that message threatens to cause physical injury to any person or damage to the property of any person; (3) to another person on an electronic mail or other computerized communication system and in that message uses any obscene, lewd, or profane language; or (4) on an electronic mail or other computerized communication system with the reasonable expectation that the other person will receive the message and in that message uses any obscene, lewd, or profane language.
California	Cal. Penal Code § 422	Any person who willfully threatens to commit a crime which will result in death or great bodily injury to another person, with the specific intent that the statement, made verbally, in writing, or by means of an electronic communication device, is to be taken as a threat, even if there is no intent of actually carrying it out, which, on its face and under the circumstances in which it is made, is so unequivocal, unconditional, immediate, and specific as to convey to the person threatened, a gravity of purpose and an immediate prospect of execution of the threat, and thereby causes that person reasonably to be in sustained fear for his or her own safety or for his or her immediate family's safety.
California	Cal. Penal Code § 653(m)	Every person who, with intent to annoy, telephones or makes contact by means of an electronic communication device with another and addresses to or about the other person any obscene language or threat to inflict injury to the person or property of the person addressed or any member of his or her family, is guilty of a misdemeanor. Every person who makes repeated telephone calls or makes repeated contact by means of an electronic communication device with intent to annoy another person at his or her residence is, whether or not conversation ensues from making the telephone call or electronic contact, guilty of a misdemeanor.
Colorado	Colo. Rev. Stat. § 18-9-111	**Harassment:** With intent to harass, initiates communication with a person, by telephone, computer, computer network, or computer system in a manner intended to harass or threaten bodily injury or property damage, or makes any comment, request, suggestion, or proposal by telephone, computer, computer network, or computer system that is obscene.
Connecticut	Conn. Gen. Stat. § 53A-182-83	A person is guilty of harassment in the first degree when, with the intent to harass, annoy, alarm or terrorize another person, he threatens to kill or physically injure that person or any other person, and communicates such threat by telephone, or by telegraph, mail, computer network, as defined in section 53a-250, or any other form of written communication, in a manner likely to cause annoyance or alarm and has been convicted of a previous felony. A person is guilty of harassment in the second degree when: (2) with intent to harass, annoy or alarm another person, he communicates with a person by telegraph or mail, by electronically transmitting a facsimile through connection with a telephone network, by computer network, as defined in section 53a-250, or by any other form of written communication, in a manner likely to cause annoyance or alarm.
Delaware	Del. Code 11 § 1311	A person is guilty of harassment when, with intent to harass, annoy or alarm another person: (2) Communicates with a person by telephone, telegraph, mail or any other form of written or electronic communication in a manner which the person knows is likely to cause annoyance or alarm.

State	Citation	Selected Statutory Language
Florida	Fla. Stat. § 784.048	**"Cyberstalk"** means to engage in a course of conduct to communicate, or to cause to be communicated, words, images, or language by or through the use of electronic mail or electronic communication, directed at a specific person, causing substantial emotional distress to that person and serving no legitimate purpose. (2) Any person who willfully, maliciously, and repeatedly follows, harasses, or cyberstalks another person commits the offense of stalking, a misdemeanor of the first degree; (3) Any person who willfully, maliciously, and repeatedly follows, harasses, or cyberstalks another person, and makes a credible threat with the intent to place that person in reasonable fear of death or bodily injury of the person, or the person's child, sibling, spouse, parent, or dependent, commits the offense of aggravated stalking, a felony of the third degree; (4) Any person who, after an injunction for protection against repeat violence, sexual violence, or dating violence, or an injunction for protection against domestic violence, or after any other court-imposed prohibition of conduct toward the subject per-son or that person's property, knowingly, willfully, maliciously, and repeatedly follows, harasses, or cyberstalks another person commits the offense of aggravated stalking, a felony of the third degree; (5) Any person who willfully, maliciously, and repeatedly follows, harasses, or cyberstalks a minor under 16 years of age commits the offense of aggravated stalking, a felony of the third degree.
Hawaii	Hawaii Rev. Stat. § 711-1106	A person commits the offense of harassment if, with intent to harass, annoy, or alarm any other person, that person: repeatedly makes telephone-calls, facsimile, or electronic mail transmissions without purpose of legit-imate communication; Repeatedly makes a communication anonymously or at an extremely inconvenient hour; repeatedly makes communications, after being advised by the person to whom the communication is directed that further communication is unwelcome; or makes a communication using offensively coarse language that would cause the recipient to reasonably believe that the actor intends to cause bodily injury to the recipient or ano-ther or damage to the property of the recipient or another.
Illinois	Ill. Comp. Stat. 720 § 135 1-2	**Harassment through electronic communications** is the use of electronic communication for any of the following purposes: (1) Making any comment, request, suggestion or proposal which is obscene with an intent to offend; (2) Interrupting, with the intent to harass, the telephone service or the electronic communication service of any person; (3) Transmitting to any person, with the intent to harass and regardless of whether the communication is read in its entirety or at all, any file, document, or other communication which prevents that person from using his or her telephone service or electronic communications device; (3.1) Transmitting an electronic communication or knowingly inducing a person to transmit an electronic communication for the purpose of harassing another person who is under 13 years of age, regardless of whether the person under 13 years of age consents to the harassment, if the defendant is at least 16 years of age at the time of the commission of the offense; (4) Threatening injury to the person or to the property of the person to whom an electronic communication is directed or to any of his or her family or household members; or (5) Knowingly permitting any electronic communications device to be used for any of the purposes mentioned in this subsection (a). "Electronic communication" means any transfer of signs, signals, writings, images, sounds, data or intelligence of any nature transmitted in whole or in part by a wire, radio, electromagnetic, photoelectric or photooptical system.

Table 3. (Continued)

State	Citation	Selected Statutory Language
Indiana	Ind. Code § 35-45-2-2	A person who, with intent to harass, annoy, or alarm another person but with no intent of legitimate communication: uses a computer network (as defined in IC 35-43-2-3(a)) or other form of electronic communication to: (A) communicate with a person; or (B) transmit an obscene message or indecent or profane words to a person.
Iowa	Iowa Code § 708.7	A person commits harassment when, with intent to intimidate, annoy, or alarm another person, the person does any of the following: Communicates with another by telephone, telegraph, writing, or via electronic commun-ication without legitimate purpose and in a manner likely to cause the other person annoyance or harm.
Maryland	Md. Code § 3-3-805	A person may not use electronic mail with the intent to harass: (1) one or more persons; or (2) by sending lewd, lascivious, or obscene material.
Massac-husetts	Mass. Gen.Laws § 265-43A	Whoever willfully and maliciously engages in a knowing pattern of conduct or series of acts over a period of time directed at a specific person, which seriously alarms that person and would cause a reasonable person to suffer substantial emotional distress, shall be guilty of the crime of criminal hara-ssment. Such conduct or acts described in this paragraph shall include, but not be limited to, conduct or acts conducted by mail or by use of a telephonic or telecommunication device including, but not limited to, electronic mail, Internet communications or facsimile communications.
Michigan	Mich. Comp. Laws § 750.411s	A person shall not post a message through the use of any medium of communication, including the Internet or a computer, computer program, computer system, or computer network, or other electronic medium of communication, without the victim's consent, if all of the following apply: (a) The person knows or has reason to know that posting the message could cause 2 or more separate noncontinuous acts of unconsented contact with the victim; (b) Posting the message is intended to cause conduct that would make the victim feel terrorized, frightened, intimidated, threatened, harassed, or molested; (c) Conduct arising from posting the message would cause a reasonable person to suffer emotional distress and to feel terrorized, frightened, intimidated, threatened, harassed, or molested; (d) Conduct arising from posting the message causes the victim to suffer emotional distress and to feel terrorized, frightened, intimidated, threatened, harassed, or molested.
.Minnesota	Minn. Stat. § 609.749	Harassment and stalking crimes. A person who harasses another by committing any of the following acts is guilty of a gross misdemeanor: directly or indirectly manifests a purpose or intent to injure the person, property, or rights of another by the commission of an unlawful act; stalks, follows, monitors, or pursues another, whether in person or through technological or other means; repeatedly mails or delivers or causes the delivery by any means, including electronically, of letters, telegrams, messages, packages, or other objects.
Mississippi	Miss. Code § 97-29-45	It shall be unlawful for any person: (a) To make any comment, request, suggestion or proposal by means of telecommunication or electronic communication which is obscene, lewd or lascivious with intent to abuse, threaten or harass any party to a telephone conversation, telecommunication or electronic communication; (b) To make a telecommunication or electronic communication with intent to terrify, intimidate or harass, and threaten to inflict injury or physical harm to any person or to his property; (c) To make a telephone call, whether or not conversation ensues, without disclosing his identity and with intent to annoy, abuse, threaten or harass any person at the called number;... (f) Knowingly to permit a computer or a telephone of any type under his control to be used for any purpose prohibited by this section.

State	Citation	Selected Statutory Language
Missouri	V.A.M.S. § 565.090	A person commits the crime of harassment if he or she: Knowingly frightens, intimidates, or causes emotional distress to another person by anonymously making a telephone call or any electronic communication.
Montana	MCA § 45-8-213	A person commits the offense of violating privacy in communications if the person knowingly or purposely: (a) with the purpose to terrify, intimidate, threaten, harass, annoy, or offend, communicates with a person by electronic communication and uses obscene, lewd, or profane language, suggests a lewd or lascivious act, or threatens to inflict injury or physical harm to the person or property of the person. The use of obscene, lewd, or profane language or the making of a threat or lewd or lascivious suggestions is prima facie evidence of an intent to terrify, intimidate, threaten, harass, annoy, or offend; (b) uses an electronic communication to attempt to extort money or any other thing of value from a person or to disturb by repeated communications the peace, quiet, or right of privacy of a person at the place where the communications are received.
New Hampshire	N.H. Rev. Stat. § 644-4	A person is guilty of a misdemeanor if such person: (d) Knowingly communicates any matter of a character tending to incite murder, assault, or arson; (e) With the purpose to annoy or alarm another, communicates any matter containing any threat to kidnap any person or to commit a violation of RSA 633:4; or a threat to the life or safety of another; or (f) With the purpose to annoy or alarm another, having been previously notified that the recipient does not desire further communication, communicates with such person, when the communication is not for a lawful purpose or constit-utionally protected. "Communicates" means to impart a message by any method of transmission, including but not limited to telephoning or personally delivering or sending or having delivered any information or material by written or printed note or letter, package, mail, courier service or electronic transmission, including electronic transmissions generated or communicated via a computer.
New Jersey	N.J.S. § 2C 33-4	A person commits a petty disorderly persons offense if, with purpose to harass another, he: Makes, or causes to be made, a communication or communications anonymously or at extremely inconvenient hours, or in offensively coarse language, or any other manner likely to cause annoyance or alarm; Subjects another to striking, kicking, shoving, or other offensive touching, or threatens to do so; or engages in any other course of alarming conduct or of repeatedly committed acts with purpose to alarm or seriously annoy such other person.
New York	N.Y. Penal Law § 240.30	**Aggravated harassment in the second degree:** A person is guilty of aggravated harassment in the second degree when, with intent to harass, annoy, threaten or alarm another person, he or she: (b) causes a communication to be initiated by mechanical or electronic means or otherwise with a person, anonymously or otherwise, by telephone, or by telegraph, mail or any other form of written communication, in a manner likely to cause annoyance or alarm.
North Carolina	N.C.G.S.A § 14-196.3	It is unlawful for a person to: (1) Use in electronic mail or electronic communication any words or language threatening to inflict bodily harm to any person or to that person's child, sibling, spouse, or dependent, or physical injury to the property of any person, or for the purpose of extorting money or other things of value from any person. (2) Electronically mail or electronically communicate to another repeatedly, whether or not conversation ensues, for the purpose of abusing, annoying, threatening, terrifying, harassing, or embarrassing any person. (3) Electronically mail or electronically communicate to another and to knowingly make any false statement concerning death, injury, illness,

Table 3. (Continued)

State	Citation	Selected Statutory Language
		disfigurement, indecent conduct, or criminal conduct of the person electronically mailed or of any member of the person's family or household with the intent to abuse, annoy, threaten, terrify, harass, or embarrass. (4) Knowingly permit an electronic communication device under the person's control to be used for any purpose prohibited by this section.
Ohio	Ohio Code §2917.21 A	No person shall knowingly make or cause to be made a telecommunication, or knowingly permit a telecommunication to be made from a telecommunications device under the person's control, to another, if the caller does any of the following: (1) Fails to identify the caller to the recipient and makes the telecommunication with purpose to harass or abuse any person at the premises, whether or not actual communication takes place between the caller and a recipient; (4) Knowingly states to the recipient that the caller intends to cause damage to or destroy public or private property, and the recipient, any member of the recipient's family, or any other person who resides at the premises has the responsibility of protecting, or insures the property that will be destroyed or damaged; (5) Knowingly makes the telecommunication to the recipient, to another person at the premises, or to those premises, and the recipient or another person at those premises previously has told the caller not to make a telecommunication to those premises or to any persons at those premises. No person shall make or cause to be made a telecommunication, or permit a telecommunication to be made from a device under the person's control, with purpose to abuse, threaten, or harass another person. "Telecommunication" means transmission over any communications system by any method, including, but not limited to electronic, digital, or analog.
Oklahoma	Okla. Stat. 21 § 1172	It shall be unlawful for a person who, by means of a electronic communication device, willfully either: 1. Makes any comment, request, suggestion, or proposal which is obscene, lewd, lascivious, filthy, or indecent; 2. Makes electronic communication with intent to terrify, intimidate or harass, or threaten to inflict injury or physical harm to any person or property of that person; 3. Makes an electronic communication, whether or not conversation ensues, with intent to put the party called in fear of physical harm or death; 4. Makes electronic communication, whether or not conversation ensues, without disclosing the identity of the person making the call or communication and with intent to annoy, abuse, threaten, or harass any person at the called number; 5. Knowingly permits any electronic communication under the control of the person to be used for any purpose prohibited by this section; and 6. In conspiracy or concerted action with other persons, makes repeated calls or electronic communications or simultaneous calls or electronic communications solely to harass any person.
Oregon	Or. Rev. Stat. § 166.065	A person commits the crime of harassment if the person intentionally harasses or annoys another person by: (1) Subjects another to alarm by conveying a telephonic, electronic or written threat to inflict serious physical injury on that person or to commit a felony involving the person or property of that person or any member of that person's family, which threat reasonably would be expected to cause alarm. (2) A person is criminally liable for harassment if the person knowingly permits any telephone or electronic device under the person's control to be used in violation of subsection (1) of this section.
Pennsy-lvania	Pa. Cons. Stat. 18 § 5504	**Harassment by communication or address:** A person commits the crime of harassment by communication or address when, with intent to harass, annoy or alarm another, the person: communicates to or about such other

State	Citation	Selected Statutory Language
		person any lewd, lascivious, threatening or obscene words, language, drawings or caricatures; or communicates repeatedly in an anonymous manner; communicates repeatedly at extremely inconvenient hours; or communicates repeatedly in a manner not covered.
South Carolina	S.C. Code § 16-3-700(a)2	**"Harassment in the second degree"** means a pattern of intentional, substantial, and unreasonable intrusion into the private life of a targeted person that serves no legitimate purpose and causes the person and would cause a reasonable person in his position to suffer mental or emotional distress. Harassment in the second degree may include, but is not limited to, verbal, written, or electronic contact that is initiated, maintained, or repeated.
South Dakota	S.D. Cod. Laws § 49-31-31	It is a Class 1 misdemeanor for a person to use a telephone or other electronic communication device for any of the following purposes: (1) To contact another person with intent to terrorize, intimidate, threaten, harass or annoy such person by using obscene or lewd language or by suggesting a lewd or lascivious act; (2) To contact another person with intent to threaten to inflict physical harm or injury to any person or property; (3) To contact another person with intent to extort money or other things of value; (4) To contact another person with intent to disturb that person by repeated anonymous telephone calls or intentionally failing to replace the receiver or disengage the telephone connection; (5) For a person to knowingly permit a telephone or other electronic communication device under his or her control to be used for a purpose prohibited by this section.
Tennessee	Tenn. Code § 39-17-308	A person commits an offense who intentionally: Threatens, by telephone, in writing, or by electronic communication, including electronic mail or Internet services, to take action known to be unlawful against any person, and by this action knowingly annoys or alarms the recipient.
Texas	Tx. Penal Code § 42.07 (Provision ruled unconstitutional by Court of Appeals of Texas April 3, 2008, *Karenev v. Texas*, 20-08 WL 02799.)	**Harassment:** A person commits an offense if, with intent to harass, annoy, alarm, abuse, torment, or embarrass another, he: (1) initiates communication by telephone, in writing, or by electronic communication and in the course of the communication makes a comment, request, suggestion, or proposal that is obscene; (2) threatens, by telephone, in writing, or by electronic communication, in a manner reasonably likely to alarm the person receiving the threat, to inflict bodily injury on the person or to commit a felony against the person, a member of his family or household, or his property ... ; (7) sends repeated electronic communications in a manner reasonably likely to harass, annoy, alarm, abuse, torment, embarrass, or offend another.
Utah	Utah code § 76-9-201	A person is guilty of electronic communication harassment if with intent to annoy, alarm, intimidate, offend, abuse, threaten, harass, frighten, or disrupt the electronic communications of another, the person: (a) makes repeated contact by means of electronic communications, whether or not a conversation ensues; or after the recipient has requested or informed the person not to contact the recipient, and the person repeatedly or continuously contacts the electronic communication device of the recipient; or causes an electronic communication device of the recipient to ring or to receive other notification of attempted contact by means of electronic communication; (b) makes contact by means of electronic

Table 3. (Continued)

State	Citation	Selected Statutory Language
		communication and insults, taunts, or challenges the recipient of the communication or any person at the receiving location in a manner likely to provoke a violent or disorderly response; (c) makes contact by means of electronic communication and threatens to inflict injury, physical harm, or damage to any person or the property of any person.
Vermont	13 V.S.A. § 1027	Disturbing peace by use of telephone or other electronic communications: A person who, with intent to terrify, intimidate, threaten, harass or annoy, makes contact by means of a telephonic or other electronic communication with another and (i) makes any request, suggestion or proposal which is obscene, lewd, lascivious or indecent; (ii) threatens to inflict injury or physical harm to the person or property of any person; or (iii) disturbs, or attempts to disturb, by repeated anonymous telephone calls or other electronic communications, whether or not conversation ensues, the peace, quiet or right of privacy of any person at the place where the communication or communications are received.
Virginia	Va. Code 18.2 § 152.7.1	**Harassment by computer:** If any person, with the intent to coerce, intimidate, or harass any person, shall use a computer or computer network to communicate obscene, vulgar, profane, lewd, lascivious, or indecent language, or make any suggestion or proposal of an obscene nature, or threaten any illegal or immoral act, he shall be guilty of a Class 1 misdemeanor.
Washington	Wash. Rev.Code § 9A.46.020	A person is guilty of harassment if: The person by words or conduct places the person threatened in reasonable fear that the threat will be carried out. "Words or conduct" includes, in addition to any other form of communication or conduct, the sending of an electronic communication.
West Virginia	W. Va. Code § 61-3C-14A	**Obscene, anonymous, harassing and threatening communications by computer:** It is unlawful for any person, with the intent to harass or abuse another person, to use a computer to: (1) Make contact with another without disclosing his or her identity with the intent to harass or abuse; (2) Make contact with a person after being requested by the person to desist from contacting them; (3) Threaten to commit a crime against any person or property; or (4) Cause obscene material to be delivered or transmitted to a specific person after being requested to desist from sending such material.
Wisconsin	Wis. Stat. § 947.0125	A person is guilty of harassment when: (a) With intent to frighten, intimidate, threaten, abuse or harass another person, sends a message to the person on an electronic communication system and in that message threatens to inflict injury or physical harm to any person or the property of any person or sends a message on an electronic communication system with the reasonable expectation that the person will receive the message and in that message threatens to inflict injury or physical harm to any person or the property of any person. (c) With intent to frighten, intimidate, threaten or abuse another person, sends a message to the person on an electronic communication system and in that message uses any obscene, lewd or profane language or suggests any lewd or lascivious act or sends a message on an electronic communication system with the reasonable expectation that the person will receive the message and in that message uses any obscene, lewd or profane language or suggests any lewd or lascivious act or sends a message to the person on an electronic communication system while intentionally preventing or attempting to prevent the disclosure of his or her own identity... (f) While intentionally preventing or attempting to prevent the disclosure of his or her identity and with intent to frighten, intimidate, threaten or abuse another person, sends a message on an electronic communication system with the reasonable expectation that the person will receive the message.

End Note

[386] Social networking sites are virtual communities where people convene to chat, instant message (IM), post pictures, share stories, etc. Currently, there is a myriad of social networking sites that are topic specific, i.e., individuals interested in certain sports or have certain medical issues and/or concerns. A social network is basically a huge community of people broken down into smaller communities where you find people of like minds or interests.

[387] Generally, assault is defined as an attempt to cause or purposely, knowing, or recklessly causing bodily injury to another. *See, e.g.*, TEXAS PENAL CODE § 22.01.

[388] *Heart of Atlanta Motel, Inc. v. United States*, 379 U.S. 241, 256 (1964)(stating that "the authority of Congress to keep the channels of interstate commerce free from immoral and injurious uses has been frequently sustained.").

[389] *Southern R. Co. v. United States*, 222 U.S. 20 (1991)(upholding amendment to the Safety Appliance Act as applied to vehicles used in intrastate commerce).

[390] *See, United States v. Lopez*, 514 U.S. 549, 558-559 (1995)(citations omitted).

[391] 18 U.S.C. § 2425.

[392] For an in-depth discussion of these laws, refer to CRS Report 95-804, *Obscenity and Indecency: Constitutional Principles and Federal Statutes,* by Henry Cohen.

[393] 15 U.S.C. §§ 6501-6506.

[394] Federal Trade Commission (FTC), How to Comply With The Children's Online Privacy Protection Rule, http://www.ftc.gov/bcp/conline/pubs/buspubs/coppa.htm. Last visited June 5, 2008.

[395] *Id.*

[396] *Id.* COPPA creates an exception for children's e-mail addresses collected for such uses as contests, online newsletters, homework help, and online postcards. In addition, COPPA contains a safe harbor provision for site operators who comply with Commission-approved self-regulatory industry guidelines.

[397] 47 U.S.C. § 231.

[398] *Id.*

[399] *American Civil Liberties Union v. Reno*, 31 F.Supp.2d 473 (E.D. Pa. 1999), *aff'd*, 217 F.3d 162 (3d Cir. 2000), *vacated and remanded sub nom. Ashcroft v. American Civil Union Liberties Union*, 535 U.S. 564 (2002), *aff'd on remand*, 322 F.3d 240 (3d Cir. 2003), *aff'd and remanded*, 542 U.S. 656 (2004).

[400] *American Civil Liberties Union v. Gonzales,* 478 F.Supp.2d 775 (E.D. Pa. 2007).

[401] *American Civil Liberties Union v. Mukasey*, 534 F.3d 181 (3rd Cir. 2008).

[402] P.L. 106-554.

[403] 20 U.S.C. § 9134(f) and 47 U.S.C. § 254(h)(6).

[404] *United States v. Am. Library Ass'n*, 539 U.S. 194 (2003)(upholding CIPA's condition imposed on institutions in exchange for government funding).

[405] Federal child pornography statutes are codified at 18 U.S.C. §§ 2251-2260. For an in-depth discussion of these laws, refer to CRS Report 95-804, Obscenity and Indecency: Constitutional Principles and Federal Statutes, by Henry Cohen.

[406] *See, e.g.*, N.M. STAT. ANN § 30-37-3.2(b); N.J. STAT. ANN. § 2C:13-6 and CAL. PENAL CODE § 272(b)(1).

[407] ALA. CODE §§ 13A-6-110, 111; ALASKA STATUTES § 11.41-452; ARIZ. REV. STAT. §§ 13-3506.01, 13-1554; ARK. STAT. § 5-27-603; CAL. PENAL CODE §§ 272(B), 288.2; COLO. REV. STAT. §§ 31-21-1001, -1002, -1003, 18-3-306, 18- 405.4; CONN. GEN. STAT. § 53A-90A; DEL. CODE. TIT. 11 § 1112A; FLA. STAT. § 847.0135; GA. CODE § 16-12-100.2; HAWAII REV. STAT. §§ 707.756, 707.757, 708.892; IDAHO CODE § 18-1509A; 720 ILCS 5/11-6; IND. CODE § 35-42-4-6; KY REV. STAT. § 510.155; LA. REV. STAT. § 14:81.3; ME. REV. STAT. TIT. 17-A § 259;9 MD. CRIMINAL LAW CODE § 3- 324, 11-207; MICH. COMP. LAWS §§ 750.145A, 750.145D; MINN. STAT. § 609.352; MISS. CODE §§ 97-5-27, 97-5-33; MO. REV. STAT. § 546.151; NEB. REV. STAT. § 28-320.02; NEV. REV. STAT. § 201.560; N.H. REV. STAT. §§ 649-B:3, 649-B:4; N.J. REV. STAT. § 2C:13-6; N.M. STAT. § 30-37-3.2; N.Y. PENAL LAW § 235.22; N.C. GEN. STAT. § 14-202.3; N.D. CENT. CODE § 12.1-20-05.1; OHIO REV. CODE § 2907.07; OKLA. STAT. TIT. 21 §§ 1040.13A, 1123; PA. CONS. STAT. TIT. 18 § 6318; R.I. GEN. LAWS § 11-37-8.8; S.D. CODIFIED LAWS § 22-24A-5; TENN. CODE ANN. § 39-13-528; TEX. PENAL CODE § 33.021; UTAH CODE § 76-4-401; VT. STAT. TIT. 13 § 2828; VA. CODE § 18.2-374.3; W. VA. CODE § 61-3C-14B; WIS. STAT. § 948.075.

[408] 18 U.S.C. § 2422(b) states that

> [w]hoever, using the mail or any facility or means of interstate or foreign commerce, or within the special maritime and territorial jurisdiction of the United States knowingly persuades, induces, entices, or coerces any individual who has not attained the age of 18 years, to engage in prostitution or any sexual activity for which any person can be charged with a criminal offense, or attempts to do so, shall be fined under this title and imprisoned not less than ten years or for life.

[409] Stalking usually refers to harassing or threatening behavior that is engaged in repeatedly. California was the first state to criminalize stalking due to several high-profile cases, including the 1982 attempted murder of actress Theresa Saldana, the 1988 massacre by Richard Farley, and the 1989 murder of actress Rebecca Schaeffer. Other states passed stalking statutes, sometimes with varying names such as criminal harassment or criminal menace. Physical stalking can include following someone, appearing at a person's home or job, making harassing telephone calls, leaving written messages and/or objects, and vandalizing one's property.

[410] These states are Alabama, Alaska, Arizona, California, Connecticut, Delaware, Hawaii, Illinois, Indiana, Maine, Massachusetts, Michigan, New Hampshire, New York, Oklahoma, and Wyoming. Arkansas and Maryland have enacted statutes that cover harassment via electronic communications outside their stalking statutes. State laws that do not include specific references to electronic communication may still apply to individuals who threaten or harass others online, but the addition of specific language might make the laws easier to enforce.

[411] CAL. PENAL CODE § 646.9.

[412] Under California law, "electronic communication device" includes telephones, cellular phones, computers, video recorders, fax machines, and pagers.

[413] 18 U.S.C. § 2261A.

[414] *See*, Violence Against Women and Department of Justice Reauthorization Act of 2005, P.L. 109-162 Tit. I, § 113, 119 Stat. 2960 (2006).

[415] See, *United States v. Kammersell*, 196 F.3d 1137 (10th Cir. 1999)(concluding that 18 U.S.C. § 875 is a general intent statute requiring the intent "to effect some change or achieve some goal through intimidation.").

[416] *See, e.g., United States v. Freeman*, 176 F.3d 575 (1st Cir. 1999).

[417] 196 F.3d 1137 (10th Cir. 1999).

[418] *See, United States v. Alkhabaz*, 104 F.3d 1492, 1495 (6th Cir. 1997).

[419] Id.

[420] Id. at 1496.

[421] 47 U.S.C. § 223 was passed in 1934, when the telephone was at the cutting edge of communication technology. It was subsequently amended in January 2006 to cover e-mail communications via the Internet. *See*, Violence Against Women and Department of Justice Reauthorization Act of 2005, P.L. 109-162 Tit. I, § 113, 119 Stat. 2960 (2006).

[422] Some use the term "cyberharassment" and "cyberbullying" interchangeably, while others use "cyberbullying" to describe situations in which a minor is both the perpetrator and victim.

[423] Courts have found the pre-Internet telephone harassment statute constitutional, but concluded that it cannot be interpreted to include political or public discourse. *See, United States v. Popa*, 187 F.3d 672 (D.C. Cir. 1999).

[424] 47 U.S.C. § 223(a)(2).

[425] 47 U.S.C. § 223(h)(C)(1)(defining "telecommunication device" as "any device or software that can be used to originate telecommunications or other types of communications that are transmitted, in whole or in part, by the Internet ..."). This definition was added by P.L. 109-162, § 113(a)(3). As such, there is no case law directed toward Internet questions as yet.

[426] 47 U.S.C. § 223(a)(1)(C).

[427] *Id.*

[428] 372 F.3d 365 (6th Cir. 2004), *vacated on other grounds*, 543 U.S. 1182 (2005).

[429] *Id.* at 372-73.

[430] *Id.* at 379.

[431] *Id.* at 380 (*citing Parker v. Levy,* 417 U.S. 733 (1974)(stating that facial invalidation is inappropriate when the remainder of the statute "covers a whole range of easily identifiable and constitutionally proscribable conduct.")).

[432] *Id.*

[433] IOWA CODE § 708.7(1).

[434] VA. CODE 18.2 § 152.7.1.

[435] *See, e.g., Mahaffey v. Aldrich*, 236 F.Supp.2d 779, 78 1-82 (E.D. Mich. 2002)(holding that a student's suspension for co-creating a website entitled "Satan's web page" violated his First Amendment right, absent proof of disruption to school by website or that the website was created on school property).

[436] *See,* Cyberbullying, http://stopcyberbullying.org/what_is_cyberbullying_exactly.html. Last visited June 3, 2008.

[437] *See, e.g.,* States Pushing for Laws to Curb Cyberbullying, at http://www.foxnews.com/story/0,2933,253259,00.html. Last visited July 23, 2008.

[438] See VT. STAT. ANN. TIT. 16 § 1 161a(a)(6).

[439] See VT. STAT. ANN. TIT. 16 § 1 1(a)(32)(A)-(C). The statute provides:

Bullying means any overt act or combination of acts directed against a student by another student or group of students and which:

(A) is repeated over time;

(B) is intended to ridicule, humiliate, or intimidate the student; and

(C) occurs during the school day on school property, on a school bus, or at a school-sponsored activity, or before or after the school day on a school bus or at a school-sponsored activity.

[440] Other states with cyberbullying policies include Idaho, Iowa, Minnesota, New Jersey, Oregon, South Carolina, and Washington.

[441] Some courts have concluded that a school district may not punish a student for out-of-school speech. *See, e.g., Killion v. Franklin Regional School Dist.*, 136 F. Supp.2d 446 (W.D.Pa. 2001)(holding that school could not punish student for list disparaging the athletic director); *Flaherty v. Keystone Oaks School Dist.*, 247 F. Supp.2d 693 (W.D.Pa. 2003)(holding that the school could not punish a student for "trash talk" about a volleyball game); *Latour v. Riverside Beaver School Dist.*, No. 05-1076, 2005 WL 2106562 (W.D.Pa. August 24, 2005)(enjoining school from punishing a student for rap song lyrics).

[442] *See, e.g.,* "Teen's Neighbor Charged in Death-Indictment for Alleged Role in MySpace Prank Sets Precedent," Washington Post, page C3, May 16, 2008.

[443] *See, e.g.,* "No charges to be filed over Meier suicide," St. Charles Journal, at http://stcharlesjournal.stltoday.com/articles/2007/12/03/news/sj2tn20071203-1203stc_meier.ii1 .txt. Last visited July 29, 2008.

[444] At the time of the hoax, Missouri's harassment statute was limited to telephone activity. However, state legislators recently passed legislation expanding the state's stalking and harassment laws to include electronic communications. In addition, the new law provides for harsher penalties for some violations. For example, harassment would be a misdemeanor unless committed by a person 21 years of age or older against a minor 17 years of age or younger. At that point, the crime would be classified as a felony. V.A.M.S. § 565.090.

[445] The Computer Fraud and Abuse Act has been previously used to address the problem of hacking. It appears that this may be the first time the statute has been used in a "harassment" or social networking case.

[446] Under the statute, a "protected computer" is one used in interstate or foreign commerce. Courts have interpreted this term very broadly. *See, United States v. Mitra*, 405 F.3d 492, 495 (8th Cir. 2005)(stating that "[e]very cell phone and cell tower is a 'computer' under this statute's definition; so is every iPod, every wireless base station in the corner coffee shop, and many another gadget.").

[447] MySpace membership requires users to agree to the terms of service (TOS). The TOS requires users to agree "to provide truthful and accurate registration information" and to refrain from "using any information obtained from MySpace services to harass, abuse, or harm other people."

[448] On November 27, 2008, jurors found the defendant guilty on three lesser charges (misdemeanors). The jury was deadlocked on the fourth felony charge of criminal conspiracy. Sentencing is scheduled for April 30, 2009.

[449] This bill is identical to H.R. 6123, introduced in the 110th Congress. Additional bills, such as H.R. 3577, H.R. 4134, H.R. 6120, S. 3016, and S. 3074 were introduced in the 110th Congress, which would have authorized educational grants for Internet crime prevention programs.

[450] The term "electronic means" includes "email, instant messaging, blogs, websites, telephones, and text messages."

[451] *44 Liquormart, Inc. v. Rhode Island*, 517 U.S. 484, 489 (1996); *Gitlow v. New York,* 268 U.S. 652, 666 (1925).

[452] *See, e.g.*, LA. CONST. ART. I § 7; MD. DECL. RTS. ART. 40.

[453] *Chaplinsky v. New Hampshire*, 315 U.S. 568, 571-72 (1942).

[454] *Gertz v. Welch*, 418 U.S. 323, 339-340 (1974).

[455] *Miller v. California*, 413 U.S. 15, 26 (1973).

[456] *See, e.g., Pope v. Illinois*, 481 U.S. 497, 500-01 (1987)(discussing how the serious value doctrine tests whether a reasonable person would find value in speech).

[457] *Brandenburg v. Ohio*, 395 U.S. 444, 447 (1969).

[458] *Watts v. United States*, 394 U.S. 705, 707 (1969).

[459] *Harper & Row, Publishers, Inc. v. Nation Enterprises*, 471 U.S. 539, 569 (1985).

[460] *R.A. V. v. City of St. Paul*, 505 U.S. 377, 388 (1992).

[461] 394 U.S. 705, 705 (1969).

[462] *Id.* at 706.

[463] *Id.* at 708 (describing the audience's reaction as that of laughter).

[464] *Id.*

[465] *Id.* at 707.

[466] *See, e.g., United States v. Alkhabaz*, 104 F.3d 1492 (6th Cir. 1997).

[467] *See, e.g., United States v. Fulmer*, 108 F.3d 1486 (1st Cir. 1997)

[468] *See, e.g., United States v. Maisonet*, 484 F.2d 1356, 1357 (4th Cir. 1973).

[469] 290 F.3d 1058 (9th Cir. 2002)(en banc), *cert denied*, 123 S.Ct. 2637.

[470] 18 U.S.C. §§ 248(a)(1) and (c)(1)(A).

[471] 90 F.3d 1058, 1065.

[472] *Id.* at 1085.

[473] *Id.*

[474] *Id.* at 1077.

[475] *See, Tinker v. Des Moines Independent Community School District*, 393 U.S. 503 (1969); Bethel School District No. 403 v. Fraser, 478 U.S. 675 (1986)(upholding suspension of a high school student for a student government nomination speech including the use of obscene, profane language and gestures); *Hazelwood School District v. Kuhlmeier*, 484 U.S. 260 (1988)(upholding a principal's authority to delete material from a high school paper); and *Morse v. Frederick*, 127 S.Ct. 2618 (2007)(holding that a principal did not violate a student's right to free speech by confiscating a banner she reasonably viewed as promoting illegal drug use).

[476] 393 U.S. 503 (1969).

[477] *Id.* at 507.

[478] *Id.* at 506.

[479] 478 U.S. 675 (1986).

[480] *Id.* at 681.

[481] *Id.*

[482] *Id.* at 683.

[483] 807 A.2d 847 (Pa. 2002).

[484] The website contained a disclaimer that stated that "[b]y clicking," or entering, the website, the visitor agreed not to disclose to any school district personnel any information regarding the website or its creator. The disclaimer, however, did not prevent access to the website. Id. at 851.

[485] *Id.*.

[486] *Id.*

[487] The math teacher testified that she was frightened and fearful that someone would attempt to kill her. In addition, she suffered "stress, anxiety, loss of appetite, loss of sleep, loss of weight, and a general sense of loss of well being as a result of viewing the website." *Id.* at 852.

[488] *Id.* at 859.

[489] *Id.* at 865.

[490] *Id.* (stating that "where speech that is aimed at a specific school and/or its personnel is brought onto the school campus or accessed at school by its originator, the speech will be considered on-campus speech.").

[491] *Id.* at 868-869.

[492] *Id.*

[493] *Id.* However, in *Emmett v. Kent School District No. 415*, the court granted a temporary restraining order in the student's favor. In this case, a high school senior posted a Web page from his home computer that contained mock obituaries of two of his friends. The obituaries were written tongue-in-cheek and inspired, in part, by a creative writing class held the previous school year in which students had been assigned to write their own obituaries. The website became a topic of discussion at the school by both faculty and students. Web page viewers were allowed to vote on who would "die" next. When a local news broadcast described the Web page as featuring a "hit list," the student was immediately placed on emergency expulsion. Subsequently, the expulsion was modified to a five-day suspension. In granting the temporary restraining order, the court found that there was no evidence that the student had intended to threaten anyone, that the site threatened anyone, or that the speech manifested any violent tendencies. 92 F. Supp.2d (1088) (W.D. Wash. 2000)

[494] 494 F.3d 34 (2nd Cir. 2007), *cert. denied*, ___ U.S. ___, 128 S.Ct. 1741 (2008).

[495] *Id.* at 35.

[496] *Id.* at 36.

[497] *Id.*

[498] *Id.* at 39.

[499] *Id.* at 40.

[500] 30 F. Supp.2d 1175 (E.D. Missouri 1998).

[501] *Id.*

[502] The absenteeism policy "drops" students' grades in each class by one letter grade for each unexcused absence in excess of 10 days. Suspension days are considered unexcused absences. *Id.* at 1178.

[503] *Id.*

[504] 496 F. Supp.2d 587 (W.D.Pa. 2007).

[505] *Id.* at 591.

[506] *Id.* at 592.

[507] *Id.* at 593.

[508] Substantive due process has generally dealt with specific subject areas, such as liberty of contract or privacy.

[509] See, e.g., *Chicago v. Morales*, 527 U.S. 41 (1999); *Kolender v. Lawson*, 461 U.S. 352 (1983).

[510] 408 U.S. 104 (1972).

[511] *Id.* at 108-09.

[512] 405 U.S. 156 (1972).

[513] *Id.* at n.1.

[514] Similarly, an ordinance making it a criminal offense for three or more persons to assemble on a sidewalk and conduct themselves in a manner annoying to passersby was found impermissibly vague and void on its face because it encroached on the freedom of assembly. *Coats v. City of Cincinnati,* 402 U.S. 611 (1971).
[515] 2008 WL 902799 (Tex. App.-Fort Worth April 3, 2008).
[516] It is worth noting that at trial, the State relied without objection on translations of the messages by an uncertified translator who was one of the wife's acquaintances. The defendant countered the translations with an Bulgarian translator.
[517] 2008 WL 902799, *2.
[518] *Id.*
[519] *Id.*
[520] TEX. PENAL CODE § 42.07.
[521] In *Kramer v. Price*, 712 F.2d 174 (5th Cir.), the court found the Texas pre-1983 harassment statute to be facially unconstitutional due to vagueness inasmuch as the words "annoy" and "alarm" were inherently vague. In addition, the court found that the statute failed to specify whose sensitivities are relevant. In *Long v. State*, 931 S.W.2d 285 (Tex. Crim. App. 1996), the court found that Texas's 1993 stalking statute suffered the same flaws denounced in *Kramer*. It is worth noting that the current harassment statute mirrors the 1993 stalking statute.
[522] 2008 WL 902799, *7. *See, Long*, 931 S.W.2d at 289.
[523] 2008 WL 902799, *7.
[524] 247 F. Supp.2d 698 (W.D. Pa. 2003).
[525] *Id.* at 700.
[526] *Id.* at 704.

In: Trends in Internet Research
Editor: B.G. Kutais

ISBN: 978-1-59454-140-7

Chapter 11

INTERNET: AN OVERVIEW OF KEY TECHNOLOGY POLICY ISSUES AFFECTING ITS USE AND GROWTH*

Lennard G. Kruger, John D. Moteff, Angele A. Gilroy, Jeffrey W. Seifert and Patricia Moloney Figliola

ABSTRACT

In the decade between 1994 and 2004, the number of U.S. adults using the Internet increased from 15% to 63%, and by 2005, stood at 78.6%. From electronic mail to accessing information to watching videos to online purchasing, the Internet touches almost every aspect of modern life. The extent to which use of the Internet continues to grow, however, may be affected by a number of technology policy issues being debated in Congress.

First is the availability of high-speed — or "broadband" — Internet access. Broadband Internet access gives users the ability to send and receive data at speeds far greater than "dial-up" Internet access over traditional telephone lines. With deployment of broadband technologies accelerating, Congress is seeking to ensure fair competition and timely broadband deployment to all sectors and geographical locations of American society.

Next are a range of issues that reflect challenges faced by those who do use the Internet, such as security, privacy (including spyware and identity theft), unsolicited commercial electronic mail ("spam"), protecting children from unsuitable material (such as pornography), and computer security, including the vulnerability of the nation's critical infrastructures to cyber attacks.

Other issues include the Internet's domain name system (DNS), which is administered by a nonprofit corporation called the Internet Corporation for Assigned Names and Numbers (ICANN). With the Department of Commerce currently exercising legal authority over ICANN, Congress continues to monitor the administration of the

---

* This is an edited, reformatted and augmented version of a Congressional Research Service Publication, Order Code 98-67, Prepared for Members and Committees of Congress, Updated January 5, 2007.

DNS, particularly with respect to issues such as privacy, governance, and protecting children on the Internet.

The evolving role of the Internet in the political economy of the United States also continues to attract congressional attention. Among the issues are what changes may be needed at the Federal Communications Commission in the Internet age, federal support for information technology research and development, provision of online services by the government ("e-government"), and availability and use of "open source" software by the government.

A number of laws already have been passed on many of these issues. Congress is monitoring the effectiveness of these laws, and assessing what other legislation may be needed. Other CRS reports referenced in this document track legislation, and the reader should consult those reports, which are updated more frequently than this one, for current information.

This report will not be updated.

INTRODUCTION

The continued growth of the Internet for personal, government, and business purposes may be affected by a number of technology policy issues being debated by Congress. Among them are access to and regulation of broadband (high-speed) Internet services, computer and Internet security, Internet privacy, the impact of "spam," concerns about what children may encounter (such as pornography) when using the Internet, management of the Internet Domain Name System, and government information technology management.

This report provides overviews of those issues, plus appendices providing a list of acronyms, and a discussion of legislation passed in earlier Congresses. Other issues that are not directly related to technology could also affect the use and growth of the Internet, such as intellectual property rights and Internet taxation. Those are not addressed in this report.

This report does not attempt to track legislation. For more timely information, see the other CRS reports identified in the following sections.

BACKGROUND: INTERNET USAGE AND E-COMMERCE STATISTICS[527]

A December 2006 survey by the Nielsen/Net Ratings market research firm found that 78% of active home Web users connected via broadband during the month of November, up 13 percentage points from 65% of active Web users a year ago. Social activities dominate broadband time online: websites for online gaming, instant messaging, e-mail and social networking all made the top 10 list when ranked by average time per person among broadband users at home. The Internet has become an integral part of everyday social life, particularly among children and teenagers.[528]

A spring 2006 Pew Internet & American Life survey found that 48 million Americans — mostly those with high-speed access at home — have posted content to the Internet.[529]

Internet Usage in the United States

Trends

The Fifth Study of the Internet by the Digital Future Project Finds Major New Trends in Online Use for Political Campaigns[530] highlights the major fmdings in the Annenberg School's Digital Future Project, which is studying the impact of the Internet on Americans. Among the fmdings are:

- Internet users are fmding growing numbers of online friends, as well as friends they first met online and then met in person. Internet users report having met an average of 4.65 friends online whom they have never met in person.
- Although more than 40% of users say that the Internet has increased the number of people with whom they stay in contact, a lower percent say that since starting to use the Internet they are communicating more with family and friends.
- While large percentages of Internet users say that going online increases contact with family and friends, almost all users report that the Internet has no effect on the time spent with close friends or family face-to-face.

Number of Users

The Federal Communications Commission (FCC) issues biannual reports on broadband Internet access service.[531] In its July 2006 report, the FCC reported that during the year 2005, high-speed lines serving residential, small business, larger business, and other subscribers increased by 33%, to 50.2 million lines. High-speed lines serving residential and small business subscribers increased by 36% during 2005, to 42.9 million lines.[532] Additional demographic information on Internet users is compiled by MRI Cyberstats.[533]

Geographic Distribution

Rural Americans are less likely to log on to the Internet at home with high-speed Internet connections than people living in other parts of the country. However, rural areas show fast growth in home broadband uptake in the past two years and the gap between rural and non-rural America in home broadband adoption, though still substantial, is narrowing. As of March 2006, 39% of adult rural Americans went online at home with high-speed Internet connections compared with 42% of adults in urban and suburban areas.[534] *A Nation Online: Entering the Broadband Age*, the sixth report released by the U.S. Department of Commerce examining Americans' use of computers, the Internet, and other information technology tools, examined the geographic differences in broadband adoption and the reasons why some Americans do not have high-speed service.[535] According to the September 2004 report, although the rate of Internet penetration among rural households (54.1%) was similar to that in urban areas (54.8%), the proportion of Internet users with home broadband connections remained much lower in rural areas than in urban areas.

International Internet Usage

There are many different estimates of international Internet usage. Some sources which compile Internet usage data are: the International Telecommunications Union (ITU), the Organisation for Economic Co-operation and Development (OECD), the CIA Fact Book, and independent market research firms such as Nielsen//NetRatings, eMarketer, and the Computer Industry Almanac.[536]

According to a January 2006 estimate from the Computer Industry Almanac, the worldwide number of Internet users is 1.08 billion.[537] The 2 billion Internet users milestone is expected to occur in 2011. Much of current and future Internet user growth is coming from highly populated countries such as China, India, Brazil, Russia, and Indonesia. In the next decade many Internet users will be accessing the Internet with mobile devices, in addition to personal computers.[538]

Broadband subscribers in the Organisation for Economic Cooperation and Development (OECD) member countries[539] reached 181 million by June 2006. Over the past year, the number of broadband subscribers in the OECD increased 33% from 136 million in June 2005 to 181 million in June 2006. This growth increased broadband penetration rates in the OECD from 11.7 in June 2005 to 15.5 subscriptions per 100 inhabitants one year later.[540] The main highlights for the first half of 2006 are:

- Northern European countries have continued their advance with high broadband penetration rates. In June 2006, six countries (Denmark, the Netherlands, Iceland, Korea, Switzerland and Finland) led the OECD in broadband penetration, each with at least 25 subscribers per 100 inhabitants.
- Denmark now leads the OECD with a broadband penetration rate of 29.3 subscribers per 100 inhabitants.
- The strongest per-capita subscriber growth comes from Denmark, Australia, Norway, the Netherlands, Finland, Luxembourg, Sweden and the United Kingdom.
- The United States has the largest total number of broadband subscribers in the OECD at 57 million representing 31% of all broadband connections in the OECD.

E-Commerce

The U.S. Census Bureau releases quarterly retail e-commerce statistics. On November 17, 2006, its estimate of U.S. retail e-commerce sales for the third quarter of 2006, adjusted for seasonal variation and holiday and trading-day differences, but not for price changes, was \$27.5 billion, an increase of 4.5% from the 2nd quarter of 2006. Total retail sales for the 4th quarter of 2006 were estimated at \$991.7 billion, an increase of 0.7% from the 2nd quarter of 2006.[541] E-commerce sales in the third quarter accounted for 2.8% of total sales.

ComScore Networks reported its e-commerce sales estimates for the first three quarters of 2006 and forecasts for the entire year. Overall, comScore forecasts that total online spending in 2006 will reach approximately \$170 billion. Of that total, the market research firm estimates that non-travel e-commerce will break the \$100 billion threshold for the first time. Through the first three quarters of 2006, total e-commerce spending rose 19 percent versus last year to $122.1 billion, buoyed by a 24% increase in non-travel spending to $69.1 billion.[542]

BROADBAND INTERNET REGULATION AND ACCESS[543]

Broadband Internet access gives users the ability to send and receive data at speeds far greater than conventional "dial up" Internet access over existing telephone lines. Broadband technologies — cable modem, digital subscriber line (DSL), satellite, wireless Internet, and fiber — are currently being deployed nationwide by the private sector. While the numbers of new broadband subscribers continue to grow, some areas of the nation — particularly rural and low-income communities — continue to lack sufficient access to high-speed broadband Internet service. In order to address this problem, the 109th Congress considered, but did not pass, legislation to address the scope and effect of federal broadband financial assistance programs (including universal service), and the impact of regulatory policies and new technologies on broadband deployment. These issues are anticipated to continue to be a focus of the broadband policy debate in the 110th Congress.

Some policymakers, believing that disparities in broadband access across American society could have adverse economic and social consequences on those left behind, assert that the federal government should play a more active role to avoid a "digital divide" in broadband access. One approach is for the federal government to provide financial assistance to support broadband deployment in underserved areas. In the 109th Congress, legislation was introduced, but not enacted, to provide financial assistance (including loans, grants, and tax incentives) to encourage broadband deployment. (For more information on federal assistance for broadband deployment, see CRS Report RL30719, *Broadband Internet Access and the Digital Divide: Federal Assistance Programs*, by Lennard G. Kruger and Angele A. Gilroy.) Others, however, question the reality of the "digital divide," and argue that federal intervention in the broadband marketplace would be premature and, in some cases, counterproductive.

The debate over access to broadband services has prompted policymakers to examine a range of other issues to ensure that broadband will be available on a timely and equal basis to all U.S. citizens. One facet of this debate focuses on whether present laws and subsequent regulatory policies are needed to ensure the development of competition and its subsequent consumer benefits, or conversely, whether such laws and regulations are overly burdensome and discourage needed investment in and deployment of broadband services. The regulatory debate focuses on a number of issues including the extent to which legacy regulations should be applied to traditional providers as they enter new markets, the extent to which legacy regulations should be imposed on new entrants as they compete with traditional providers in their markets, and the treatment of new and converging technologies.

For example, present law requires all incumbent local exchange (telephone) carriers (ILECs), such as Verizon or SBC, to open up their networks to enable competitors to lease out parts of the incumbent's network. These unbundling and resale requirements, which are detailed in Section 251 of the Telecommunications Act of 1996, were enacted in an attempt to open up the local telephone network to competitors. Whether such "open access" regulations should be applied to ILECs when they offer new non-dominant services such as broadband connections, or to new market entrants such as cable television companies when they offer services (such as voice and broadband) remains under debate. Whether regulators should play a role to ensure that the Internet remains open to all, often referred to as "net neutrality" became a major part of and is expected to continue to be, a major focus of the ongoing Congressional debate. Equally contentious is the debate over whether legacy regulations, such as the requirement that cable television companies obtain a local franchise as a prerequisite for offering video service, be extended to other entrants, such as telephone companies, if they choose to enter the video market. A third and related debate surrounds the appropriate regulatory framework that should be imposed on new technologies such as voice over Internet Protocol (VoIP) and other Internet Protocol services as well as bundled service offerings.

The regulatory treatment of broadband technologies — whether offered by traditional or emerging providers, or incumbent or new entrants — remains a major focus of the policy debate. Cities, counties, and states have taken up the issue of whether to mandate open access requirements on local cable franchises. In June 1999, a federal judge ruled that the city of Portland, Oregon had the right to require open access to the Tele-Communications Incorporated (TCI) broadband network as a condition for transferring its local cable television franchise to AT&T. On March 14, 2002, the FCC adopted a Declaratory Ruling which classified cable modem service as an "interstate information service," subject to FCC jurisdiction and largely shielded from local regulation. After a series of conflicting court decisions the US Supreme Court in a June 27, 2005 action (*National Cable and Telecommunications Association v. Brand X Internet Services*), ruled that the FCC should be given deference in its decision that cable broadband service should be classified as an "interstate information service." The classification of cable modem service as an "interstate information service" will result in FCC treatment under the less rigorous Title I of the 1934 Communications Act. Similarly, in an August 5, 2005 action, the FCC ruled that the regulatory treatment of wireline broadband services will be granted regulatory parity. The FCC ruled that, subject to a one-year transition period, which expired in August 2006, wireline broadband Internet access services (commonly delivered by DSL technology) are defined as information services, thereby placing telephone company DSL services on an equal regulatory footing with cable modem services. Regulatory parity was also granted to broadband over power line (BPL) service, when the FCC, in a November 2006 decision, determined that such service would also be classified as an "interstate information service" subject to Title I regulation.

Finally, emerging broadband technologies — such as fiber, wireless (including "3G", "wi-fi" and "Wimax"), and BPL — continue to be developed and/or deployed, and have the potential to affect the regulatory and market landscape of broadband deployment. The 110th Congress and the FCC will likely consider policies to address the emergence of these and other new broadband technologies. In addition, how and to what extent "social regulations" such as 911 requirements, disability access, law enforcement obligations, and universal service support, should be applied to emerging technologies is also under debate. A related issue, the emergence of municipal broadband networks (primarily wireless and fiber based) and the debate over whether such networks constitute unfair competition with the private sector has become a significant policy issue (for more information on municipal broadband, see CRS Report RS20993, *Wireless Technology and Spectrum Demand: Advanced Wireless Services*, by Linda K. Moore).

COMPUTER AND INTERNET SECURITY[544]

On October 21, 2002, all 13 of the Internet's root Domain Name System servers were targeted by a distributed denial of service attack. While the attack had little overall effect on the performance of the Internet, a more sophisticated and sustainable attack might have had a more deleterious impact. As use of the Internet grows, so has concern about security of and security on the Internet. A long list of security-related incidents that have received wide-ranging media coverage (e.g. Melissa virus, the Love Bug, and the Code Red, Nimda, Slammer, and Blaster worms) represents the tip of the iceberg. More recently, hackers using Trojan horses and other techniques, were able to place keylogging software on the personal computers of people with online trading accounts to surreptitiously acquire their personal account information. The hackers used the information to access these personal accounts to buy little known stocks in which they (the hackers) had invested, driving up the price. The thieves then dumped their shares for a profit.[545] Every day, persons gain access, or try to gain access, to someone else's computer without authorization to read, copy, modify, or destroy the information contained within. These persons range from juveniles to disgruntled (ex) employees, to criminals, to competitors, to politically or socially motivated groups, to agents of foreign governments.

The extent of the problem is unknown. Much of what gets reported as computer "attacks" are probes, often conducted automatically with software widely available for even juveniles to use. But the number of instances where someone has actually gained unauthorized access is not known. Not every person or company whose computer system has been compromised reports it either to the media or to authorities. Sometimes the victim judges the incident not to be worth the trouble. Sometimes the victim may judge that the adverse publicity would be worse. Sometimes the affected parties do not even know their systems have been compromised. There is some evidence to suggest, however, that the number of incidents is increasing. According to the Computer Emergency Response Team (CERT) at Carnegie-Mellon University, the number of incidents reported to it has grown just about every year since the team's establishment — from 132 incidents in 1989 to over 137,000 incidents in 2003. Since many attacks are now coordinated and cascade throughout the Internet, CERT no longer tracks the number of incidents reported to them. While the total number of incidents may be rising exponentially, it is interesting to note that, according to the Computer Crime and Security Survey, the percentage of respondents that reported unauthorized use of their computer systems over the previous 12 months has declined since the year 2000.[546]

The impact on society from the unauthorized access or use of computers is also unknown. Again, some victims may choose not to report losses. In many cases, it is difficult or impossible to quantify the losses. But social losses are not zero. Trust in one's system may be reduced. Proprietary and/or customer information (including credit card numbers) may be compromised. Any unwanted code must be found and removed. The veracity of the system's data must be checked and restored if necessary. Money may be stolen from accounts or extorted from the victim If disruptions occur, sales may be lost. If adverse publicity occurs, future sales may be lost and stock prices may be affected. Estimates of the overall financial losses due to unauthorized access vary and are largely speculative. Estimates typically range in the billions of dollars per major event like the Love Bug virus or the series of denial¬of-service attacks of February 2000.[547] Similar estimates have been made for the Code Red worms. Estimates of losses internationally range up to the tens of billions of dollars. In the 2005 Computer Crime and Security Survey, 687 responders (out of a total of 700) estimated financial losses totaling $130 million in the previous 12 months. According to the survey, viruses accounted for the most financial losses ($43 million), followed by loss of proprietary information. Denial of service attacks accounted for $7 million in losses. Two of the online brokers whose customers' accounts were used in the "pump-and-dump" scheme mentioned above reported spending $22 million to compensate their customers.[548] For more discussion on the economic impact of attacks against computer systems, and the difficulties in measuring it, see CRS Report RL32331, *The Economic Impact of Cyber-Attacks*, by Brian Cashell, Will D. Jackson, Mark Jickling, and Baird Webel.

Aside from the losses discussed above, there is also growing concern that unauthorized access to computer systems could pose an overall national security risk should it result in the disruption of the nation's critical infrastructures (e.g., transportation systems, banking and finance, electric power generation and distribution). These infrastructures rely increasingly on computer networks to operate, and are themselves linked by computer and communication networks. In February 2003, the President's Critical Infrastructure Board (established by President George W. Bush through E.O. 13231 but later dissolved by E.O. 13286) released a *National Strategy to Secure Cyberspace. The Strategy* assigned a number of responsibilities for coordinating the protection of the nation's information infrastructure to the Department of Homeland Security. Most of the Department's efforts in cybersercurity are managed by the National Cyber Security Division (NCSD) within in the Preparedness Directorate. As part of the *Strategy*, the NCSD has assumed a major role in raising awareness of the risks associated with computer security among all users, from the home user to major corporations, and to facilitate information exchange between all parties. To this end numerous cooperative and coordinating groups and fora have been established. One such activity is U.S.-CERT, a cooperative effort by the National Cyber Security Division and Carnegie Mellon's CERT, which among other services and activities, produces alerts of new and existing attacks and guidelines for preventing or responding to them.

Congress has shown, and continues to show, a strong interest in the security of computers and the Internet. Over the years this interest has been manifested in numerous hearings by a multitude of committees and subcommittees, in both the House and the Senate. Legislation has also been passed. The federal Computer Fraud and Abuse statute (18 U.S.C. 1030) was initially added as part of the Comprehensive Crime Control Act of 1984 (P.L. 98-473). This act, as amended, makes it a federal crime to gain unauthorized access to, damage, or use in an illegal manner, protected computer systems (including federal computers, bank computers, computers used in interstate and foreign commerce).[549] Legislation specifically requiring system owners/operators to take actions to protect their computer systems has been confined to executive federal agencies (most recently, the Federal Information Security Management Act of 2002, P.L. 107-347, Title III). Other legislation is primarily aimed at protecting privacy by protecting certain personal information held by government and private sector entities and affects computer security indirectly. For example, the Gramm-Leach-Bliley Act (P.L. 106-102, Title V) and the Health Insurance Portability and Accountability Act of 1996 (HIPPA, P.L. 104-191, Title II, Subtitle F) require that entities have in place programs that protect the fmancial and health-related information, respectively, in their possession. The Sarbanes-Oxley Act of 2002 (P.P. 107-204) also indirectly affects private sector computers and networks, by requiring certain firms to certify the integrity of their financial control systems as part of their annual financial reporting requirements. To the extent that this information resides on computer systems, these requirements extend to those systems. Congress also supports a number of programs that help develop computer security education, training, and research at selected universities. For an overview of federal legislation and other federal documents associated with computer and internet security, see CRS Report RL32357, *Computer Security: A Summary of Selected Federal Laws, Executive Orders, and Presidential Directives*, by John Moteff.

It is not clear how these efforts have affected the overall security of the Internet. Given the perceived rise in security threats and attacks, there is a general sense that more must be done. Aside from the inherent vulnerabilities associated with highly interconnected information networks, two major sources of vulnerabilities exist: software, and network configuration and management. Operating systems and applications developers say they are paying greater attention to designing better security into their software products. But it is still common to have vulnerabilities found in products after they have been put on the market. In some cases, patches have had to be offered at the same time a new product is brought onto the market. Although patches typically are offered to fix these vulnerabilities, many system administrators do not keep their software/configurations current. Many intrusions take advantage of software vulnerabilities noted many months earlier, for which fixes have already been offered.

There are as yet no agreed upon industry standards for determining how secure a firm's computer system should be or for assessing how secure it is in fact. Some observers speculate that it is only a matter of time before owners of computer systems are held responsible for damage done to a third-party computer as a result of inadequately protecting their own systems.[550] Nor are there any agreed upon standards on how secure a vendor's software product should be. The federal government, in cooperation with a number of other countries, has developed a set of International Common Criteria for Information Technology Security Evaluation, to allow certified laboratories to test security products and rate their level of security for government use. These criteria may evolve into industry standards for certifying security products. Some in the security community feel that security will not improve without some requirements imposed upon the private sector. However, both users and vendors of computer software suggest that the market is sufficient to address security in the most cost-effective manner The Bush Administration, as the Clinton Administration before it, has chosen to use engagement and not regulation to encourage the private sector to improve security. However, both Administrations did not rule out the use of regulation if necessary. For a discussion of the difficulties associated with setting standards, see CRS Report RL32777, *Creating a National Framework for Cybersecurity: An Analysis oflssues and Options*, by Eric A. Fischer.

During the 109th Congress, legislation was introduced that, again, primarily addressed privacy issues with indirect impact on computer security. In light of large losses of personal information through fraud, lost records, and unauthorized access, a number of bills were introduced that extended the requirements to safeguard and protect personal information, similar to that found in Gramm-Leach-Bliley and HIPPA, to "information brokers" and/or required any organization engaged in interstate commerce holding personal information to inform consumers of any security breach that may have compromised their information. Bills commonly referred to as "Spyware" legislation were also introduced. These topics are discussed in the next section of this report. The theft of a laptop computer from the home of a employee of the Department of Veterans Affairs in May 2006, containing personal information of over 20 million military veterans, while not an Internet-related incident, renewed focus on the ability of federal agencies to enforce their own information security policies and procedures and to hold agency officials accountable. Such concern led the House to pass the Veterans Identity and Credit Security Act of 2006 (H.R. 5835) that included amendments to the Federal Information Security Management Act. The Senate did not take up the bill. Similar activity is expected in the 110th Congress.

INTERNET PRIVACY

Concerns related to Internet privacy encompass a wide range of issues. At the center of these issues is how networks can facilitate the collection and transfer of data inexpensively and on a large scale. While such data transfers can improve the efficiency and effectiveness of services, they can also pose great risk if the information is not appropriately protected. One example is the surreptitious installation of software ("spyware") by website operators to collect personally identifiable information (PII) and share that information with third parties, usually without the knowledge or consent of the people concerned. Another example is identity theft, which is a form of fraud in which the personal identifying information of an individual, such as a Social Security number, name, or date of birth, is co-opted by another person to facilitate committing a criminal or fraudulent act by impersonating the victim.

Spyware[551]

Spyware is another focus of congressional concern. There is no firm definition of spyware, but the most common example is software products that include a method by which information is collected about the use of the computer on which the software is installed, and the user. When the computer is connected to the Internet, the software periodically relays the information back to the software manufacturer or a marketing company. Some spyware traces a user's Web activity and causes advertisements to suddenly appear on the user's monitor — called "pop-up" ads — in response. Typically, users have no knowledge that the software they obtained included spyware and that it is now resident on their computers. A central point of the debate is whether new laws are needed, or if industry self-regulation, coupled with enforcement actions under existing laws such as the Federal Trade Commission Act, is sufficient. Most recently, the 109th Congress passed the Undertaking Spam, Spyware, And Fraud Enforcement With Enforcers beyond Borders Act of 2005 (US SAFE WEB) (P.L. 109-455). The bill allows the FTC and parallel foreign law enforcement agencies to share information while investigating allegations of "unfair and deceptive practices" that involve foreign commerce.

Identity Theft and "Phishing"[552]

Identity theft is a form of fraud in which the personal identifying information of an individual, such as a Social Security number, name, or date of birth, is co-opted by another person to facilitate committing a criminal or fraudulent act by impersonating the victim.

Identity theft, also sometimes referred to as identity fraud, does not usually occur as a stand-alone crime. Instead, identity theft is often committed as part of some other fraud or white-collar crime, such as illegally obtaining credit, taking over existing financial accounts, or establishing cellular phone service in the victim's name An identity thief could also take other actions on behalf of the victim, such as establishing residency/citizenship, securing employment, obtaining government benefits, and committing other crimes in the victim's name In addition, identity theft can play a facilitating role in potentially more violent crimes such as drug trafficking, people smuggling, and international terrorism.[553]

While identity theft is not solely an Internet issue, a number of high profile data breaches involving the personally identifiable information (PII) of citizens and consumers has drawn significant attention to the issue. Among the most recent incidents was the theft of a laptop containing the names, dates of birth, and other information of more than 26 million veterans. Although the laptop was eventually recovered and it is believed that the data was not accessed, the incident highlighted the ease with which the PII of large numbers of people could be taken at one time.

Another way identity theft can happen is through "phishing." Phishing refers to a practice where someone misrepresents their identity or authority in order to induce another person to provide PII over the Internet. Some common phishing scams involve e-mails that purport to be from a financial institution, ISP, or other trusted company claiming that a person's record has been lost. The e-mail directs the person to a website that mimics the legitimate business' website and asks the person to enter a credit card number and other PII so the record can be restored. In fact, the e-mail or website is controlled by a third party who is attempting to extract information that will be used in identity theft or other crimes. The FTC issued a consumer alert on phishing in June 2004.[554]

Several laws restrict the disclosure of consumer information and require companies to ensure the security and integrity of the data in certain contexts — Section 5 of the Federal Trade Commission Act, the Fair Credit Reporting Act (FCRA), and Title V of the Gramm-Leach-Bliley Act. Congress also has passed several laws specifically related to identity theft: the 1998 Identity Theft and Assumption Deterrence Act; the 2003 Fair and Accurate Credit Transactions (FACT) Act; and the 2004 Identity Theft Penalty Enhancement Act. Those laws are summarized in CRS Report RL31919, *Remedies Available to Victims of Identity Theft*, by Angie A. Welborn. For information on state laws and pending federal legislation, see CRS Report RS22484, *Identity Theft Laws: State Penalties and Remedies and Pending Federal Bills*, by Kristin Thornblad.

"Spam": Unsolicited Commercial Electronic Mail[555]

One aspect of increased use of the Internet for electronic mail (e-mail) has been the advent of unsolicited advertising, also called "unsolicited commercial e-mail (UCE)," "unsolicited bulk e-mail," "junk e-mail, "or "spam." Complaints focus on the fact that some spam contains or has links to pornography, that much of it is fraudulent, that it is a nuisance, and the volume is increasing. Although consumers are most familiar with spam on their personal computers, it also is becoming an issue in text messaging on wireless telephones and personal digital assistants (PDAs).

In 2003, Congress passed a federal anti-spam law, the CAN-SPAM Act (P.L. 108-187), which became effective on January 1, 2004. The act preempts state laws that specifically address spam but not state laws that are not specific to e-mail, such as trespass, contract, or tort law, or other state laws to the extent they relate to fraud or computer crime. It does not ban unsolicited commercial e-mail. Rather, it allows marketers to send commercial e-mail as long as it conforms with the law, such as including a legitimate opportunity for consumers to "opt-out" of receiving future commercial e-mails from that sender. It does not require a centralized "do not e-mail" registry to be created by the Federal Trade Commission (FTC), similar to the National Do Not Call registry for telemarketing. The law requires only that the FTC develop a plan and timetable for establishing a "Do Not E-mail" registry and to inform Congress of any concerns it has with regard to establishing it. The FTC reported to Congress in June 2004 that without a technical system to authenticate the origin of e-mail messages, a registry would not reduce the amount of spam, and, in fact, might increase it. Authentication is a technical approach that could be used to control spam that is under study by a number of groups, including ISPs, who are attempting to develop a single authentication standard for the industry. Additionally, the CAN-SPAM Act included a provision requiring the FCC to establish regulations to protect wireless consumers from spam.[556]

Many argue that technical approaches, such as authentication, and consumer education, are needed to solve the spam problem — that legislation alone is insufficient. Nonetheless, there is considerable interest in assessing how effective the CAN-SPAM Act is in reducing spam. The effectiveness of the law may be difficult to determine, however, if for no other reason than there are various definitions of spam. Proponents of the law argue that consumers are most irritated by fraudulent e-mail, and that the law should reduce the volume of such e-mail because of the civil and criminal penalties included therein. Skeptics counter that consumers object to unsolicited commercial e-mail, and since the bill legitimizes commercial e-mail (as long as it conforms with the law's provisions), consumers actually may receive more, not fewer, unsolicited commercial e-mail messages. Thus, whether "spam" is reduced depends in part on how it is defined.

In December 2005, the FTC submitted a report to Congress, as required under the CAN-SPAM Act, on the act's effectiveness and enforcement, and whether any changes are needed.[557] Based on information from ISPs, the general public, e-marketers, law enforcers, and technologists, the report concluded that the act has been effective in two areas: legitimate online marketers have adopted the "best practices" mandated by the act, and the act provides an additional tool for law enforcement officials and ISPs to bring suits against spammers. However, it also concluded that some aspects of the spam problem have not changed, such as its international dimension. It also reported on a number of "troubling" changes in the e-mail landscape, such as the inclusion of malicious content ("malware") in spam messages. The report outlined three steps to further improve the effectiveness of the act: passage of legislation to improve the FTC's ability to trace spammers and sellers who operate outside U.S. borders; continued consumer education; and continued improvement in anti-spam technologies, especially domain-level authentication.

Most recently, the 109th Congress passed the Undertaking Spam, Spyware, And Fraud Enforcement With Enforcers beyond Borders Act of 2005 (US SAFE WEB) (P.L. 109-455). The bill allows the FTC and parallel foreign law enforcement agencies to share information while investigating allegations of "unfair and deceptive practices" that involve foreign commerce, but raised some privacy concerns because the FTC would not be required to make public any of the information it obtained through foreign sources.

PROTECTING CHILDREN FROM UNSUITABLE MATERIAL[558]

Preventing children from encountering unsuitable material as they use the Web has been a major congressional concern for many years.[559] In response to this concern, Congress has passed such laws as the 1996 Communications Decency Act (CDA), the 1998 Child Online Protection Act (COPA), and the 2000 Children's Internet Protection Act (CIPA), all of which dealt in some way with the content found on the Internet. More recently, however, additional attention has been given to protecting children from exploitation and predators on the Internet. For example, in the last few years, social networking sites, such as MySpace, have become popular with teenagers and young adults. Unfortunately, there have been a number of incidents recently in which children were abducted and/or lured to meet adults over these services. Because of these incidents, Congress began exploring ways to limit children's access to these sites, or at least to limit the ability of adults to contact children. During the 109th Congress, H.R. 5319, the Deleting Online Predators Act of 2006 (DOPA), would have amended the Communications Act of 1934 to prohibit schools and libraries receiving "E-Rate" funding from providing access to these types of websites to minors. The proposal was controversial because the definition of social networking sites could potentially limit access to a wide range of websites, including many with harmless or educational material. Although this bill did not pass, this issue is likely to receive continued attention in the 110th Congress.

"Data retention" is another topic that is likely to receive continued attention from policymakers in the 110th Congress. Data retention is the practice of ISPs maintaining electronic records of subscriber activity, regardless of whether those records have been identified as being needed for an ongoing investigation. At this time, ISPs typically discard records that log subscriber activity when those records are no longer required for business purposes (e.g., network monitoring, billing disputes). However, law enforcement agencies have expressed that they would like data to be retained for longer periods – in general, the time periods suggested have ranged from one to two years – to ensure they can successfully prosecute online child predators and individuals producing and downloading child pornography. Proposals that have been discussed range from simply maintaining records of what websites subscribers visit to requiring the storage of the contents of e-mail messages and individual web pages visited. ISPs have expressed a number of concerns, including the cost of retaining the data, web content being included in data retention legislation, and the privacy and security risks of having such a massive data warehouse available. Opponents of such legislation note that current law already allows law enforcement agencies to mandate data retention for 90-days;[560] further, privacy advocates are concerned that police would potentially be able to obtain records of e-mail chatter, Web browsing, or chat room activity that normally are discarded.

INTERNET DOMAIN NAMES[561]

The 110th Congress will continue to monitor issues related to the Internet domain name system (DNS). Internet domain names were created to provide users with a simple location name for computers on the Internet, rather than using the more complex, unique Internet Protocol (IP) number that designates their specific location. As the Internet has grown, the method for allocating and designating domain names has become increasingly controversial.

Background

The Internet originated with research funding provided by the Department of Defense Advanced Research Projects Agency (DARPA) to establish a military network. As its use expanded, a civilian segment evolved with support from the National Science Foundation (NSF) and other science agencies. No formal statutory authorities or international agreements govern the management and operation of the Internet and the DNS. Prior to 1993, NSF was responsible for registration of nonmilitary generic Top Level Domains (gTLDs) such as .com, .org, and .net. In 1993, the NSF entered into a five-year cooperative agreement with Network Solutions, Inc. (NSI) to operate Internet domain name registration services. With the cooperative agreement between NSI and NSF due to expire in 1998, the Clinton Administration, through the Department of Commerce (DOC), began exploring ways to transfer administration of the DNS to the private sector.

In the wake of much discussion among Internet stakeholders, and after extensive public comment on a previous proposal, the DOC, on June 5, 1998, issued a final statement of policy, *Management of Internet Names and Addresses* (also known as the "White Paper"). The White Paper stated that the U.S. government was prepared to recognize and enter into agreement with "a new not-for-profit corporation formed by private sector Internet stakeholders to administer policy for the Internet name and address system." On October 2, 1998, the DOC accepted a proposal for an Internet Corporation for Assigned Names and Numbers (ICANN). On November 25, 1998, DOC and ICANN signed an official Memorandum of Understanding (MOU), whereby DOC and ICANN agreed to jointly design, develop, and test the mechanisms, methods, and procedures necessary to transition management responsibility for DNS functions to a private-sector not-for-profit entity.

The White Paper also signaled DOC's intention to ramp down the government's Cooperative Agreement with NSI, with the objective of introducing competition into the domain name space while maintaining stability and ensuring an orderly transition. During this transition period, government obligations will be terminated as DNS responsibilities are transferred to ICANN. Specifically, NSI committed to a timetable for development of a Shared Registration System that permits multiple registrars to provide registration services within the .com, .net., and .org gTLDs. NSI (now VersiSign) will continue to administer the root server system until receiving further instruction from the government.

Significant disagreements between NSI on the one hand, and ICANN and DOC on the other, arose over how a successful and equitable transition would be made from NSI's previous status as exclusive registrar of .com, org. and net. domain names, to a system that allows multiple and competing registrars. On November 10, 1999, ICANN, NSI, and DOC formally signed an agreement which provided that NSI (now VeriSign) was required to sell its registrar operation by May 10, 2001 in order to retain control of the dot-com registry until 2007. In April 2001, arguing that the registrar business is now highly competitive, VeriSign reached a new agreement with ICANN whereby its registry and registrar businesses would not have to be separated. With DOC approval, ICANN and VeriSign signed the formal agreement on May 25, 2001. On September 17, 2003, ICANN and the Department of Commerce agreed to extend their MOU until September 30, 2006. The MOU specified transition tasks which ICANN has agreed to address, including implementing an objective process for selecting new Top Level Domains; implementing an effective strategy for multi¬lingual communications and international outreach; and developing a contingency plan, consistent with the international nature of the Internet, to ensure continuity of operations in the event of a severe disruption of operations.

On June 30, 2005, Michael Gallagher, Assistant Secretary of Commerce for Communications and Information and Administrator of the National Telecommunications and Information Administration (NTIA), stated the U.S. Government's principles on the Internet's domain name system. Specifically, NTIA states that the U.S. Government "intends to preserve the security and stability" of the DNS, and that "the United States is committed to taking no action that would have the potential to adversely impact the effective and efficient operation of the DNS and will therefore maintain its historic role in authorizing changes or modifications to the authoritative root zone file."[562] The NTIA statement also says that governments have legitimate interests in the management of their country code top level domains, that ICANN is the appropriate technical manager of the DNS, and that dialogue related to Internet governance should continue in relevant multiple fora. On May 23, 2006, NTIA announced an inquiry and public meeting seeking comment on the progress of the transition of the technical coordination and management of the DNS to the private sector. The public meeting was held on July 26, 2006.

On September 29, 2006, DOC announced a new Joint Project Agreement with ICANN which continues the transition to the private sector of the coordination of technical functions relating to management of the DNS. The Joint Project Agreement extends through September 30, 2009, and focuses on institutionalizing transparency and accountability mechanisms within ICANN.

Issues

Congressional Committees (primarily the Senate Committee on Commerce, Science and Transportation and the House Committee on Energy and Commerce) maintain oversight on how the Department of Commerce manages and oversees ICANN' s activities and policies. Some issues of current concern are discussed below.

Governance

The United Nations (UN), at the December 2003 World Summit on the Information Society (WSIS), debated and agreed to study the issue of how to achieve greater international involvement in the governance of the Internet and the domain name system in particular. The study was conducted by the UN's Working Group on Internet Governance (WGIG). On July 14, 2005, the WGIG released its report, stating that no single government should have a preeminent role in relation to international Internet governance, calling for further internationalization of Internet governance, and proposing the creation of a new global forum for Internet stakeholders. Four possible models were put forth, including two involving the creation of new Internet governance bodies linked to the UN. Under three of the four models, ICANN would either be supplanted or made accountable to a higher intergovernmental body. The report's conclusions were scheduled to be considered during the second phase of the WSIS to be held in Tunis in November 2005. U.S. officials stated their opposition to transferring control and administration of the domain name system from ICANN to any international body. Similarly, the 109th Congress expressed its support for maintaining U.S. control over ICANN. On November 16, 2005, the House unanimously passed H.Con.Res. 268, which expresses the sense of the Congress that the current system for management of the domain name system works, and that "the authoritative root zone server should remain physically located in the United States and the Secretary of Commerce should maintain oversight of ICANN so that ICANN can continue to manage the day-to-day operation of the Internet's domain name and addressing system well, remain responsive to all Internet stakeholders worldwide, and otherwise fulfill its core technical mission." A similar resolution, S.Res. 323, was passed by the Senate on November 18, 2005 and calls on the President to "continue to oppose any effort to transfer control of the Internet to the United Nations or any other international entity."

The European Union (EU) initially supported the U.S. position. However, during September 2005 preparatory meetings, the EU seemingly shifted its support towards an approach which favored an enhanced international role in governing the Internet. Conflict at the WSIS Tunis Summit over control of the domain name system was averted by the announcement, on November 15, 2005, of an Internet governance agreement between the U.S., the EU, and over 100 other nations. Under this agreement, ICANN and the U.S. will remain in control of the domain name system. A new international group under the auspices of the UN will be formed — the Internet Governance Forum — which will provide an ongoing forum for all stakeholders (both governments and nongovernmental groups) to discuss and debate Internet policy issues. The Internet Governance Forum is slated to run for five years and will not have binding authority. The group held its first meeting on October 30-November 2, 2006 in Athens, Greece. The issue of ICANN and international DNS governance was not formally addressed by the conference.

ICANN-Verisign Agreement and the .com Registry

As part of a legal settlement of a long-running dispute between ICANN and Verisign, on February 28, 2006, the ICANN Board of Directors approved (by a vote of 9-5) a new .com registry agreement with Verisign. Under this settlement, Verisign will run the .com registry until 2012 (with a presumption that the agreement will be renewed beyond that date), and will be able to raise domain registration fees by 7% in four of the next six years. These registration fees refer to the current $6 fee that a registrar (such as GoDaddy or Register.com) pays the .com registry operator (Verisign) for each .com domain name registration purchased by the consumer. Under the agreement, Verisign will pay ICANN a one-time sum of $625,000 to implement the agreement, as well as a yearly registry fee, starting at $6 million per year, and going up over the next two years to approximately $12 million.

Critics of the ICANN-Verisign settlement assert that the agreement is anticompetitive, giving Verisign a virtually permanent monopoly over the lucrative .com registry, while also enabling Verisign to raise registration fees without justification. Defenders of the settlement argue that the agreement is necessary to ensure the stability and security of the Internet by ensuring the fmancial stability of ICANN, and by allowing Verisign the flexibility to raise revenue for upgrading its infrastructure. On June 7, 2006, the House Small Business Committee held a hearing on the ICANN-Verisign .com agreement entitled, "Contracting the Internet: Does ICANN create a barrier to small business?"

The ICANN-Verisign .com agreement was approved by NTIA/DOC on November 30, 2006. As a condition of its approval, NTIA retains oversight over any changes to the pricing provisions of, or renewals of, the new .com registry agreement. Approval of any renewal will occur if NTIA concludes that the approval will serve the public interest in the continued security and stability of the DNS, and in the operation of the .com registry at reasonable prices, terms and conditions.

Protecting Children on the Internet

In the 107th Congress, legislation sought to create a "kids-friendly top level domain name" that would contain only age-appropriate content. The Dot Kids Implementation and Efficiency Act of 2002 was signed into law on December 4, 2002 (P.L. 107-317), and authorizes the National Telecommunications and Information Administration (NTIA) to require the .us registry operator (currently NeuStar) to establish, operate, and maintain a second level domain within the .us TLD that is restricted to material suitable for minors.

In the 108th Congress, P.L. 108-21/S. 151 (PROTECT Act) contains a provision (Section 108: Misleading Domain Names on the Internet) which makes it a punishable crime to knowingly use a misleading domain name with the intent to deceive a person into viewing obscenity on the Internet. Increased penalties are provided for deceiving minors into viewing harmful material. In the 109th Congress, the Adam Walsh Child Protection and Safety Act of 2006 (P.L. 109-248), signed into law on July 27, 2006, increases the maximum sentence from four years to ten years for deceiving minors into viewing harmful material.

Meanwhile, on June 1, 2005, ICANN announced that it had entered into commercial and technical negotiations with a registry company (ICM Registry) to operate a new ".xxx" domain, which would be designated for use by adult websites. Registration by adult websites into the .xxx domain would be purely voluntary, and those sites would not be required to give up their existing sites. Announcement of a .xxx domain has proven controversial. With the ICANN Board scheduled to consider final approval of the .xxx domain on August 16, 2005, the Department of Commerce sent a letter to ICANN requesting that adequate additional time be provided to allow ICANN to address the objections of individuals expressing concerns about the impact of pornography on families and children and opposing the creation of a new top level domain devoted to adult content. ICANN's Government Advisory Committee (GAC) also requested more time before the final decision. At the March 2006 Board meeting in New Zealand, the ICANN Board authorized ICANN staff to continue negotiations with ICM Registry to address concerns raised by the DOC and the GAC. However, on May 10, 2006, the Board voted voted 9-5 against accepting the proposed agreement, but did not rule out accepting a revised agreement. Subsequently, on January 5, 2007, ICANN published for public comment a proposed revised agreement with ICM Registry to establish a .xxx domain The revised agreement would include additional safeguards intended to protect children online[563]

Meanwhile in the 109th Congress, on March 16, 2006, Senator Baucus introduced the Cyber Safety for Kids Act of 2006 (S. 2426), which would require NTIA to compel ICANN to establish a new top level domain name — such as .xxx—exclusively for material harmful to minors. Websites with material harmful to minors would be required to switch to the new domain Those that do not would face civil penalties from NTIA.[564] S. 2426 was ultimately not enacted by the 109th Congress.

Trademark Disputes

The increase in conflicts over property rights to certain trademarked names has resulted in a number of lawsuits. The White Paper called upon the World Intellectual Property Organization (WIPO) to develop a set of recommendations for trademark/domain name dispute resolutions, and to submit those recommendations to ICANN. At ICANN's August 1999 meeting in Santiago, the board of directors adopted a dispute resolution policy to be applied uniformly by all ICANN-accredited registrars. Under this policy, registrars receiving complaints will take no action until receiving instructions from the domain-name holder or an order of a court or arbitrator. An exception is made for "abusive registrations" (i.e., cybersquatting and cyberpiracy), whereby a special administrative procedure (conducted largely online by a neutral panel, lasting 45 days or less, and costing about $1000) will resolve the dispute. Implementation of ICANN's Domain Name Dispute Resolution Policy commenced on December 9, 1999. Meanwhile, the 106th Congress passed the Anticybersquatting Consumer Protection Act (incorporated into P.L. 106-113, the FY2000 Consolidated Appropriations Act). The act gives courts the authority to order the forfeiture, cancellation, and/or transfer of domain names registered in "bad faith" that are identical or similar to trademarks, and provides for statutory civil damages of at least $1,000, but not more than $100,000, per domain name identifier.

Privacy

Any person or entity who registers a domain name is required to provide contact information (phone number, address, email) which is entered into a public online database (the "WHOIS" database). The scope and accessibility of WHOIS database information has been an issue of contention. Privacy advocates have argued that access to such information should be limited, while many businesses, intellectual property interests, law enforcement agencies, and the U.S. Government have argued that complete and accurate WHOIS information should continue to be publicly accessible. Over the past several years, ICANN has debated this issue through its Generic Names Supporting Organization (GNSO). The GNSO—composed of stakeholder constituencies — is developing policy recommendations on what data should be publicly available through the WHOIS database.

On April 12, 2006, the GNSO approved an official "working definition" for the purpose of the public display of WHOIS information. The GNSO supported a narrow technical defmition favored by privacy advocates, registries, registrars, and non-commercial user constituencies, rather then a more expansive definition favored by intellectual property interests, business constituencies, Internet service providers, law enforcement agencies, and the Department of Commerce (through its participation in ICANN's Governmental Advisory Committee). At ICANN's June 2006 meeting, opponents of limiting access to WHOIS data continued urging ICANN to reconsider the working definition. The GNSO will next decide what data should be available for public access in the context of the working definition.[565] On July 18, 2006, the House Committee on Financial Services, Subcommittee on Financial Institutions and Consumer Credit held a hearing on ICANN and the WHOIS database.

Meanwhile, over the past several years, with the WHOIS database continuing to be publically accessible, registrants who wish to maintain their privacy have been able to register anonymously using a proxy service offered by some registrars. In February 2005, the National Telecommunications and Information Administration (NTIA) — which has authority over the .us domain name — notified Neustar (the company that administers .us) that proxy or private domain registrations will no longer be allowed for .us domain name registrations, and that registrars must provide correct WHOIS information for all existing customers by January 26, 2006. According to NTIA, this action will provide an assurance of accuracy to the American public and to law enforcement officials. The NTIA policy is opposed by privacy groups and registrars (such as Go Daddy) who argue that the privacy, anonymity, and safety of people registering .us domain names will be needlessly compromised.

In a related development, during the 108th Congress, the Fraudulent Online Identity Sanctions Act was incorporated as Title II of H.R. 3632, the Intellectual Property Protection and Courts Amendments Act of 2004, signed by the President on December 23, 2004 (P.L. 108-482). The act increases criminal penalties for those who submit false contact information when registering a domain name that is subsequently used to commit a crime or engage in copyright or trademark infringement.

Government Information Technology Management[566]

The evolving role of the Internet in the political economy of the United States continues to attract increased congressional attention to government information technology management issues. Interest has been further heightened by national information infrastructure development efforts, e-government projects, and homeland security initiatives. Although wide-ranging, some of the most significant information technology management challenges facing the federal government include FCC regulation of converging technologies, funding for information technology research and development, ongoing development and oversight of electronic government (e-government) initiatives, and the growing use of open source software by federal agencies.

The Federal Communications Commission[567]

One of the most significant issues facing the FCC is the evolution of the communications industry towards an all-digital, broadband world that has blurred the distinctions between services, also called "convergence." The FCC has restructured over the past few years to better reflect the realities of convergence, but the agency is still required to adhere to the statutory requirements of its governing legislation, the Communications Act of 1934. Thus, while convergence has made distinguishing among types of data increasingly difficult, the FCC must continue to differentiate among services based on the distinctions drawn in the 1934 Act. Unfortunately, when all data looks the same and functionally similar services are provided by companies governed by different titles of the 1934 Act, questions of fairness and competitive advantage may arise. As newer technologies and services are developed and deployed, applying legacy regulations to them may begin to appear more strained.

The FCC has continued to address a number of issues directly related to convergence: the regulatory classification of services via the Internet protocol (e.g., voice over Internet Protocol [VoIP]) and law enforcement's ability to conduct wiretaps effectively (i.e., using the Communications Assistance for Law Enforcement Act [CALEA]). During the 110th Congress, as there was during the 109th Congress, there may be legislation to enact a national franchising system for video service providers. If so, this will likely require additional attention from the FCC as well.

The FCC will also remain focused on broadband deployment. The agency will continue to monitor its policies to encourage new providers to roll out new services (e.g., power companies will be deploying broadband over powerlines [BPL]) as well as continue to promote deployment to underserved areas and populations, i.e., rural and low-income communities, through universal service and other programs (e.g., the E-Rate).

One of the difficulties in addressing the issues facing the FCC is that so many of them now intersect. So many of the broadband issues are inter-related that it is often difficult to sort out where one issue ends and another begins. For example, VoIP, CALEA, and BPL are all tied to the concept of broadband convergence and reliance on the Internet for information and it becomes difficult, if not impossible, to discuss one without touching on the others. Effectively addressing these types of issues may well be the greatest challenge facing both the FCC and Congress in the near future.

Information Technology R&D[568]

At the federal level, almost all of the funding for information science and technology and Internet development is part of a single government-wide initiative, the Networking and Information Technology Research and Development program (NITRD). This program was previously (1997-2000) called the Computing, Information, and Communications program (CIC) and, prior to that (1992-1997), the High Performance Computing and Communications program (HPCC). The NITRD is an interagency effort to coordinate key advances in information technology (IT) research and leverage funding into broader advances in computing and networking technologies. Under the NITRD, participating agencies receive support for high- performance computing science and technology, information technology software and hardware, networks and Internet-driven applications, and education and training for personnel. The FY2007 budget calls for $3.074 billion for the NITRD Program, an increase of $0.21 billion over the FY2006 budget estimate of $2.855 billion.

Research emphases are focused on eight program component areas (also called PCAs): High-End Computing (HEC) Infrastructure and Applications, HEC Research and Development, Cyber Security and Information Assurance, Human Computer Interaction and Information Management, Large Scale Networking, Software Design and Productivity, High Confidence Software and Systems, and Social, Economic, and Workforce Implications of IT and IT Workforce Development. Key issues facing congressional policymakers include whether NITRD is accomplishing its goals and objectives to enhance U.S. information technology research and development, whether the funding level is appropriate or should be changed to reflect changing U.S. priorities, and defining the private sector's role in this initiative.

Electronic Government (E-Government)[569]

Electronic government (e-government) is an evolving concept, meaning different things to different people. However, it has significant relevance to four important areas of governance: (1) delivery of services (government-to-citizen, or G2C); (2) providing information (also G2C); (3) facilitating the procurement of goods and services (government-to-business, or G2B, and business-to-government, or B2G); and (4) facilitating efficient exchanges within and between agencies (government-to-government, or G2G). For policymakers concerned about e-government, a central area of concern is developing a comprehensive but flexible strategy to coordinate the disparate e-government initiatives across the federal government.

The movement to put government online raises as many issues as it provides new opportunities. Some of these issues include, but are not limited to: security, privacy, management of governmental technology resources, accessibility of government services (including "digital divide" concerns as a result of a lack of skills or access to computers, discussed earlier), and preservation of public information (maintaining comparable freedom of information procedures for digital documents as exist for paper documents). Although these issues are neither new nor unique to e-government, they do present the challenge of performing governance functions online without sacrificing the accountability of, or public access to, government that citizens have grown to expect. Some industry groups have also raised concerns about the U.S. government becoming a publicly funded market competitor through the provision of fee-for-services such as the U.S. Postal Service's now-discontinued eBillPay service, which allowed consumers to schedule and make payments to creditors online [http://www.usps.com/paymentservices/ops_discontinued.htm].

E-government initiatives vary significantly in their breadth and depth from state to state and agency to agency. Perhaps one of the most well-known federal examples is the FirstGov website [http://www.firstgov.gov], which first went online on September 22, 2000. FirstGov is a Web portal designed to serve as a single locus point for finding federal government information on the Internet. The FirstGov site also provides access to a variety of state and local government resources. Another example is the Grants.gov initiative [http://www.grants.gov/], which is designed to provide a single portal for all available federal grants, enabling users to search, download applications, and apply for grants online At the Department of Treasury, the Internal Revenue Service (IRS) administers the Free File initiative [http://www.irs.goviefile/article/0,,id=11 89 86,00.html], which has partnered with industry to provide free online tax preparation and electronic filing services for eligible taxpayers.

Pursuant to the July 18, 2001, OMB Memorandum M-01-28, an E-Government Task Force was established to create a strategy for achieving the Bush Administration's e-government goals.[570] In doing so, the Task Force identified 23 interagency initiatives designed to better integrate agency operations and information technology investments. These initiatives, sometimes referred to as the Quicksilver projects, are grouped into four categories; government-to-citizen, government-to-government, government-to-business, and internal effectiveness and efficiency. Examples of these initiatives include an e-authentication project led by the General Services Administration (GSA) to increase the use of digital signatures, the eligibility assistance online project (also referred to as GovBenefits.gov) led by the Department of Labor to create a common access point for information regarding government benefits available to citizens, and the Small Business Administration's One-Stop Business Compliance project, being designed to help businesses navigate legal and regulatory requirements. A 24th initiative, a government wide payroll process project, was subsequently added by the President's Management Council. In 2002 the e-Clearance initiative, originally included as part of the Enterprise Human Resources Integration project, was established as a separate project, for a total of 25 initiatives. Since that time, the Bush Administration has reclassified the e-Authentication initiative as "a separate initiative that provides secure and robust authentication services to the 24 [i]nitiatives," bringing the official tally again to 24 initiatives.[571]

As the initial round of e-government projects has matured, OMB has focused attention on initiatives that consolidate information technology systems in nine functional areas, or Lines of Business (LoB). These include financial management, human resource management, grants management, case management, federal health architecture, information security, budget formulation and evaluation, geospatial systems, and information technology infrastructure. These initiatives were chosen, in part, because they represent core business functions common to many departments and agencies, and/or have the potential to reap significant efficiency and efficacy gains. These LoB initiatives are anticipated to create $5 billion in savings over 10 years.

On December 17, 2002, President Bush signed the E-Government Act of 2002 (P.L. 107-347) into law. The law contains a variety of provisions related to federal government information technology management, information security, and the provision of services and information electronically. One of the most recognized provisions involves the creation of an Office of Electronic Government within OMB. The Office is headed by an Administrator, who is responsible for carrying out a variety of information resources management (IRM) functions, as well as administering the interagency E-Government Fund provided for by the law.

For the 110th Congress, continued oversight of the Quicksilver projects, the implementation of the E-Government Act, and the development and funding of the second generation Lines of Business e-government initiatives are the primary oversight issues. Other issues include ongoing efforts to develop a federal enterprise architecture, which serves as a blueprint of the business functions of an organization, and the technology used to carry out these functions [http://www.whitehouse.gov/omb/egov/a-1-fea.html]; the recruitment and retention of IT managers, at both the chief information officer (CIO) and project manager levels; and balancing the sometimes competing demands of e-government and homeland security.

Open Source Software[572]

The use of open source software by the federal government has been gaining attention as organizations continue to search for opportunities to enhance their information technology (IT) operations while containing costs. A growing number of state and local governments have also been exploring the official adoption of open source software. Likewise, open source software may also play a role in the growth of regional health information organizations (RHIOs), as part of an effort to spread the use of e-health records. For the federal government and Congress, the debate over the use of open source software intersects several other issues, including, but not limited to, the development of homeland security and e-government initiatives, improving government information technology management practices, strengthening computer security, and protecting intellectual property rights. In the 110th Congress, the debate over open source software is anticipated to revolve primarily around information security and intellectual property rights, including the possible development of a legal definition of open source software. However, issues related to cost and quality are likely to be raised as well.

Open source software refers to a computer program whose source code, or programming instructions, is made available to the general public to be improved or modified as the user wishes. Some examples of open source software include the Linux operating system and Apache Web server software. In contrast, *closed source*, or proprietary, programs are those whose source code is not made available and can only be altered by the software manufacturer. In the case of closed source software, updates to a program are usually distributed in the form of a patch or as a new version of the program that the user can install but not alter. Some examples of closed source software include Microsoft Word and Corel WordPerfect. The majority of software products most commonly used, such as operating systems, word processing programs, and databases, are closed source programs.

For proponents, open source software is often viewed as a means to reduce an organization's dependence on the software products of a few companies while possibly improving the security and stability of one's computing infrastructure. For critics, open source software is often viewed as a threat to intellectual property rights with unproven cost and quality benefits. So far there appear to be no systematic analyses available that have conclusively compared closed source to open source software on the issue of security. In practice, computer security is highly dependent on how an application is configured, maintained, and monitored. Similarly, the costs of implementing an open source solution are dependent upon factors such as the cost of acquiring the hardware/software, investments in training for IT personnel and end users, maintenance and support costs, and the resources required to convert data and applications to work in the new computing environment. Consequently, some computer experts suggest that it is not possible to conclude that either open source or closed source software is inherently more secure or more cost efficient.

The official U.S. federal government policy regarding the use of open source software by government agencies is described in a July 2004 Office of Management and Budget (OMB) memorandum on software acquisition, M-04-16 Memoranda for Senior Procurement Executives, Chief Information Officers, *Software Acquisition*. The memorandum states that the policies guiding government information technology investment decisions are "technology and vendor neutral" and that agencies' technology choices "must be consistent with the agency's enterprise architecture and the Federal Enterprise Architecture."[573] Agencies are also instructed to take into account a number of other merit-based factors, including information security, licensing requirements, and total cost of ownership. Implicit in these requirements is an expectation that agencies will also make choices based on the quality of the product.

The growing emphasis on improved information security and critical infrastructure protection overall, will likely be an influential factor in future decisions to implement open source solutions. The rapidly changing computer environment may also foster the use of a combination of open source and closed source applications, rather than creating a need to choose one option at the exclusion of another.

APPENDIX A: LIST OF ACRONYMS

Alphabetical Listing

B2B	Business-to-Business
B2G	Business-to-Government
BOC	Bell Operating Company
CIO	Chief Information Officer
DMA	Direct Marketing Association
DNS	Domain Name System
DOC	Department of Commerce
DSL	Digital Subscriber Line
FBI	Federal Bureau of Investigation
FCC	Federal Communications Commission
FTC	Federal Trade Commission
G2B	Government-to-Business
G2C	Government-to-Citizen
G2G	Government-to-Government
GAO	Government Accountability Office (formerly General Accounting Office)
GSA	General Services Administration
gTLD	generic Top Level Domain
ICANN	Internet Corporation for Assigned Names and Numbers
ILEC	Incumbent Local Exchange Carrier
IP	Internet Protocol
ISP	Internet Service Provider
IT	Information Technology
LATA	Local Access and Transport Area
LEC	Local Exchange Carrier
MOU	Memorandum of Understanding
NGI	Next Generation Internet
NIST	National Institute for Standards and Technology (part of Department of Commerce)
NSI	Network Solutions, Inc,
NSF	National Science Foundation
NTIA	National Telecommunications and Information Administration (part of Department of Commerce)
OMB	Office of Management and Budget
OPA	Online Privacy Alliance
OS S	Open Source Software
SSN	Social Security Number
TLD	Top Level Domain
UCE	Unsolicited Commercial E-mail
WIPO	World Intellectual Property Organization

Categorical Listing

U.S. Government Entities	
DOC	Department of Commerce
FBI	Federal Bureau of Investigation
FCC	Federal Communications Commission
FTC	Federal Trade Commission
GAO	Government Accountability Office (formerly General Accounting Office)
GSA	General Services Administration
NIST	National Institute of Standards and Technology (part of Department of Commerce)
NSF	National Science Foundation
NTIA	National Telecommunications and Information Administration (part of Department of Commerce)
OMB	Office of Management and Budget
Private Sector Entities	
BOC	Bell Operating Company
DMA	Direct Marketing Association
ICANN	Internet Corporation for Assigned Names and Numbers
ILEC	Incumbent Local Exchange Carrier
ISP	Internet Service Provider
LEC	Local Exchange Carrier
NSI	Network Solutions, Inc.
General Types of Internet Services	
B2B	Business-to-Business
B2G	Business-to-Government
G2B	Government-to-Business
G2C	Government-to-Citizen
G2G	Government-to-Government
Internet and Telecommunications Terminology	
CIO	Chief Information Officer
DNS	Domain Name System
DSL	Digital Subscriber Line
gTLD	generic Top Level Domain
IP	Internet Protocol
IT	Information Technology
LATA	Local Access and Transport Area
NGI	Next Generation Internet
OSS	Open Source Software
TLD	Top Level Domain
UCE	Unsolicited Commercial E-mail
Other	
MOU	Memorandum of Understanding
SSN	Social Security Number
WIPO	World Intellectual Property Organization

Appendix B: Legislation Passed by the 105th-109th Congresses

During the years that this report has been published (since the 105th Congress), various topics have been covered based on congressional interest and action. Some of those issues continue to be of interest to Congress and are discussed in this edition of the report. Others, however, appear to be resolved from a congressional point of view, and therefore are not discussed in the main text. Nevertheless, it appears useful to retain information about legislation that passed on those subjects. Following is such a summary of all laws that have been tracked in this report over the years, by topic. Tables showing which laws were passed in each Congress appear at the end of this section.

Broadband Internet Access

The **Farm Security and Rural Investment Act of 2002 (P.L. 107-171, Section 6103)** authorizes the Secretary of Agriculture to make loans and loan guarantees to eligible entities for facilities and equipment providing broadband service in rural communities. **The National Science Foundation Authorization Act of 2002 (P.L. 107-368, Section 18(d))** directs the National Science Foundation to conduct a study of broadband network access for schools and libraries.

The **Commercial Spectrum Enhancement Act (Title II of H.R. 5419, P.L. 108-494)** seeks to make more spectrum available for wireless broadband and other services by facilitating the reallocation of spectrum from government to commercial users.

The **Deficit Reduction Act of 2005 (P.L. 109-171)**, Title III sets a hard deadline for the digital television transition, thereby reclaiming analog television spectrum to be auctioned for commercial applications such as wireless broadband.

Computer Security

The **Computer Crime Enforcement Act (P.L. 106-572)** establishes Department of Justice grants to state and local authorities to help them investigate and prosecute computer crimes. The law authorizes the expenditure of $25 million for the grant program through FY2004. **The FY2001 Department of Defense Authorization Act (P.L. 106-398)** includes language that originated in S. 1993 to modify the Paperwork Reduction Act and other relevant statutes concerning computer security of government systems, codifying agency responsibilities regarding computer security.

Internet Privacy (Including Identity Theft)

The **Identity Theft and Assumption Deterrence Act (P.L. 105-318)** sets penalties for persons who knowingly, and with the intent to commit unlawful activities, possess, transfer, or use one or more means of identification not legally issued for use to that person.

Language in the **FY2001 Transportation Appropriations Act (P.L. 106-246)** and the **FY2001 Treasury-General Government Appropriations Act** (included as part ofthe FY2001 Consolidated Appropriations Act, P.L. 106-554) addresses website information collection practices by departments and agencies. Section 501 of the FY2001 Transportation Appropriations Act prohibits funds in the FY2001 Treasury-General Government Appropriations Act from being used by any federal agency to collect, review, or create aggregate lists that include personally identifiable information (PII) about an individual's access to or use of a federal website, or enter into agreements with third parties to do so, with exceptions. Section 646 of the FY2001 Treasury-General Government Appropriations Act requires Inspectors General of agencies or departments covered in that act to report to Congress within 60 days of enactment on activities by those agencies or departments relating to the collection of PII about individuals who access any Internet site of that department or agency, or entering into agreements with third parties to obtain PII about use of government or non-government websites.

The **Internet False Identification Prevention Act (P.L. 106-578)** updates existing law against selling or distributing false identification documents to include those sold or distributed through computer files, templates, and disks. It also requires the Attorney General and Secretary of the Treasury to create a coordinating committee to ensure that the creation and distribution of false IDs is vigorously investigated and prosecuted.

The **USA PATRIOT Act (P.L. 107-56)**, passed in the wake of the September 11, 2001 terrorist attacks, *inter alia* expands law enforcement's authority to monitor Internet activities. **The Cyber Security Enhancement Act**, included as section 225 of the Homeland Security Act (P.L. 107-296), amends the USA PATRIOT Act to further loosen restrictions on Internet Service Providers (ISPs) as to when, and to whom, they can voluntarily release information about subscribers.

Prior to the terrorist attacks, concern had focused on the opposite issue — whether law enforcement officials might be overstepping their authority when using a software program named Carnivore (later renamed DCS 1000) to monitor Internet activities. Although the USA PATRIOT Act expands law enforcement's authority to monitor Internet activities, Congress also passed a provision in the **21st Century Department of Justice Authorization Act (P.L. 107-273, section 305)** requiring the Justice Department to notify Congress about its use of Carnivore or similar systems.

The **E-Government Act (P.L. 107-347),** *inter alia*, sets requirements on government agencies as to how they assure the privacy of personal information in government information systems and establishes guidelines for privacy policies for federal websites.

The **Intelligence Reform and Terrorism Protection Act (P.L. 108-458)** was passed largely in response to recommendations from the 9/11 Commission, which investigated the September 11, 2001 terrorist attacks. Among its many provisions, the act creates a Privacy and Civil Liberties Oversight Board (Section 1061), composed of five members, two of whom (the chairman and vice-chairman) must be confirmed by the Senate. The Board's mandate is to ensure that privacy and civil liberties are not neglected when implementing terrorism-related laws, regulations, and policies. The 9/11 Commission had recommended creation of such a Board because of concern that the USA PATRIOT Act, enacted soon after the attacks, shifts the balance of power to the government.

Spam: Unsolicited Commercial E-Mail

The **CAN-SPAM Act, P.L. 108-187**, sets civil or criminal penalties if senders of commercial e-mail do not provide a legitimate opportunity for recipients to "opt-out" of receiving further commercial e-mail from the sender, if they use deceptive subject headings, if they use fraudulent information in the header of the message, if they "harvest" e-mail addresses from the Internet or use "dictionary attacks" to create e-mail addresses, if they access someone else's computer without authorization and use it to send multiple commercial e-mail messages, or engage in certain other activities connected with sending "spam." Spam is variously defined by participants in the debate as unsolicited commercial e-mail, unwanted commercial e-mail, or fraudulent commercial e-mail. The CAN-SPAM Act preempts state laws that specifically regulate electronic mail, but not other state laws, such as trespass, contract, or tort law, or other state laws to the extent they relate to fraud or computer crime. It authorizes, but does not require, the Federal Trade Commission to establish a centralized "do not e-mail" list similar to the National Do Not Call list for telemarketing. The FTC has concluded that a do not e-mail list is not feasible at this time.

The **Undertaking Spam, Spyware, And Fraud Enforcement With Enforcers beyond Borders Act of 2005 (US SAFE WEB), P.L. 109-455** would allow the Federal Trade Commission and parallel foreign law enforcement agencies to share information while investigating allegations of "unfair and deceptive practices" that involve foreign commerce.

Internet Domain Names

The **Next Generation Internet Research Act (P.L. 105-305)** directs the National Academy of Sciences to conduct a study of the short- and long-term effects on trademark rights of adding new generation top-level domains and related dispute resolution procedures.

The **Anticybersquatting Consumer Protection Act** (part of the FY2000 Consolidated Appropriations Act, **P.L. 106-113**) gives courts the authority to order the forfeiture, cancellation, and/or transfer of domain names registered in "bad faith" that are identical or similar to trademarks. The act provides for statutory civil damages of at least $1,000, but not more than $100,000 per domain name identifier.

The **Dot Kids Implementation and Efficiency Act of 2002 (P.L. 107-317)** directs the National Telecommunications and Information Administration of the Department of Commerce to require the .us registry operator to establish, operate, and maintain a second level domain that is restricted to material suitable for minors.

The **PROTECT Act (P.L. 108-21)** contains a provision (Sec. 108, Misleading Domain Names on the Internet) that makes it a punishable crime to knowingly use a misleading domain name with the intent to deceive a person into viewing obscenity on the Internet. Increased penalties are provided for deceiving minors into viewing harmful material. (CRS Report RS21328, *Internet: Status Report on Legislative Attempts to Protect Children from Unsuitable Material on the Web*, by Patricia Moloney Figliola, provides further information on this and other legislative efforts to protect children from unsuitable material on the Internet.)

The **Fraudulent Online Identity Sanctions Act** (Title II of the Intellectual Property Protection and Courts Amendments Act of 2004, **P.L. 108-482**) increases criminal penalties for those who submit false contact information when registering a domain name that is subsequently used to commit a crime or engage in copyright or trademark infringement.

The **Adam Walsh Child Protection and Safety Act of 2006 (P.L. 109-248)** increases the penalty from 4 to 10 years imprisonment for persons who knowingly use a misleading domain name with the intent to deceive a minor into viewing harmful material.

Protecting Children from Unsuitable Material and Predators on the Internet

The **Child Online Protection Act**, Title XIV of Division C of the FY1999 Omnibus Appropriations Act, **P.L. 105-277**), made it a crime to send material over the Web that is "harmful to minors" to children. Similar language was also included in the Internet Tax Freedom Act (Title XI of Division C of the same act). Called "CDA II" by some in reference to the Communications Decency Act that passed Congress in 1996, but was overturned by the Supreme Court, the bill restricted access to commercial material that is "harmful to minors" distributed on the World Wide Web to those 17 and older. This act also was challenged in the courts. See CRS Report 98-670, *Obscenity, Child Pornography, and Indecency: Recent Developments and Pending Issues*, by Henry Cohen, for a summary of court actions.

The **Children's Online Privacy Protection Act** (Title XIII of Division C of the FY1999 Omnibus Appropriations Act, **P.L. 105-277**), requires verifiable parental consent for the collection, use, or dissemination of personally identifiable information from children under 13.

The **Protection of Children from Sexual Predators Act (P.L. 105-314)** is a broad law addressing concerns about sexual predators. Among its provisions are increased penalties for anyone who uses a computer to persuade, entice, coerce, or facilitate the transport of a child to engage in prohibited sexual activity, a requirement that Internet service providers report to law enforcement if they become aware of child pornography activities, a requirement that federal prisoners using the Internet be supervised, and a requirement for a study by the National Academy of Sciences on how to reduce the availability to children of pornography on the Internet.

The **Children's Internet Protection Act** (Title XVII of the FY2001 Labor-HITS Appropriations Act, included in the FY2001 Consolidated Appropriations Act, **P.L. 106-554**) requires most schools and libraries that receive federal funding through Title III of the Elementary and Secondary Education Act, the Museum and Library Services Act, or "E-rate" subsidies from the universal service fund, to use technology protection measures (filtering software or other technologies) to block certain websites when computers are being used by minors, and in some cases, by adults. When minors are using the computers, the technology protection measure must block access to visual depictions that are obscene, child pornography, or harmful to minors. When others are using the computers, the technology must block visual depictions that are obscene or are child pornography. The technology protection measure may be disabled by authorized persons to enable access for bona fide research or other lawful purposes.

E-Government

The **E-Government Act of 2002 (P.L. 107-347)** amends Title 44 U.S.C. by adding Chapter 36 — Management and Promotion of Electronic Government Services, and Chapter 37 — Information Technology Management Program, which includes a variety of provisions related to information technology management and the provision of e-government services. Among its provisions, the law establishes an Office of Electronic Government in the Office of Management and Budget to be headed by an Administrator appointed by the President. It also authorizes $345 million through FY2006 for an E-Government Fund to support initiatives, including interagency and intergovernmental projects, that involve the "development and implementation of innovative uses of the Internet or other electronic methods, to conduct activities electronically." Additionally, the law includes language that re-authorizes and amends the Government Information Security Reform Act (GISRA), establishes an information technology worker exchange program between the federal government and the private sector, promotes the use of Share-In-Savings procurement contracts, and establishes coordination and oversight policies for the protection of confidential information and statistical efficiency (the Confidential Information Protection and Statistical Efficiency Act of 2002).

Intellectual Property

Congress passed the **Digital Millennium Copyright Act (P.L. 105-304)** implementing the World Intellectual Property Organization (WIPO) treaties regarding protection of copyright on the Internet. The law also limits copyright infringement liability for online service providers that serve only as conduits of information.

Electronic and Digital Signatures

The **Government Paperwork Elimination Act** (Title XVII of Division C of the Omnibus Appropriations Act, **P.L. 105-277**) directs the Office of Management and Budget to develop procedures for the use and acceptance of "electronic" signatures (of which digital signatures are one type) by executive branch agencies.

The **Millennium Digital Commerce Act (P.L. 106-229)** regulates Internet electronic commerce by permitting and encouraging its continued expansion through the operation of free market forces, including the legal recognition of electronic signatures and electronic records.

Table 1. Summary of Legislation Passed by the 105th Congress

Title	Public law number
FY1999 Omnibus Consolidated and Emergency Supplemental Appropriations Act	P.L. 105-277
Internet Tax Freedom Act	Division C, Title XI
Children's Online Privacy Protection Act	Division C, Title XIII
Child Online Protection Act	Division C, Title XIV
Government Paperwork Elimination Act	Division C, Title XVII
Protection of Children from Sexual Predators Act	P.L. 105-314
Identity Theft and Assumption Deterrence Act	P.L. 105-318
Digital Millennium Copyright Act	P.L. 105-304
Next Generation Internet Research Act	P.L. 105-305

Electronic Commerce

The **Internet Tax Nondiscrimination Act (P.L. 107-75)** extended the Internet tax moratorium through November 1, 2003. Facing expiration of that moratorium, Congress passed the **Internet Tax Non-Discrimination Act of 2003 (P.L. 108-435)**. Among its provisions, the act: 1) extended the e-commerce tax moratorium for four years, from November 1, 2003 through November 1, 2007; 2) expanded the definition of Internet access to include both providers and buyers of Internet access; 3) grandfathered through November 1, 2007, Internet access taxes enforced before October 1, 1998; 4) similarly grandfathered through November 1, 2005 Internet access taxes enforced before November 1, 2003; and 5) excluded Voice Over Internet Protocol (VoIP) and similar voice services.

Table 2. Summary of Legislation Passed by the 106th Congress

Title	Public law number
Millennium Digital Commerce Act	P.L. 106-229
Computer Crime Enforcement Act	P.L. 106-572
FY2001 Transportation Appropriations Act, section 501	P.L. 106-246
FY2001 Treasury-General Government Appropriations Act, section 646 (enacted by reference in the FY2001 Consolidated Appropriations Act)	P.L. 106-554
Internet False Identification Prevention Act	P.L. 106-578
Children's Internet Protection Act (Title XVII of the FY2001 Labor-HHS Appropriations Act, enacted by reference in the FY2001 Consolidated Appropriations Act)	P.L. 106-554
Anticybersquatting Consumer Protection Act (enacted by reference in the FY2000 Consolidated Appropriations Act)	P.L. 106-113

Table 3. Summary of Legislation Passed by the 107th Congress

Title	Public law number
Uniting and Strengthening America by Providing Appropriate Tools to Intercept and Obstruct Terrorism (USA PATRIOT) Act	P.L. 107-56
Internet Tax Nondiscrimination Act	P.L. 107-75
Farm Security and Rural Investment Act (Section 6103)	P.L. 107-171
Cyber Security Enhancement Act (Section 225 of the Homeland Security Act)	P.L. 107-296
21st Century Department of Justice Authorization Act (Section 305)	P.L. 107-297
Dot Kids Implementation and Efficiency Act	P.L. 107-317
E-Government Act	P.L. 107-347
National Science Foundation Authorization Act of 2002 (Section 18d)	P.L. 107-368

Table 4. Summary of Legislation Passed by the 108th Congress

Title	Public law number
PROTECT Act (Section 108, Misleading Domain Names on the Internet)	P.L. 108-21
CAN-SPAM Act	P.L. 108-187
Internet Tax Non-Discrimination Act of 2003	P.L. 108-435
Intelligence Reform and Terrorism Protection Act (Section 1061)	P.L. 108-458
Fraudulent Online Identity Sanctions Act (Title II of the Intellectual Property Protection and Courts Amendments Act of 2004)	P.L. 108-482
Commercial Spectrum Enhancement Act (Title II of the ENHANCE 911 Act)	P.L. 108-494

Table 5. Summary of Legislation Passed by the 109th Congress

Title	Public law number
Deficit Reduction Act of 2005 (Title III, Digital Television Transition and Public Safety)	P.L. 109-171
Adam Walsh Child Protection and Safety Act of 2006	P.L. 109-248
Undertaking Spam, Spyware, And Fraud Enforcement With Enforcers beyond Borders Act of 2005 (US SAFE WEB)	P.L. 109-455

End Notes

[527] By Rita Tehan, Knowledge Services Group.

[528] Nielsen/NetRatings press release, *Over Three-fourths of U.S. Active Internet Users Connect via Broadband at Home in November, According to Nielsen/Netratings*, December 12, 2006. See [http://www.nielsen-netratings.com/pr/pr 061212.pdfl.

[529] Pew Internet and American Life. *Home Broadband Adoption* 2006, May 28, 2006. See [http://www.pewinternet.org/PPF/r/184/report display.asp].

[530] USC Annenberg School, Center for the Digital Future. *Online World As Important to Internet Users as Real World?*, November 29, 2006. See [http://www.digitalcenter.org/pages/news content.asp?intGloballd=212&intTypeld=1].

[531] For the purposes of the FCC report, broadband means high-speed lines that deliver services exceeding 200 kilobits (kb) per second in at least one direction. Broadband Internet issues are discussed later in this report.

[532] FCC. Federal Communications Commission Releases Data on High-Speed Services for Internet Access. Press release, July 26, 2006. Available at [http://hraunfoss.fcc.gov/edocs_public/attachmatch/DOC-266593Al.pdf].

[533] MRI Cyberstats, *Internet Access and Usage in the U.S.*, Spring 2006. See [http://www.infoplease.com/ipa/A0908398.html]

[534] Pew Internet & American Life, *Home Broadband Adoption* 2006, May 28, 2006. See [http://www.pewinternet.org/PPF/r/176/report display.asp].

[535] U.S. Department of Commerce. A Nation Online. Entering the Broadband Age. September 2004. See [http://www.ntia.doc.gov/reports/anol/index.html]. Rural/urban geographic distribution figures are on pp. 15-19.

[536] One source of comparative data is: *Internet Usage Statistics - The Big Picture World Internet Users and Population Stats*. See [http://internetworldstats.com/stats.htm].

[537] ClickZ Stats, *Web Worldwide*, See: [http://www.clickz.com/showPage.html?page=stats/web worldwide].

[538] Computer Industry Almanac, *Worldwide Internet Users Top 1 Billion in 2005*, January 4, 2006. See [http://www.c-i-a.com/pr0106.htm].

[539] OECD member countries include include Australia, Austria, Belgium, Canada, the Czech Republic, Denmark, Finland, France, Germany, Greece, Hungary, Iceland, Ireland, Italy, Japan, Korea, Luxembourg, Mexico, The Netherlands, New Zealand, Norway, Poland, Portugal, Slovak Republic, Spain, Sweden, Switzerland, Turkey, United Kingdom, and the United States.

[540] OECD Broadband Statistics to June, 2006. See [http://www.oecd.org/stifict/broadband].

[541] U.S. Census Bureau. *Quarterly Retail E-commerce Sales, 1" quarter 2006*, May 18, 2006. See [http://www.census.gov/mrts/www/ecomm.html].

[542] comScore press release, "U.S. Non-Travel E-Commerce Spending By Consumers Increased 23 Percent in Q3 2006 Versus Year Ago, According to comScore Networks," October 26, 2006. See [http://www.comscore.com/press/release.asp?press=959].

[543] By Angele A. Gilroy and Lennard G. Kruger, Resources, Science, and Industry Division. See also CRS Report RL33542, *Broadband Internet Regulation and Access: Background and Issues*, by Angele A. Gilroy and Lennard G. Kruger, which is updated more frequently than this report.

[544] By John D. Moteff, Resources, Science, and Industry Division.

[545] See, Computerworld. ID Thefts Slam Online Brokers, by Eric Lai. Vol. 40. No. 44. Oct. 30, 2006. p.1,43.

[546] The Computer Crime and Security Survey is conducted by the Computer Security Institute (CSI) in cooperation with the San Francisco Federal Bureau of Investigation's Computer Intrusion Squad. The CSI/FBI Survey, as it has become known, has been conducted annually since 1996, and surveys U.S. corporations, government agencies, financial and medical institutions and universities. The 2005 Survey indicated a slight increase, after four straight years of decline. Still over 50% of the respondents have reported unauthorized use. The CSI/FBI survey does not represent a statistical sampling of the nation's computer security practitioners. The survey can be found at [http://www.gocsi.com] . This website was last viewed on July 10, 2006.

[547] This refers to the series of attacks, in February 2000, directed at online giants Yahoo, eBay, Amazon, E Trade, DATEK, Excite, ZDNEt, buy.com, and CNN.

[548] Computerworld. Op. cit.

[549] Some of the penalties under this statute have been increased by both the USA PATRIOT Act (P.L. 107-56, Section 814) and the Homeland Security Act of 2002 (P.L. 107-296, Sectiom 225(g)).

[550] See "IT Security Destined for the Courtroom," *Computerworld*, May 21, 2001, vol. 35, no. 21, pp. 1, 73.

[551] By Patricia Moloney Figliola, Resources, Science, and Industry Division.

[552] By Jeffrey W. Seifert, Resources, Science, and Industry Division.

[553] General Accounting Office, *Identity Fraud: Prevalence and Links to Alien Illegal Activities*, GAO-02-830T, 25 June 2002, p. 10.

[554] FTC. "How Not to Get Hooked by a Thishing' Scam." June 2004. See [http://www.ftc.gov/bcp/conline/pubs/alerts/phishingalrt.pdf].

[555] By Patricia Moloney Figliola, Resources, Science, and Industry Division. See also CRS Report RL31953, *Spam: An Overview of Issues Concerning Commercial Electronic Mail*, by Patricia Moloney Figliola, which is updated more frequently than this report.

[556] The FCC issued those rules in August 2004. See also CRS Report RL31636, *Wireless Privacy and Spam: Issues for Congress*, by Patricia Moloney Figliola, for more on wireless privacy and wireless spam.

[557] FTC. "Effectiveness and Enforcement of the CAN-SPAM Act: A Report to Congress." December 2005. See [http://www.ftc.gov/reports/canspam05/051220canspamrpt.pdf].

[558] By Patricia Moloney Figliola, Resources, Science, and Industry Division.

[559] Several laws have been passed related to this issue: Communications Decency Act (CDA) (1996), Child Online Protection Act (COPA) (1998), Children's Internet Protection Act (CIPA) (2000), "Dot Kids" Act (2002), Amber Alert Act (2003), and the Adam Walsh Act (2006).

---

[560] Under 18 USC §2703(f), any governmental entity can require any service provider (telephone company, ISP, cable company, university) to immediately preserve any records in its possession for up to 90 days, renewable indefinitely.

[561] By Lennard G. Kruger, Resources, Science, and Industry Division. See also CRS Report 97-868, *Internet Domain Names: Background and Policy Issues*, by Lennard G. Kruger, which is updated more frequently than this report.

[562] Gallagher, Michael, Assistant Secretary of Commerce for Communications, Remarks to the Wireless Communications Association, June 30, 2005. Available at [http://www.ntia.doc.gov/ntiahome/domainname/USDNSprinciples 06302005.pdf].

[563] For more information, see: [http://www.icann.orgiannouncementsiannouncement-05jan07.htm]

[564] See CRS Report RL33224, *Constitutionality of Requiring Sexually Explicit Material on the Internet to be Under a Separate Domain Name*, by Henry Cohen.

[565] See ICANN "Whois Services" page, available at [http://www.icann.org/topics/whois-services/]

[566] See also CRS Report RL30661, *Government Information Technology Management: Past and Future Issues (the Clinger-Cohen Act)*, by Jeffrey W. Seifert.

[567] By Patricia Moloney Figliola, Resources, Science, and Industry Division. For more information, see CRS Report RL32589, *The Federal Communications Commission: Current Structure and its Role in the Changing Telecommunications Landscape*, by Patricia Moloney Figliola; and CRS Report RL33542, *Broadband Internet Access: Background and* Issues by Angele A. Gilroy and Lennard G. Kruger, both of which are updated more frequently than this report.

[568] By Patricia Moloney Figliola, Resources, Science, and Industry Division. See also CRS Report RL33586, *The Federal Networking and Information Technology Research and Development Program: Funding Issues and Activities*, by Patricia Moloney Figliola, which is updated more frequently than this report.

[569] By Jeffrey W. Seifert, Resources, Science, and Industry Division. See also CRS Report RL31057, *A Primer on E-Government: Sectors, Stages, Opportunities, and Challenges of Online Governance*, by Jeffrey W. Seifert, which is updated more frequently than this report.

[570] See [http://www.whitehouse.gov/omb/inforeg/egovstrategy.pdf].

[571] See [http://www.whitehouse.gov/omb/egov/c-presidential.html].

[572] By Jeffrey W. Seifert, Resources, Science, and Industry Division. See also CRS Report RL31627, *Computer Software and Open Source Issues: A Primer*, by Jeffrey W. Seifert.

[573] For more information about enterprise architectures generally, and the Federal Enterprise Architecture (FEA) specifically, see CRS Report RL33417, *Federal Enterprise Architecture and E-Government: Issues for Information Technology Management*, by Jeffrey W. Seifert.

INDEX

B

C

D

E

F

G

H

I

J

K

L

M

N

O

P

Q

R

T

U

V

W

Y

Z